CECIL and JORDAN
in new york
stories by
GABRIELLE BELL

Cecil and Jordan in New York: Stories by Gabrielle Bell
ISBN 978-1-897299-57-9

First Printing: March 2009
Printed in Singapore
10987654321

Library and Archives Canada Cataloguing in Publication
Bell, Gabrielle
Cecil and Jordan in New York: Stories / by Gabrielle Bell
ISBN 978-1-897299-57-9
I. Title. II. Title.
PN6727.B3775C4 2008 741.5'973 C2008-901255-0

Drawn & Quarterly
Post Office Box 48056
Montreal, Quebec
Canada H2V 4S8
www.drawnandquarterly.com

Distributed in the USA and abroad by:
Farrar, Straus and Giroux
18 West 18th Street
New York, NY 10011
Orders: 888 330 8477

Distributed in Canada by:
Raincoast Books
9050 Shaughnessy Street
Vancouver, BC V6P 6E5
Orders: 800-663-5714

CECIL AND JORDAN IN NEW YORK
STORIES BY GABRIELLE BELL

Cecil and Jordan

in New York

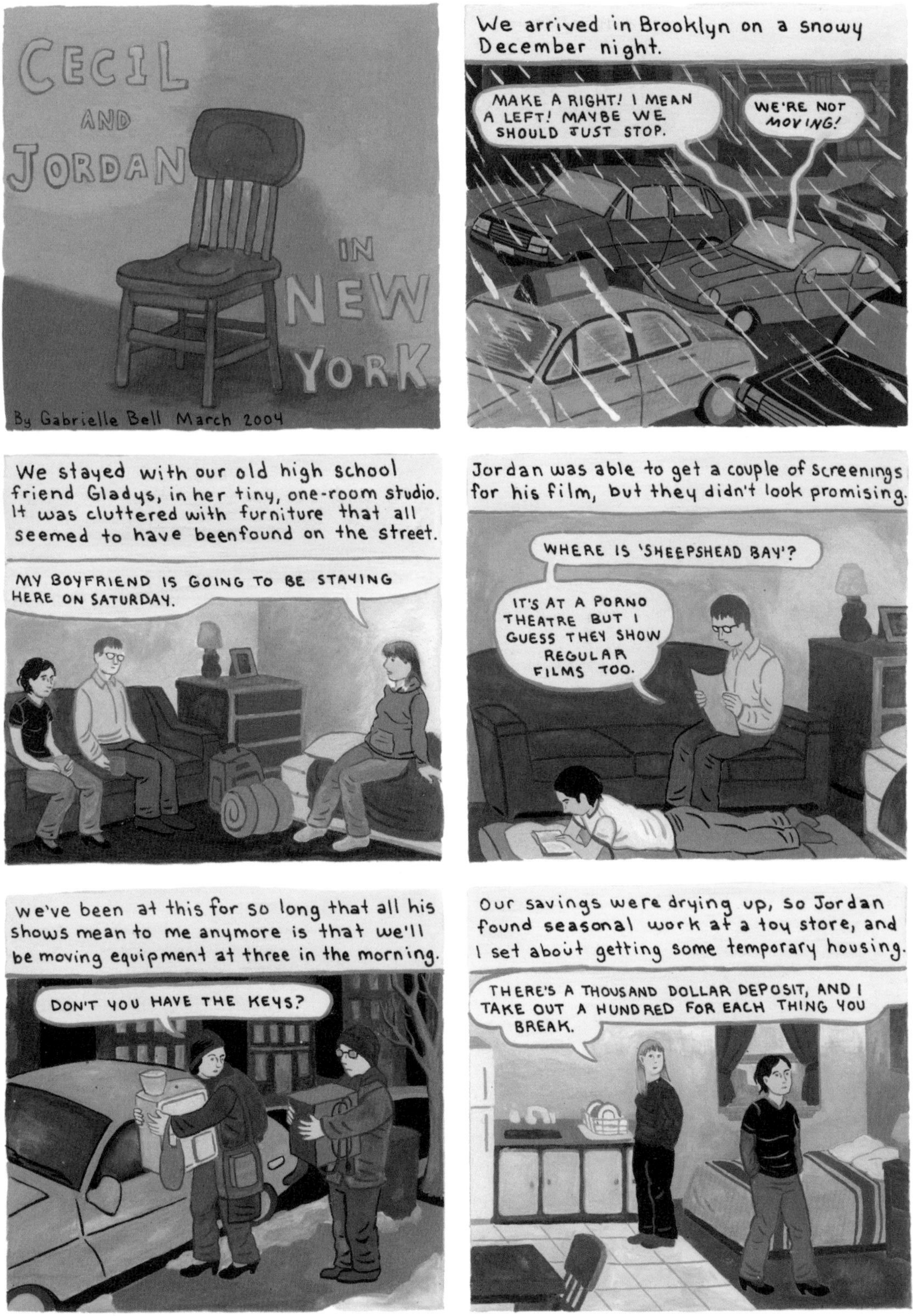
CECIL AND JORDAN IN NEW YORK
By Gabrielle Bell March 2004
We arrived in Brooklyn on a snowy December night.
MAKE A RIGHT! I MEAN A LEFT! MAYBE WE SHOULD JUST STOP.
WE'RE NOT MOVING!
We stayed with our old high school friend Gladys, in her tiny, one-room studio. It was cluttered with furniture that all seemed to have beenfound on the street.
MY BOYFRIEND IS GOING TO BE STAYING HERE ON SATURDAY.
Jordan was able to get a couple of screenings for his film, but they didn't look promising.
WHERE IS 'SHEEPSHEAD BAY'?
IT'S AT A PORNO THEATRE BUT I GUESS THEY SHOW REGULAR FILMS TOO.
we've been at this for so long that all his shows mean to me anymore is that we'll be moving equipment at three in the morning.
DON'T YOU HAVE THE KEYS?
Our savings were drying up, so Jordan found seasonal work at a toy store, and I set about getting some temporary housing.
THERE'S A THOUSAND DOLLAR DEPOSIT, AND I TAKE OUT A HUNDRED FOR EACH THING YOU BREAK.

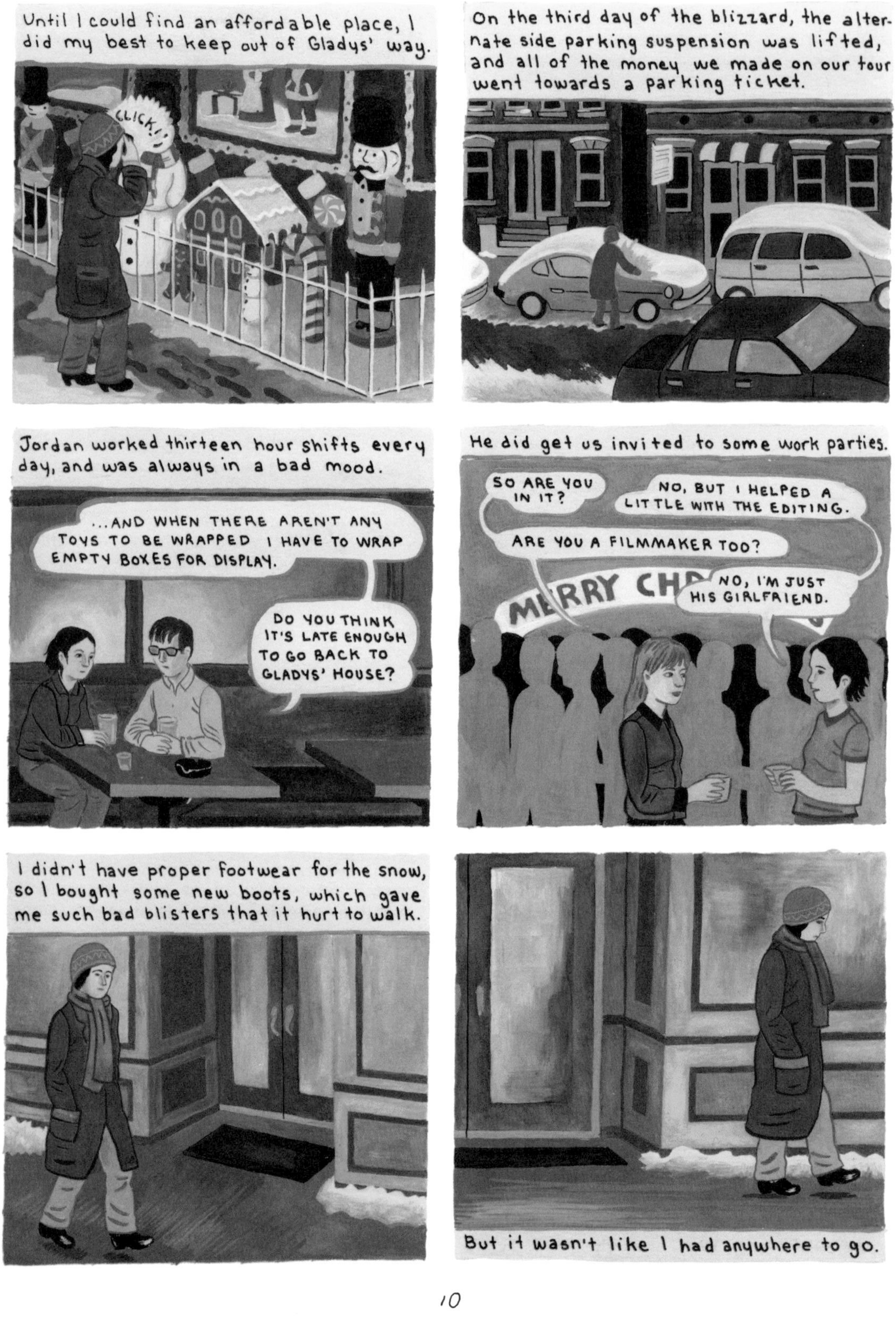
Until I could find an affordable place, I did my best to keep out of Gladys' way.
CLICK!
On the third day of the blizzard, the alternate side parking suspension was lifted, and all of the money we made on our tour went towards a parking ticket.
Jordan worked thirteen hour shifts every day, and was always in a bad mood.
...AND WHEN THERE AREN'T ANY TOYS TO BE WRAPPED I HAVE TO WRAP EMPTY BOXES FOR DISPLAY.
DO YOU THINK IT'S LATE ENOUGH TO GO BACK TO GLADYS' HOUSE?
He did get us invited to some work parties.
SO ARE YOU IN IT?
NO, BUT I HELPED A LITTLE WITH THE EDITING.
ARE YOU A FILMMAKER TOO?
NO, I'M JUST HIS GIRLFRIEND.
I didn't have proper footwear for the snow, so I bought some new boots, which gave me such bad blisters that it hurt to walk.
But it wasn't like I had anywhere to go.

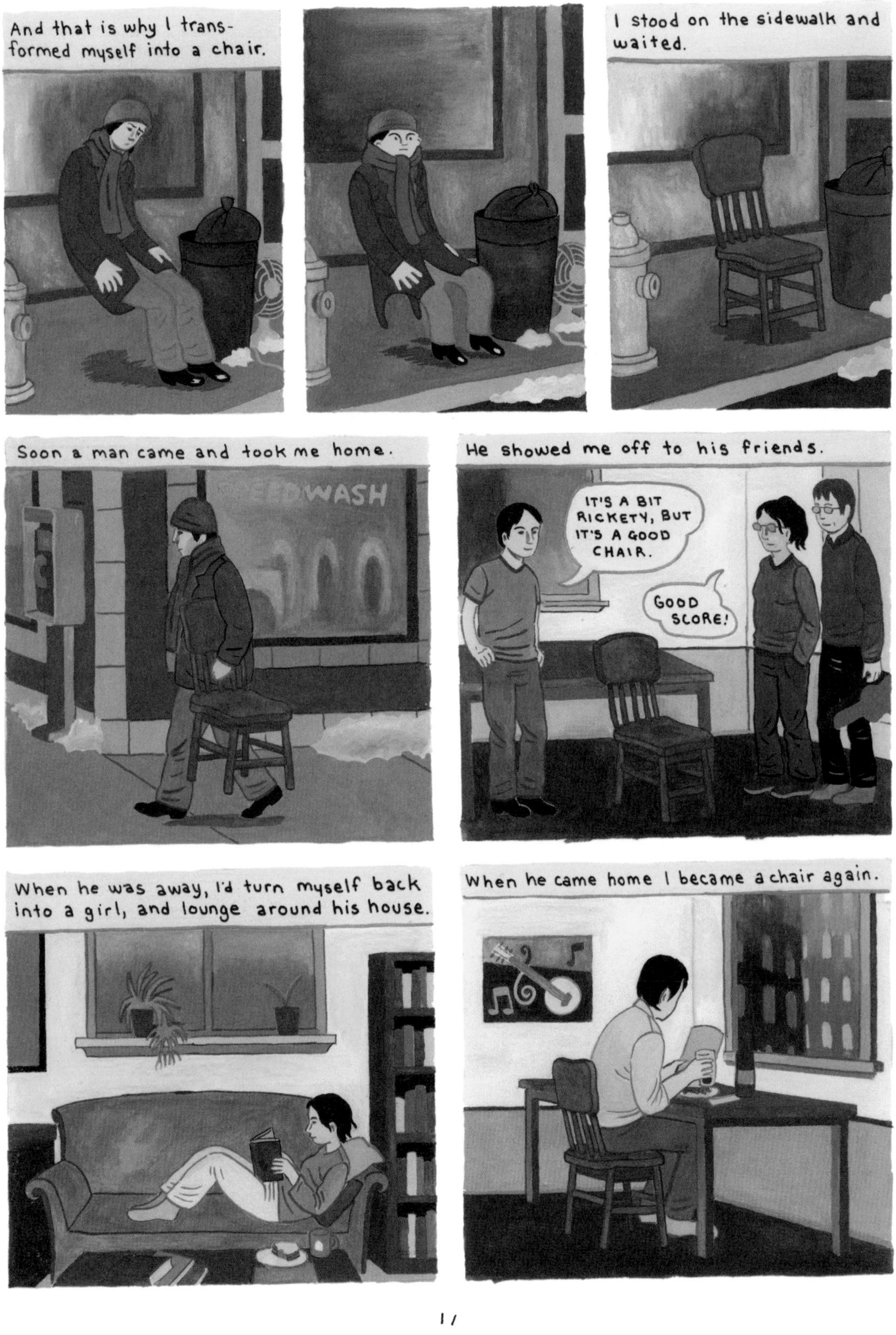
And that is why I transformed myself into a chair.
I stood on the sidewalk and waited.
Soon a man came and took me home.
WASH
He showed me off to his friends.
IT'S A BIT RICKETY, BUT IT'S A GOOD CHAIR.
GOOD SCORE!
When he was away, I'd turn myself back into a girl, and lounge around his house.
When he came home I became a chair again.

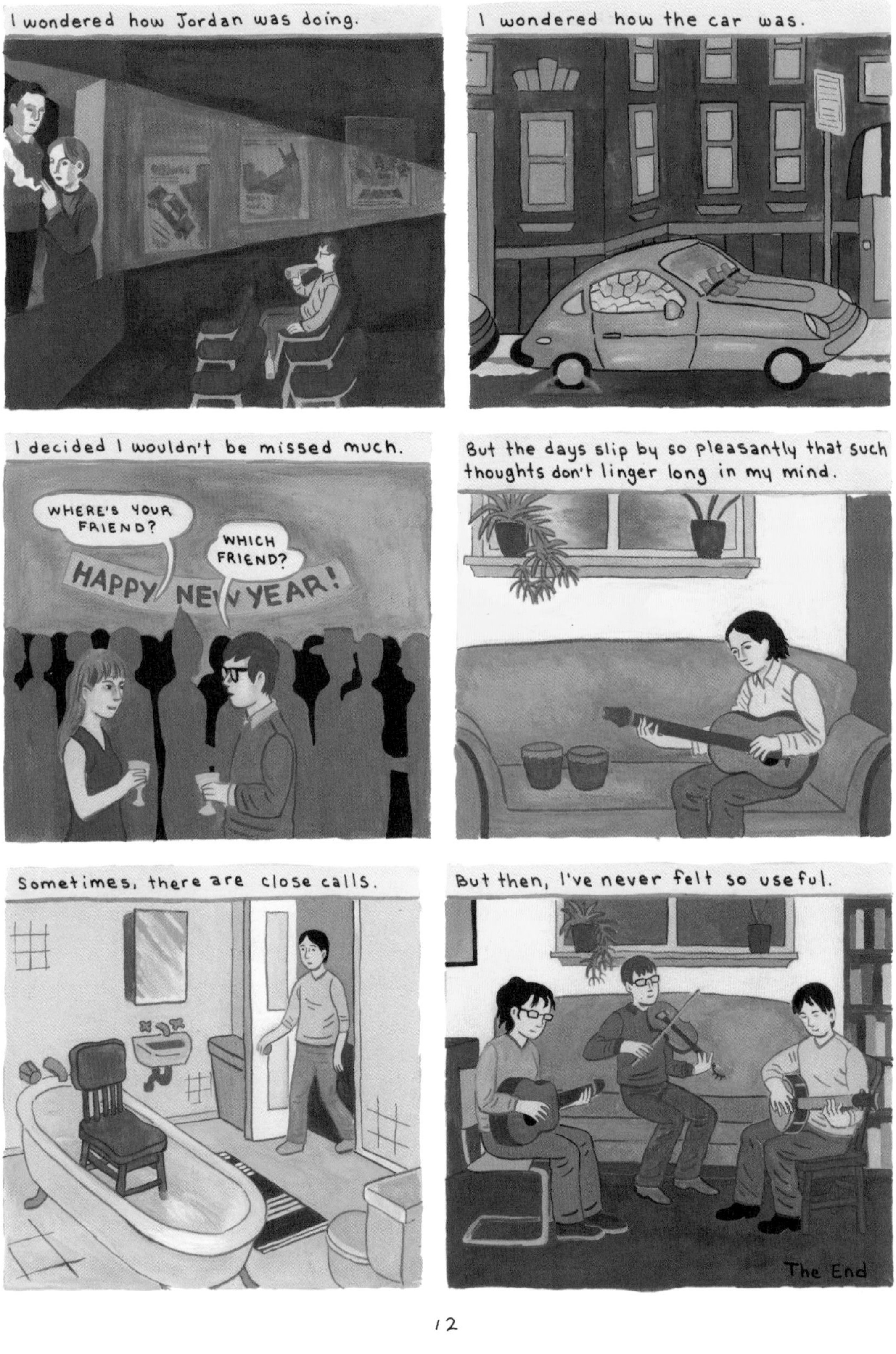
I wondered how Jordan was doing.
I wondered how the car was.
I decided I wouldn't be missed much.
WHERE'S YOUR FRIEND?
WHICH FRIEND?
HAPPY NEW YEAR!
But the days slip by so pleasantly that such thoughts don't linger long in my mind.
Sometimes, there are close calls.
But then, I've never felt so useful.
The End

I Feel Nothing

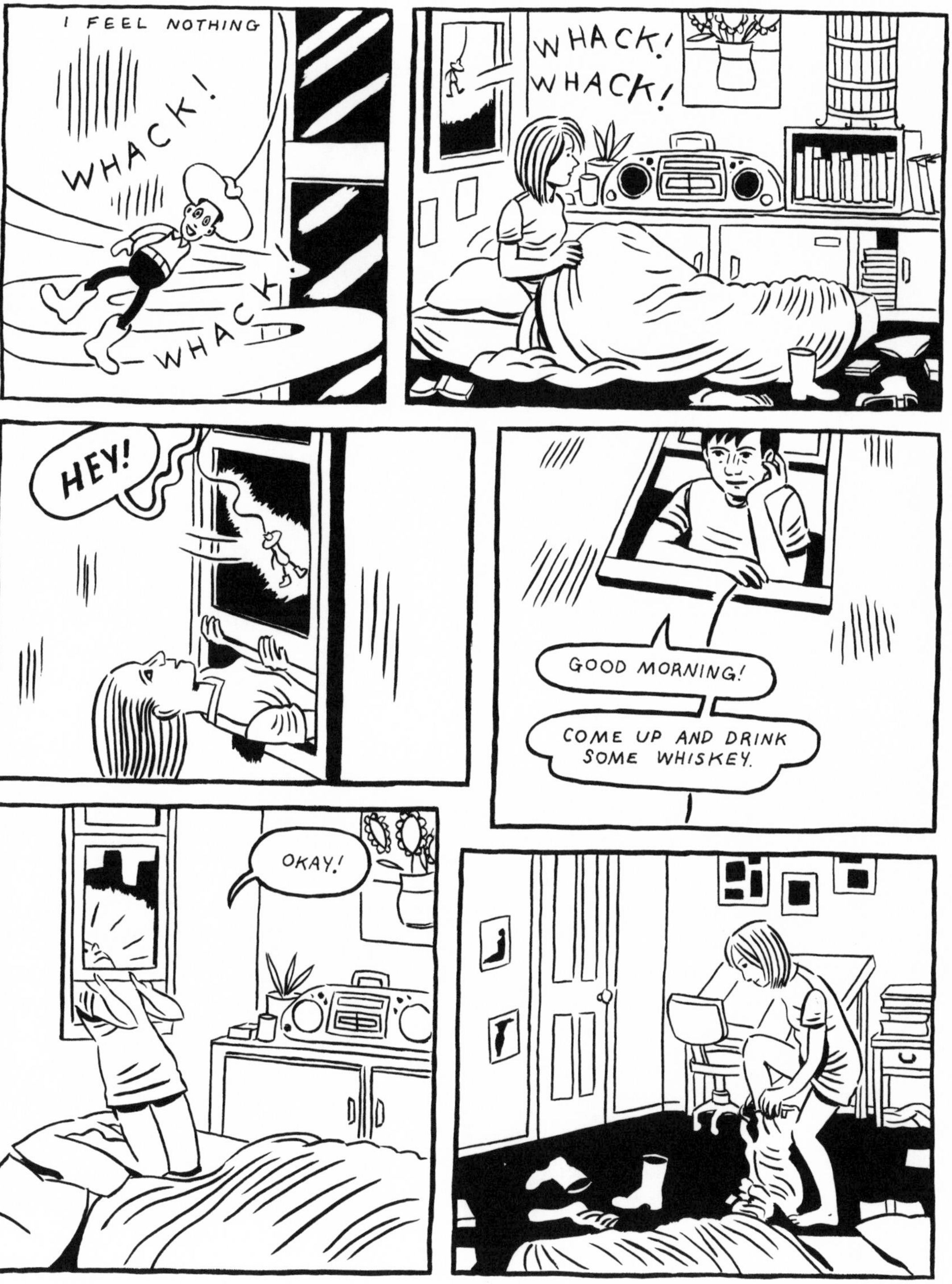
I FEEL NOTHING
WHACK!
WHACK
WHACK
WHACK!
WHACK!
HEY!
GOOD MORNING!
COME UP AND DRINK SOME WHISKEY.
OKAY!

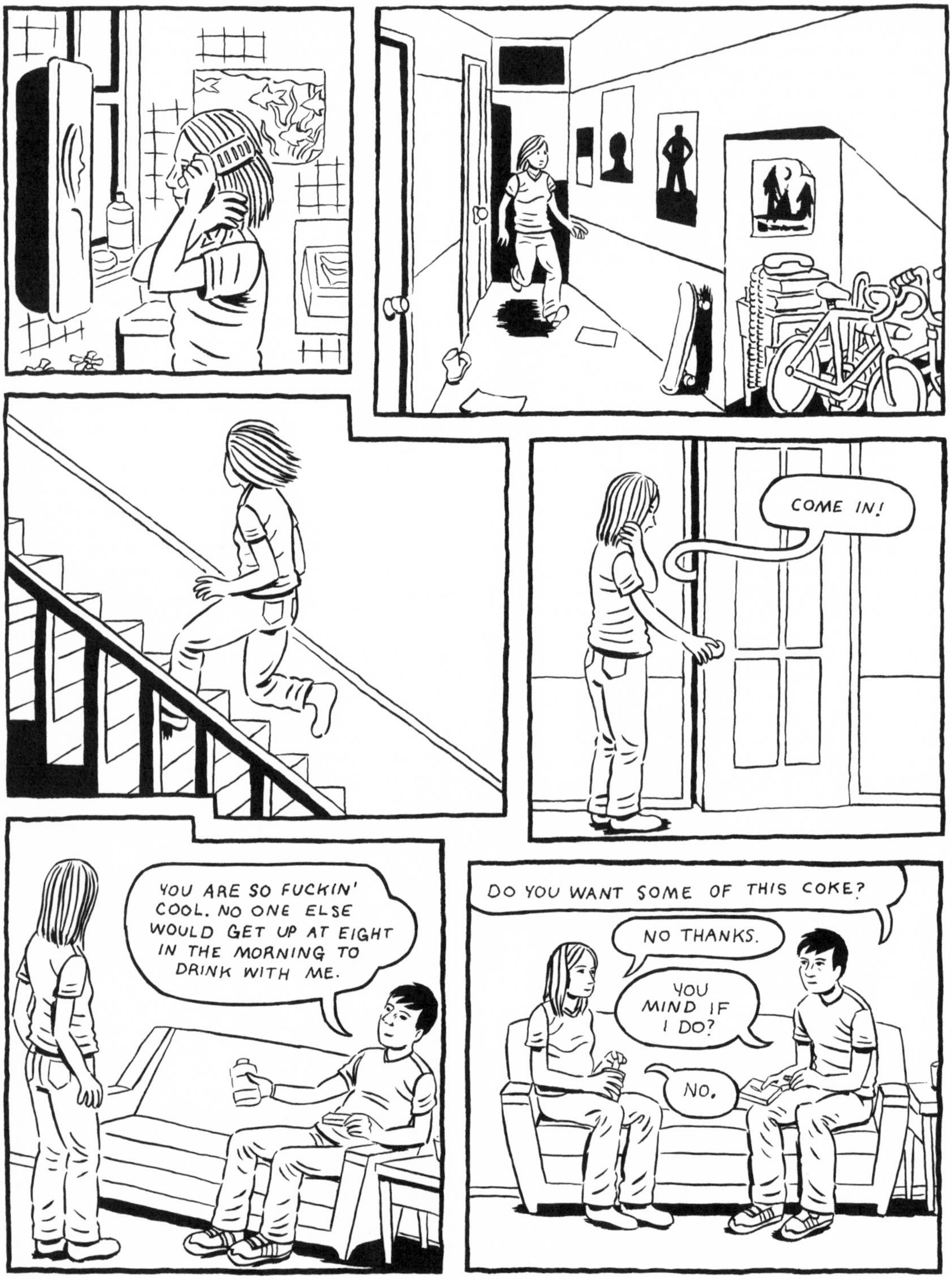
COME IN!
YOU ARE SO FUCKIN' COOL. NO ONE ELSE WOULD GET UP AT EIGHT IN THE MORNING TO DRINK WITH ME.
DO YOU WANT SOME OF THIS COKE?
NO THANKS.
YOU MIND IF I DO?
NO.

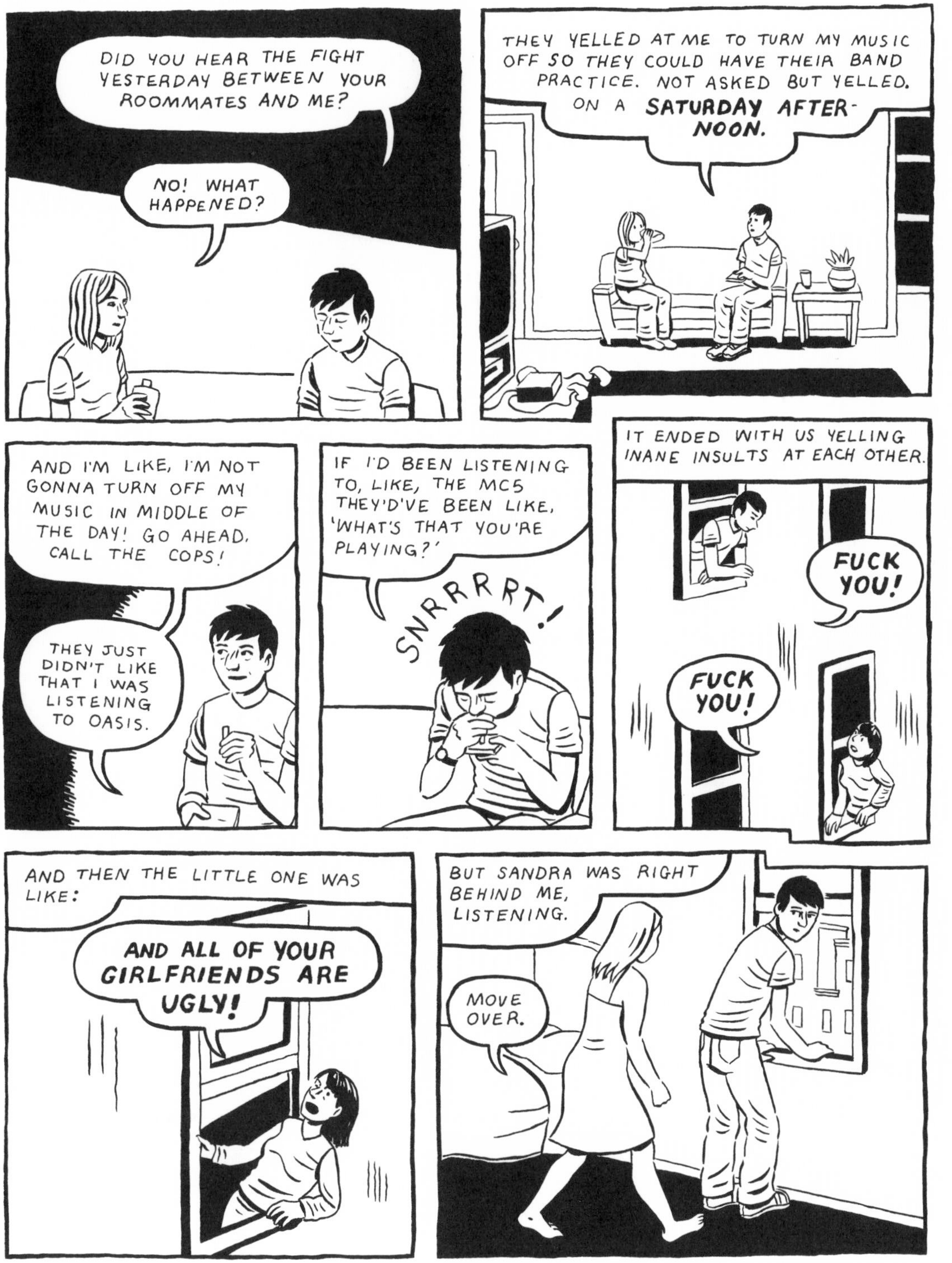
DID YOU HEAR THE FIGHT YESTERDAY BETWEEN YOUR ROOMMATES AND ME?
NO! WHAT HAPPENED?
THEY YELLED AT ME TO TURN MY MUSIC OFF SO THEY COULD HAVE THEIR BAND PRACTICE. NOT ASKED BUT YELLED. ON A SATURDAY AFTER-NOON.
AND I'M LIKE, I'M NOT GONNA TURN OFF MY MUSIC IN MIDDLE OF THE DAY! GO AHEAD, CALL THE COPS!
THEY JUST DIDN'T LIKE THAT I WAS LISTENING TO OASIS.
IF I'D BEEN LISTENING TO, LIKE, THE MC5 THEY'D'VE BEEN LIKE, 'WHAT'S THAT YOU'RE PLAYING?'
SNRRRRT!
IT ENDED WITH US YELLING INANE INSULTS AT EACH OTHER.
FUCK YOU!
FUCK YOU!
AND THEN THE LITTLE ONE WAS LIKE:
AND ALL OF YOUR GIRLFRIENDS ARE UGLY!
BUT SANDRA WAS RIGHT BEHIND ME, LISTENING.
MOVE OVER.

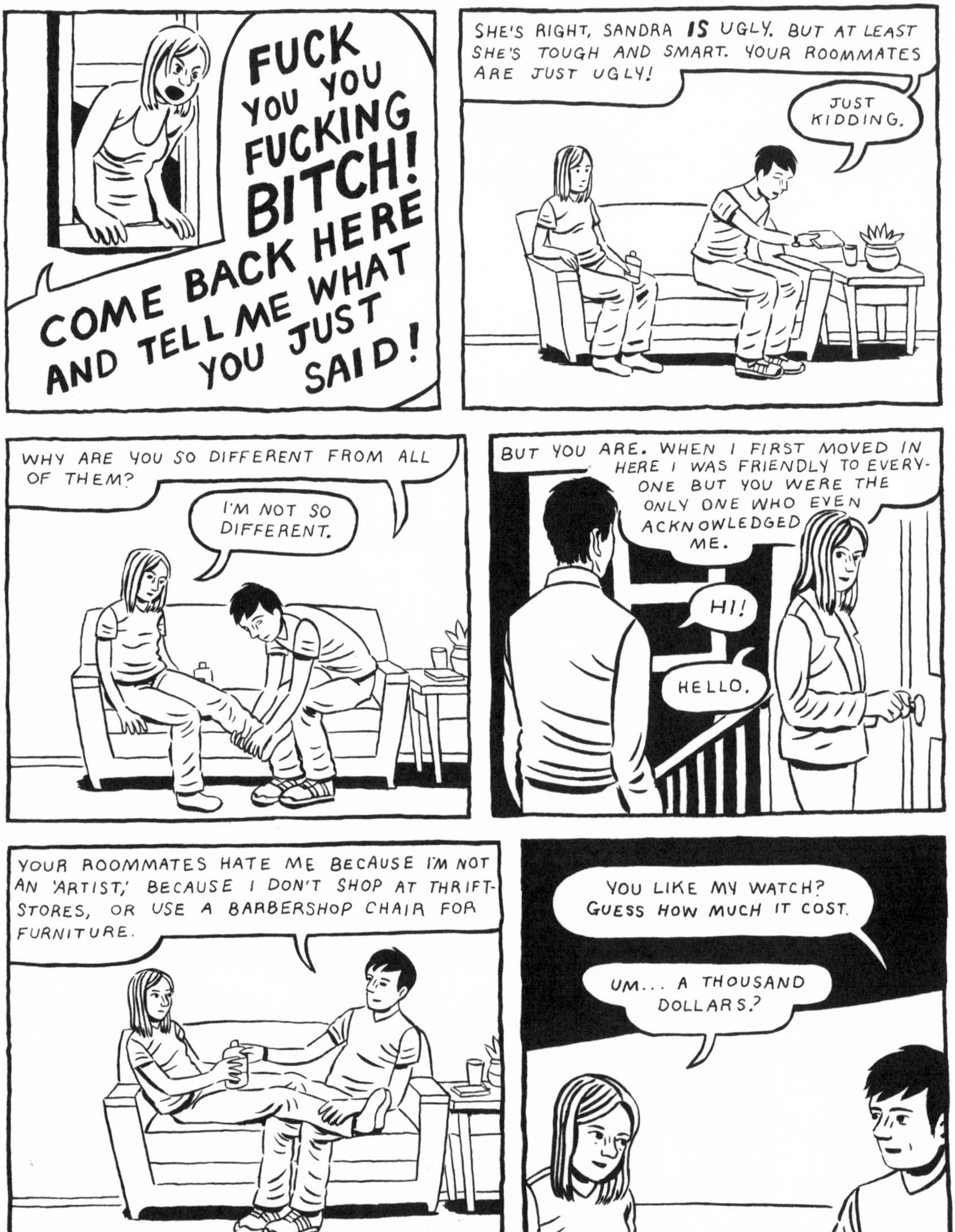
FUCK YOU YOU FUCKING BITCH!
COME BACK HERE AND TELL ME WHAT YOU JUST SAID!
SHE'S RIGHT, SANDRA IS UGLY. BUT AT LEAST SHE'S TOUGH AND SMART. YOUR ROOMMATES ARE JUST UGLY!
JUST KIDDING.
WHY ARE YOU SO DIFFERENT FROM ALL OF THEM?
I'M NOT SO DIFFERENT.
BUT YOU ARE. WHEN I FIRST MOVED IN HERE I WAS FRIENDLY TO EVERYONE BUT YOU WERE THE ONLY ONE WHO EVEN ACKNOWLEDGED ME.
HI!
HELLO.
YOUR ROOMMATES HATE ME BECAUSE I'M NOT AN 'ARTIST,' BECAUSE I DON'T SHOP AT THRIFT-STORES, OR USE A BARBERSHOP CHAIR FOR FURNITURE.
YOU LIKE MY WATCH? GUESS HOW MUCH IT COST.
UM... A THOUSAND DOLLARS?

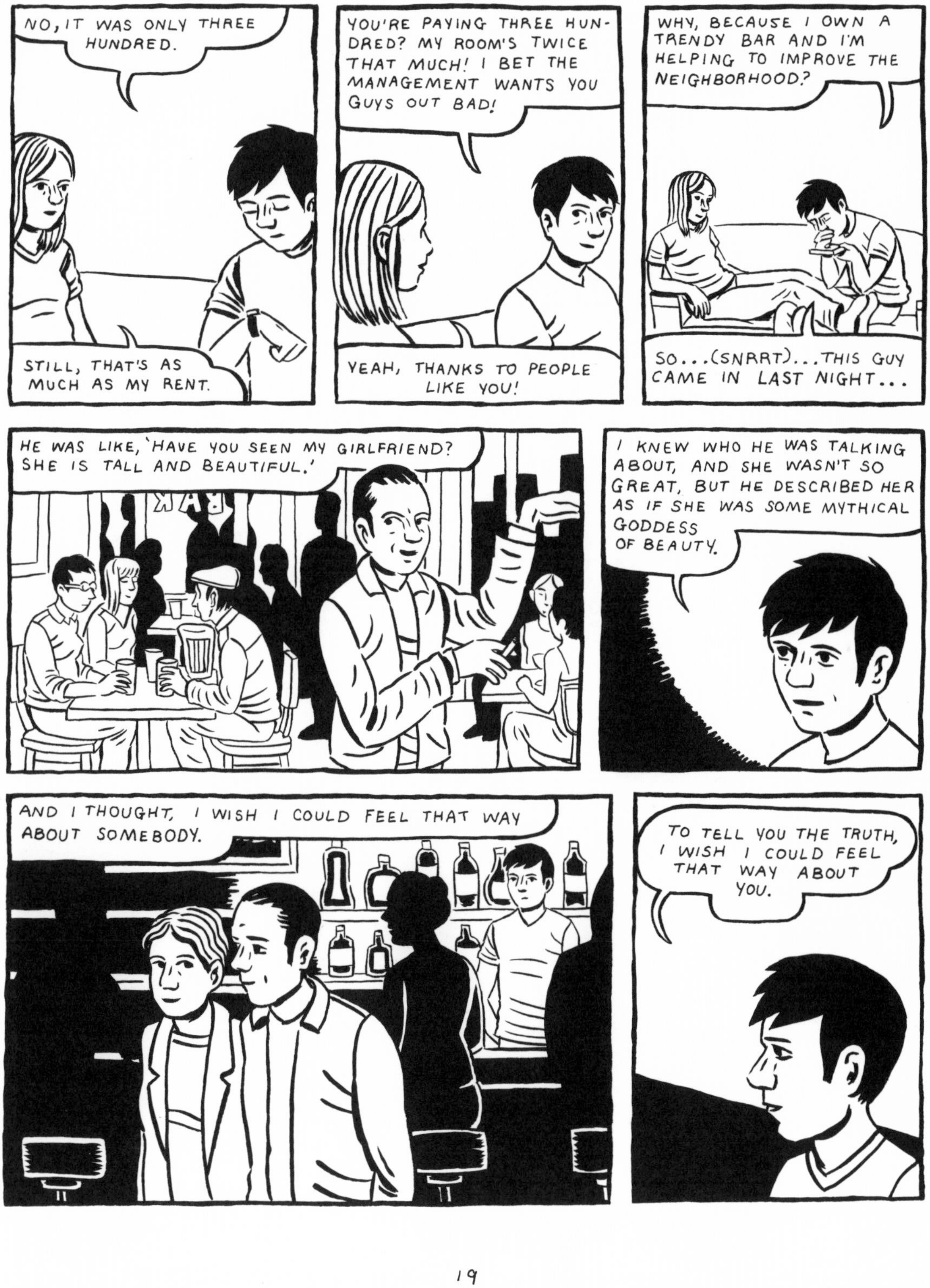
NO, IT WAS ONLY THREE HUNDRED.
STILL, THAT'S AS MUCH AS MY RENT.
YOU'RE PAYING THREE HUNDRED? MY ROOM'S TWICE THAT MUCH! I BET THE MANAGEMENT WANTS YOU GUYS OUT BAD!
YEAH, THANKS TO PEOPLE LIKE YOU!
WHY, BECAUSE I OWN A TRENDY BAR AND I'M HELPING TO IMPROVE THE NEIGHBORHOOD?
SO...(SNRRT)...THIS GUY CAME IN LAST NIGHT...
HE WAS LIKE, 'HAVE YOU SEEN MY GIRLFRIEND? SHE IS TALL AND BEAUTIFUL.'
I KNEW WHO HE WAS TALKING ABOUT, AND SHE WASN'T SO GREAT, BUT HE DESCRIBED HER AS IF SHE WAS SOME MYTHICAL GODDESS OF BEAUTY.
AND I THOUGHT, I WISH I COULD FEEL THAT WAY ABOUT SOMEBODY.
TO TELL YOU THE TRUTH, I WISH I COULD FEEL THAT WAY ABOUT YOU.

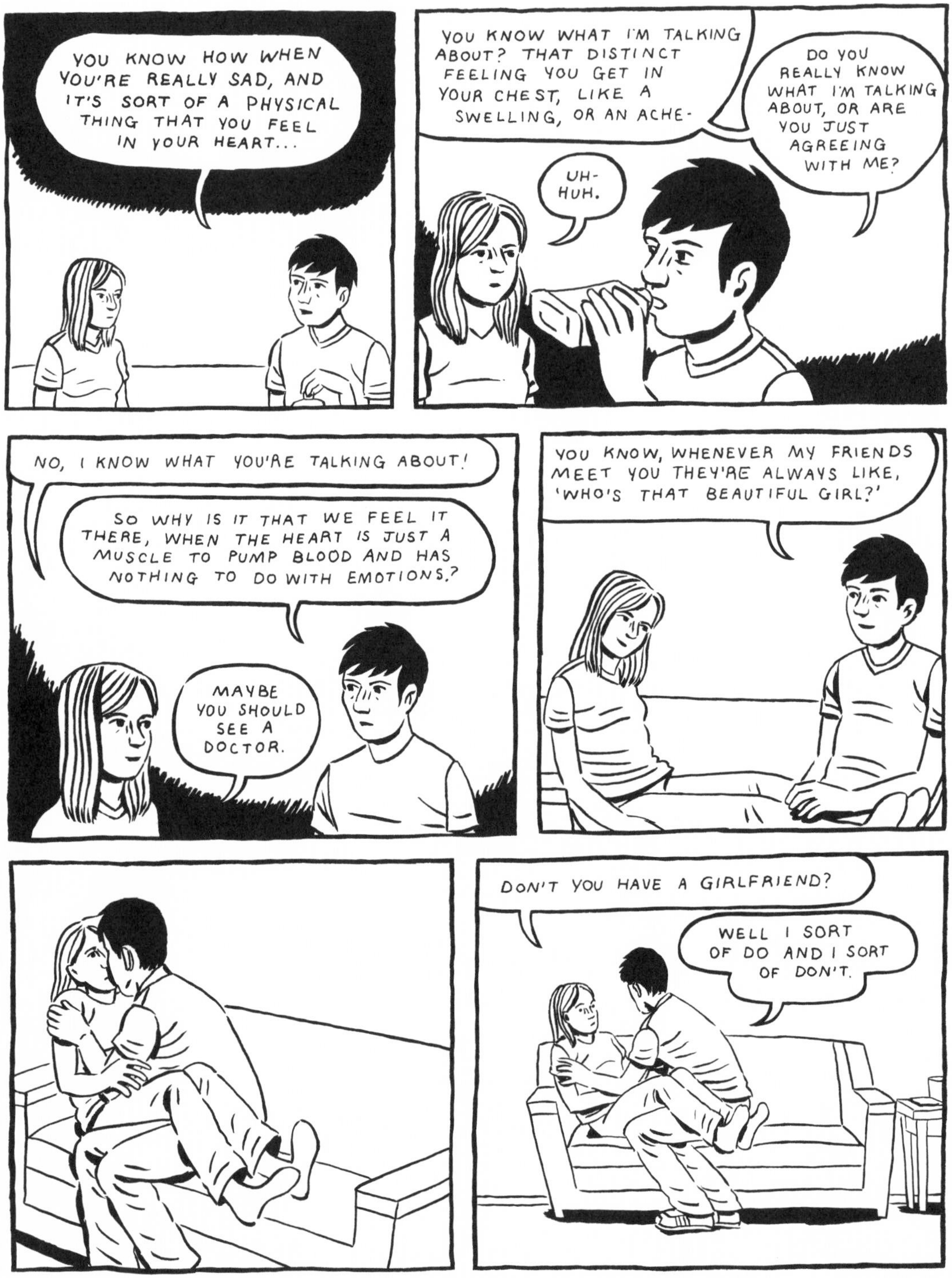
YOU KNOW HOW WHEN YOU'RE REALLY SAD, AND IT'S SORT OF A PHYSICAL THING THAT YOU FEEL IN YOUR HEART...
YOU KNOW WHAT I'M TALKING ABOUT? THAT DISTINCT FEELING YOU GET IN YOUR CHEST, LIKE A SWELLING, OR AN ACHE-
UH-HUH.
DO YOU REALLY KNOW WHAT I'M TALKING ABOUT, OR ARE YOU JUST AGREEING WITH ME?
NO, I KNOW WHAT YOU'RE TALKING ABOUT!
SO WHY IS IT THAT WE FEEL IT THERE, WHEN THE HEART IS JUST A MUSCLE TO PUMP BLOOD AND HAS NOTHING TO DO WITH EMOTIONS?
MAYBE YOU SHOULD SEE A DOCTOR.
YOU KNOW, WHENEVER MY FRIENDS MEET YOU THEY'RE ALWAYS LIKE, 'WHO'S THAT BEAUTIFUL GIRL?'
DON'T YOU HAVE A GIRLFRIEND?
WELL I SORT OF DO AND I SORT OF DON'T.

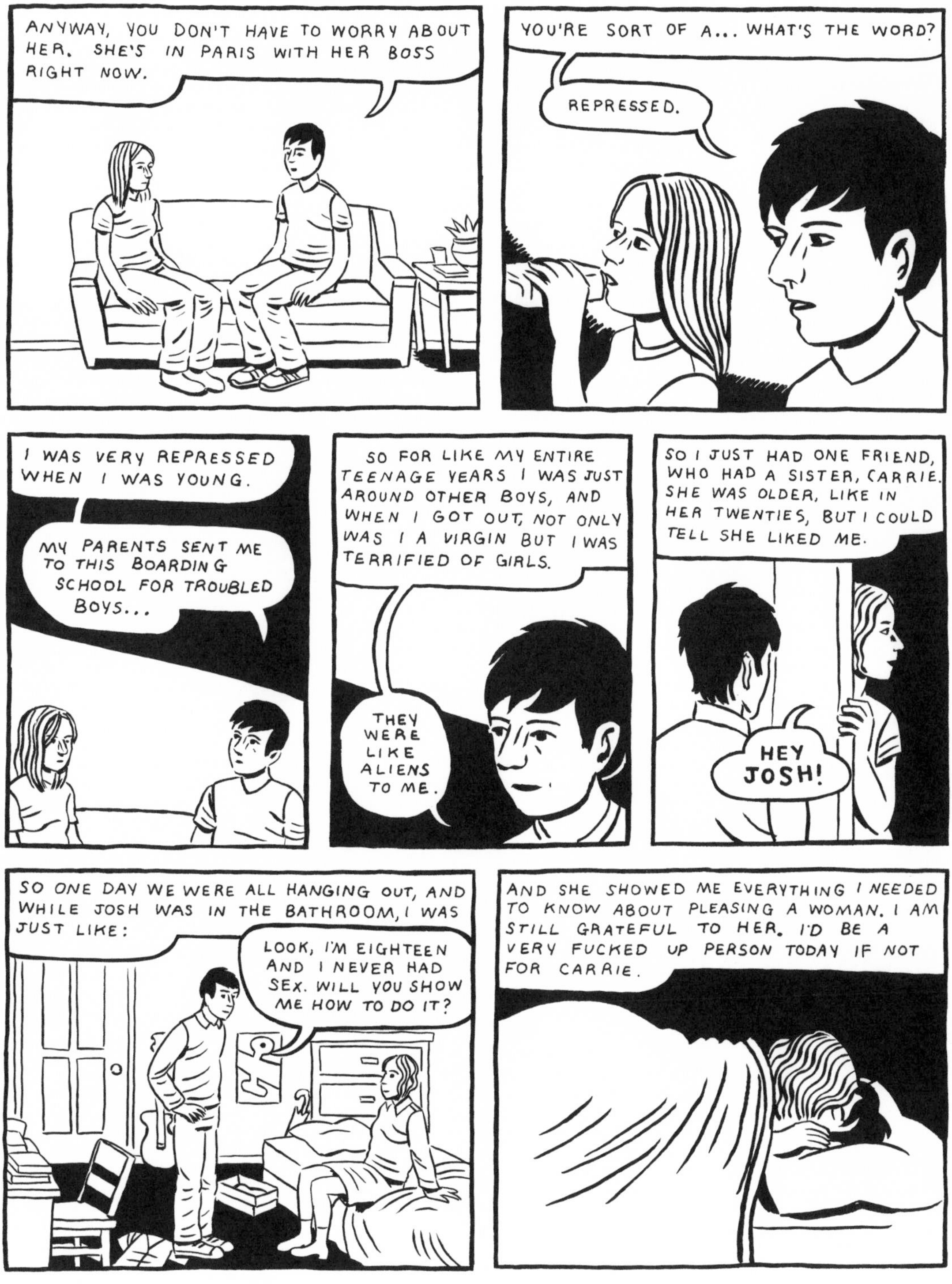
ANYWAY, YOU DON'T HAVE TO WORRY ABOUT HER. SHE'S IN PARIS WITH HER BOSS RIGHT NOW.
YOU'RE SORT OF A... WHAT'S THE WORD?
REPRESSED.
I WAS VERY REPRESSED WHEN I WAS YOUNG.
MY PARENTS SENT ME TO THIS BOARDING SCHOOL FOR TROUBLED BOYS...
SO FOR LIKE MY ENTIRE TEENAGE YEARS I WAS JUST AROUND OTHER BOYS, AND WHEN I GOT OUT, NOT ONLY WAS I A VIRGIN BUT I WAS TERRIFIED OF GIRLS.
THEY WERE LIKE ALIENS TO ME.
SO I JUST HAD ONE FRIEND, WHO HAD A SISTER, CARRIE. SHE WAS OLDER, LIKE IN HER TWENTIES, BUT I COULD TELL SHE LIKED ME.
HEY JOSH!
SO ONE DAY WE WERE ALL HANGING OUT, AND WHILE JOSH WAS IN THE BATHROOM, I WAS JUST LIKE:
LOOK, I'M EIGHTEEN AND I NEVER HAD SEX. WILL YOU SHOW ME HOW TO DO IT?
AND SHE SHOWED ME EVERYTHING I NEEDED TO KNOW ABOUT PLEASING A WOMAN. I AM STILL GRATEFUL TO HER. I'D BE A VERY FUCKED UP PERSON TODAY IF NOT FOR CARRIE.

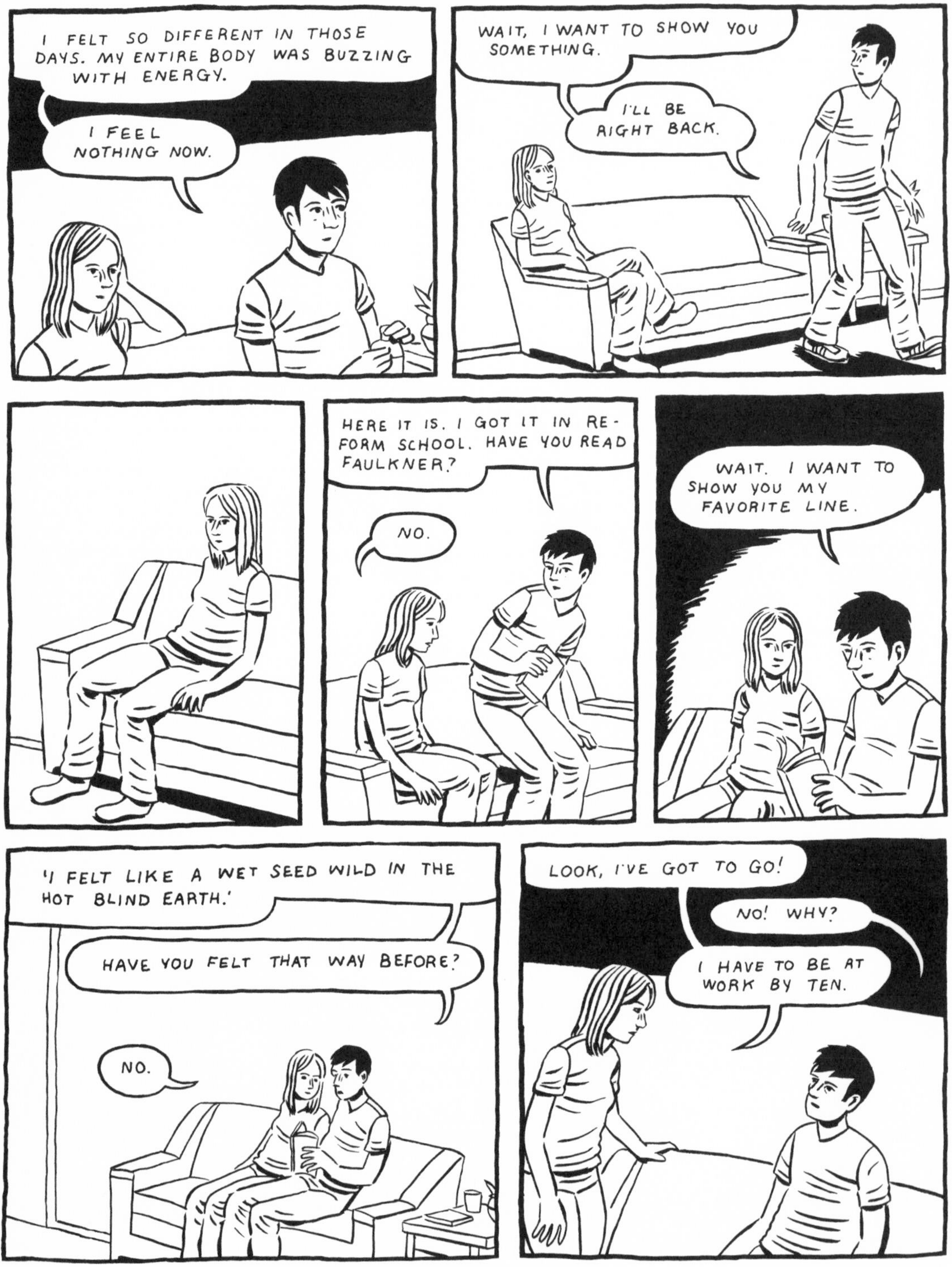
I FELT SO DIFFERENT IN THOSE DAYS. MY ENTIRE BODY WAS BUZZING WITH ENERGY.
I FEEL NOTHING NOW.
WAIT, I WANT TO SHOW YOU SOMETHING.
I'LL BE RIGHT BACK.
HERE IT IS. I GOT IT IN RE-FORM SCHOOL. HAVE YOU READ FAULKNER?
NO.
WAIT. I WANT TO SHOW YOU MY FAVORITE LINE.
'I FELT LIKE A WET SEED WILD IN THE HOT BLIND EARTH.'
HAVE YOU FELT THAT WAY BEFORE?
NO.
LOOK, I'VE GOT TO GO!
NO! WHY?
I HAVE TO BE AT WORK BY TEN.

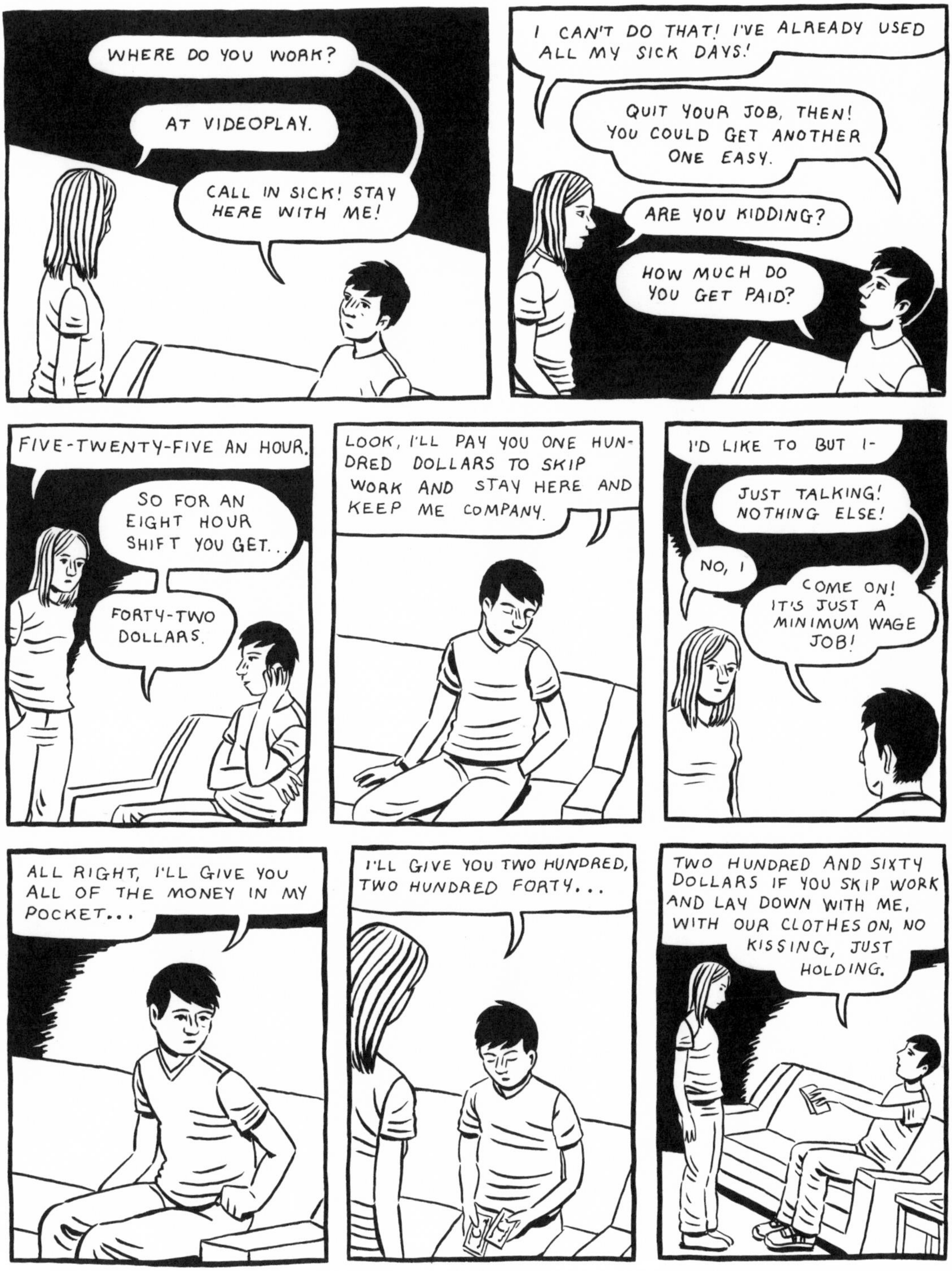
WHERE DO YOU WORK?
AT VIDEOPLAY.
CALL IN SICK! STAY HERE WITH ME!
I CAN'T DO THAT! I'VE ALREADY USED ALL MY SICK DAYS!
QUIT YOUR JOB, THEN! YOU COULD GET ANOTHER ONE EASY.
ARE YOU KIDDING?
HOW MUCH DO YOU GET PAID?
FIVE-TWENTY-FIVE AN HOUR.
SO FOR AN EIGHT HOUR SHIFT YOU GET...
FORTY-TWO DOLLARS.
LOOK, I'LL PAY YOU ONE HUNDRED DOLLARS TO SKIP WORK AND STAY HERE AND KEEP ME COMPANY.
I'D LIKE TO BUT I-
JUST TALKING! NOTHING ELSE!
NO, I
COME ON! IT'S JUST A MINIMUM WAGE JOB!
ALL RIGHT, I'LL GIVE YOU ALL OF THE MONEY IN MY POCKET...
I'LL GIVE YOU TWO HUNDRED, TWO HUNDRED FORTY...
TWO HUNDRED AND SIXTY DOLLARS IF YOU SKIP WORK AND LAY DOWN WITH ME, WITH OUR CLOTHES ON, NO KISSING, JUST HOLDING.

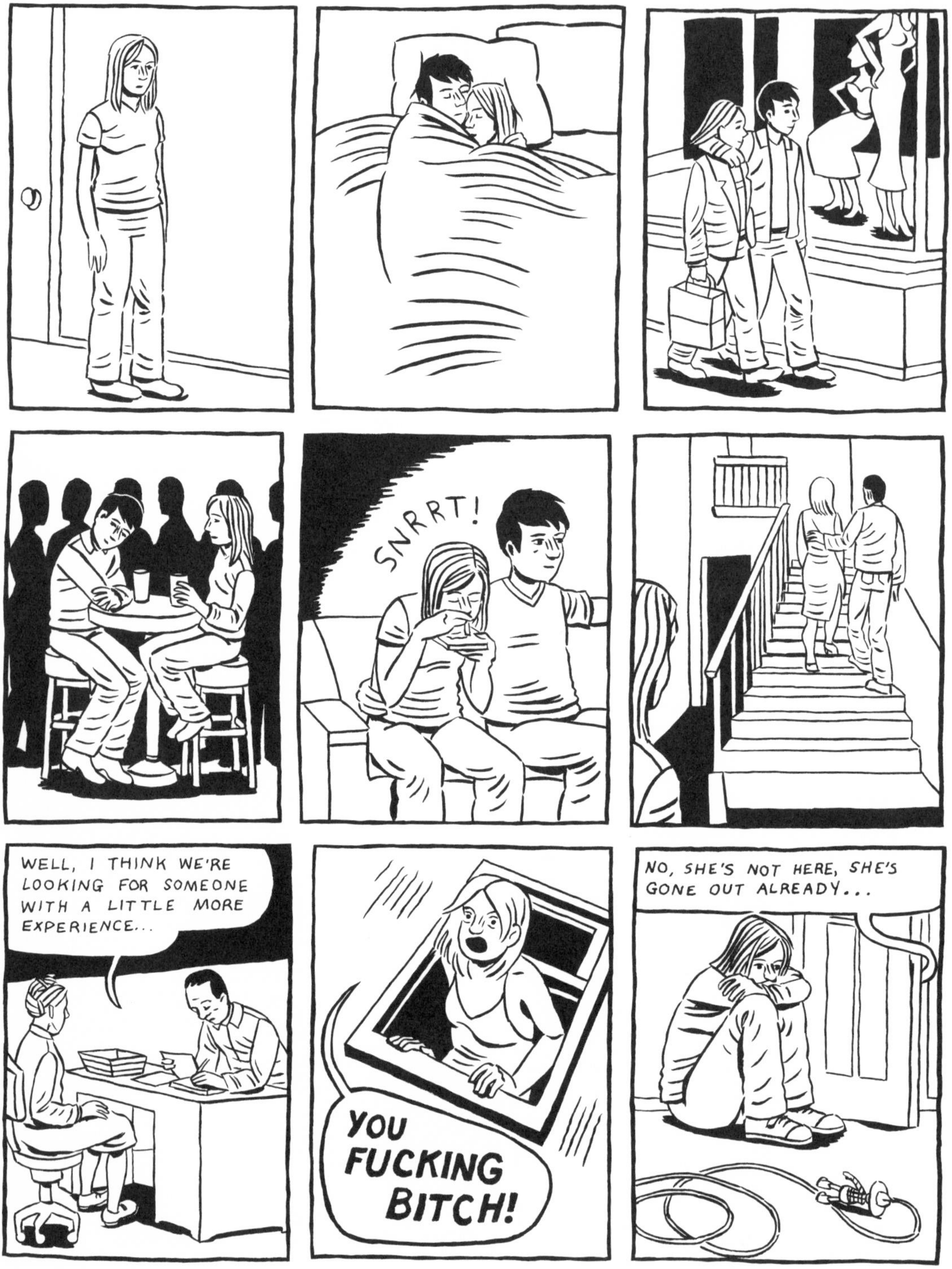
SNRRT!
WELL, I THINK WE'RE LOOKING FOR SOMEONE WITH A LITTLE MORE EXPERIENCE...
YOU FUCKING BITCH!
NO, SHE'S NOT HERE, SHE'S GONE OUT ALREADY...

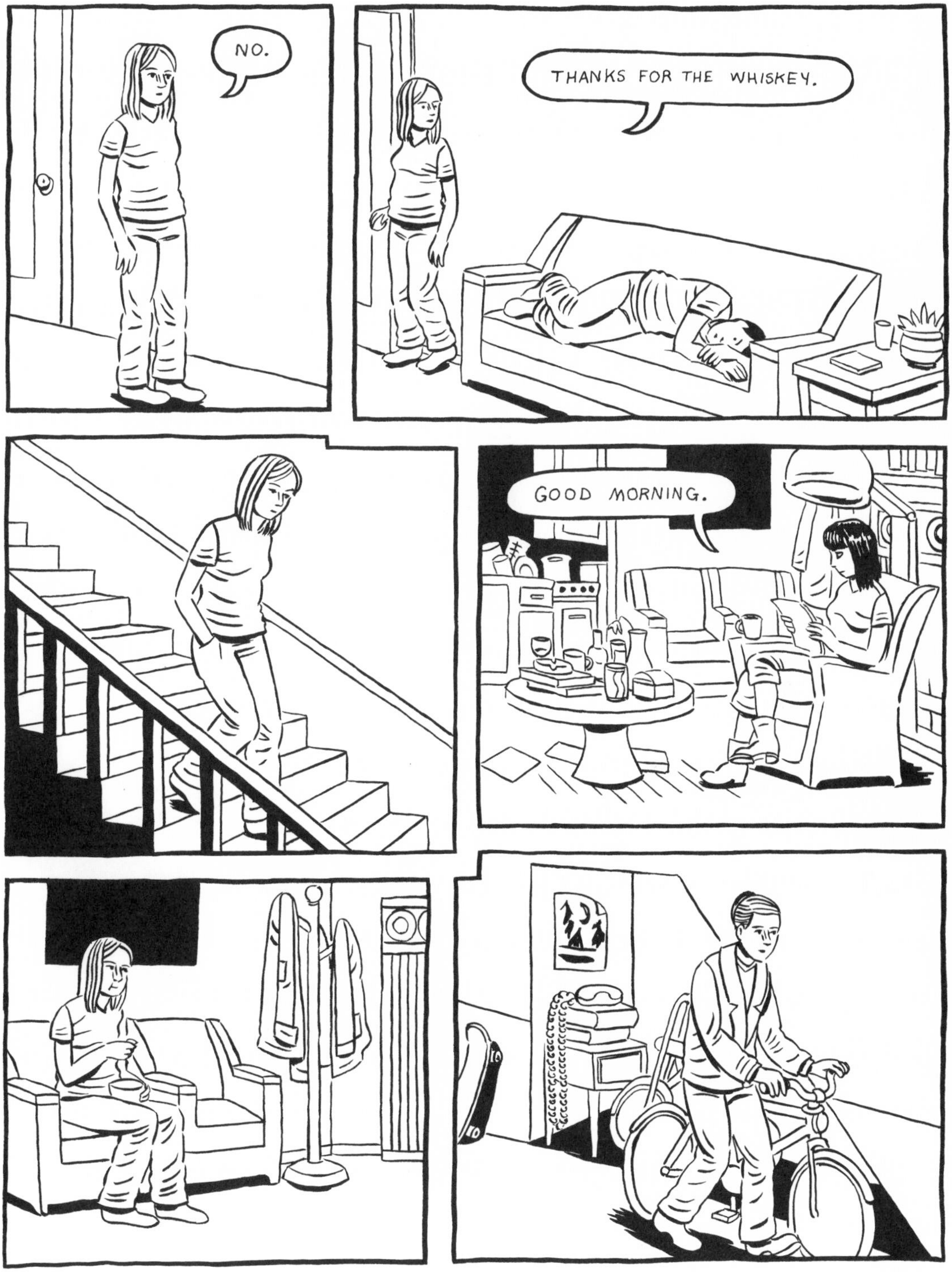
NO.
THANKS FOR THE WHISKEY.
GOOD MORNING.

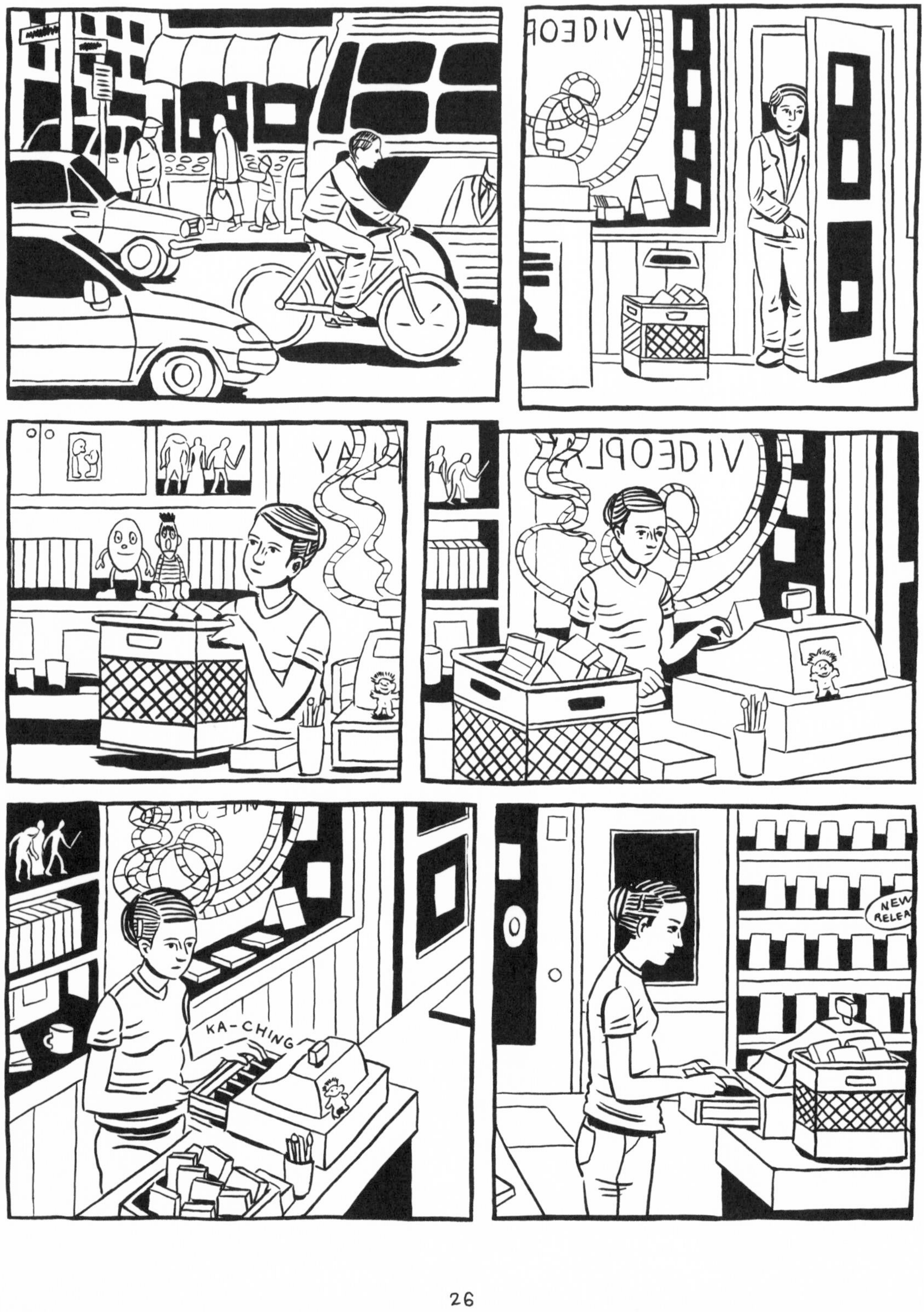
KA-CHING
NEW RELEA

Year of the Arowana

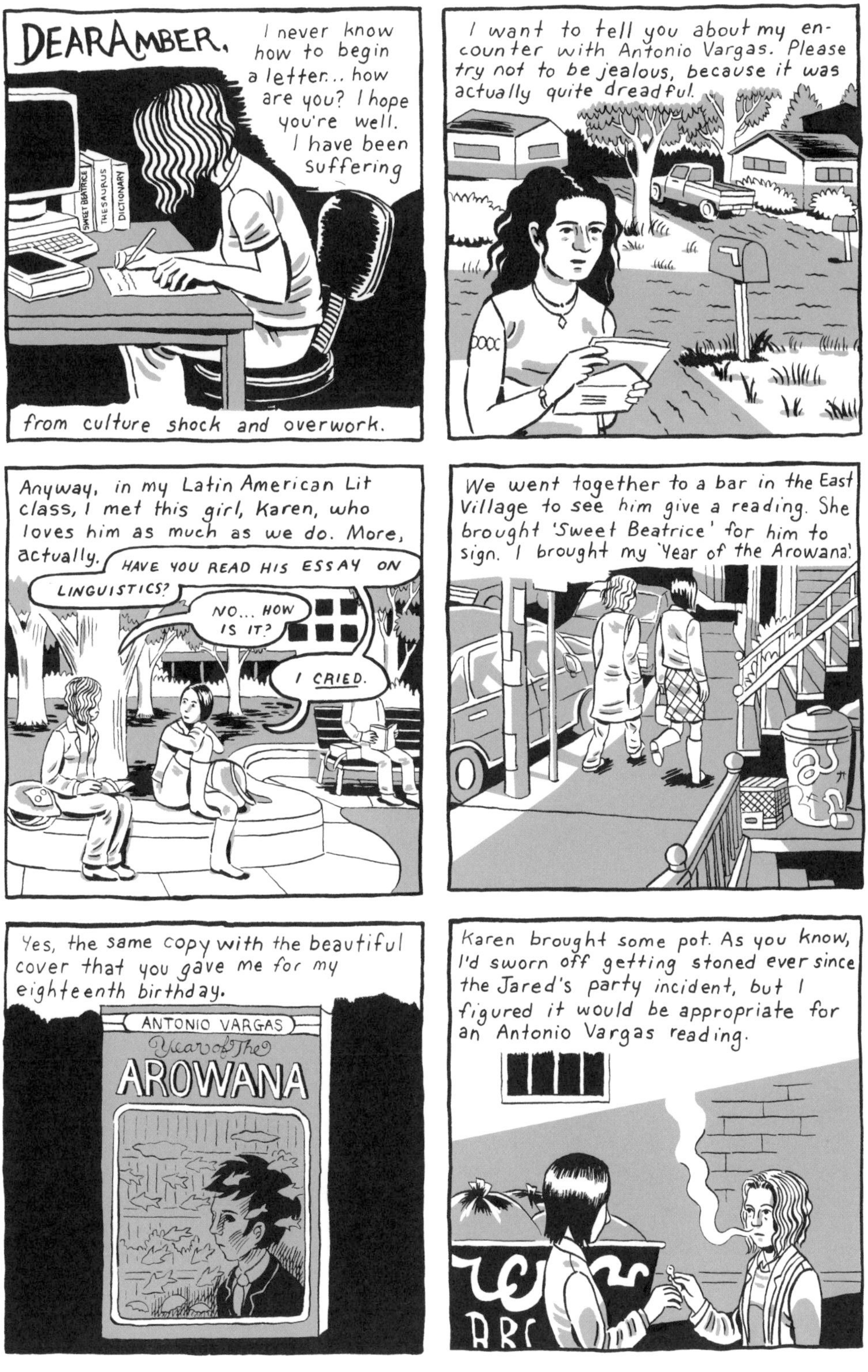
DEAR AMBER,
I never know how to begin a letter... how are you? I hope you're well. I have been suffering
SWEET BEATRICE
THESAURUS
DICTIONARY
from culture shock and overwork.
I want to tell you about my encounter with Antonio Vargas. Please try not to be jealous, because it was actually quite dreadful.
Anyway, in my Latin American Lit class, I met this girl, Karen, who loves him as much as we do. More, actually.
HAVE YOU READ HIS ESSAY ON LINGUISTICS?
NO... HOW IS IT?
I CRIED.
We went together to a bar in the East Village to see him give a reading. She brought 'Sweet Beatrice' for him to sign. I brought my 'Year of the Arowana'.
Yes, the same copy with the beautiful cover that you gave me for my eighteenth birthday.
ANTONIO VARGAS
Year of The
AROWANA
Karen brought some pot. As you know, I'd sworn off getting stoned ever since the Jared's party incident, but I figured it would be appropriate for an Antonio Vargas reading.

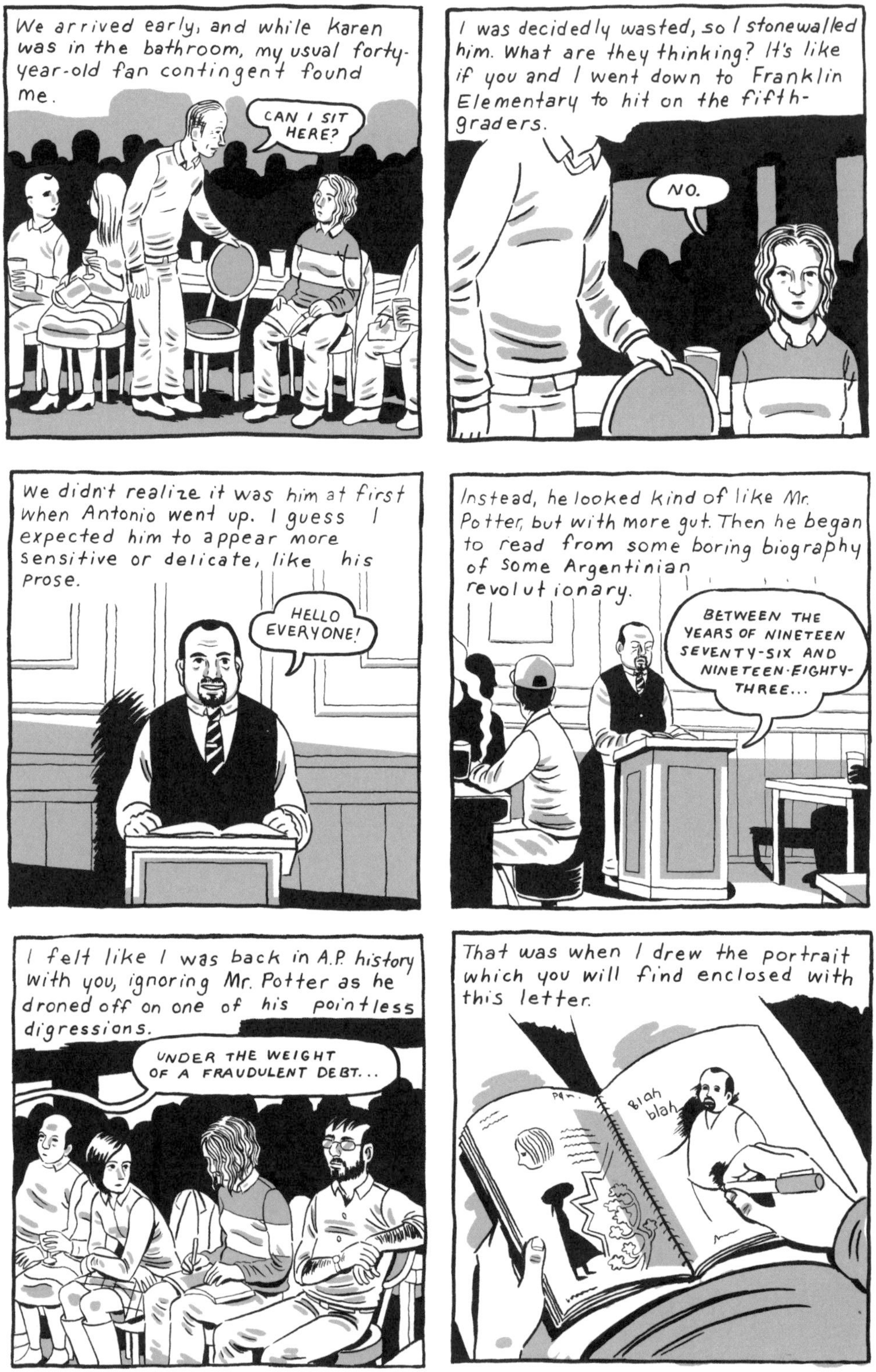
We arrived early, and while Karen was in the bathroom, my usual forty-year-old fan contingent found me.
CAN I SIT HERE?
I was decidedly wasted, so I stonewalled him. What are they thinking? It's like if you and I went down to Franklin Elementary to hit on the fifth-graders.
NO.
We didn't realize it was him at first when Antonio went up. I guess I expected him to appear more sensitive or delicate, like his prose.
HELLO EVERYONE!
Instead, he looked kind of like Mr. Potter, but with more gut. Then he began to read from some boring biography of some Argentinian revolutionary.
BETWEEN THE YEARS OF NINETEEN SEVENTY-SIX AND NINETEEN-EIGHTY-THREE...
I felt like I was back in A.P. history with you, ignoring Mr. Potter as he droned off on one of his pointless digressions.
UNDER THE WEIGHT OF A FRAUDULENT DEBT...
That was when I drew the portrait which you will find enclosed with this letter.
blah blah

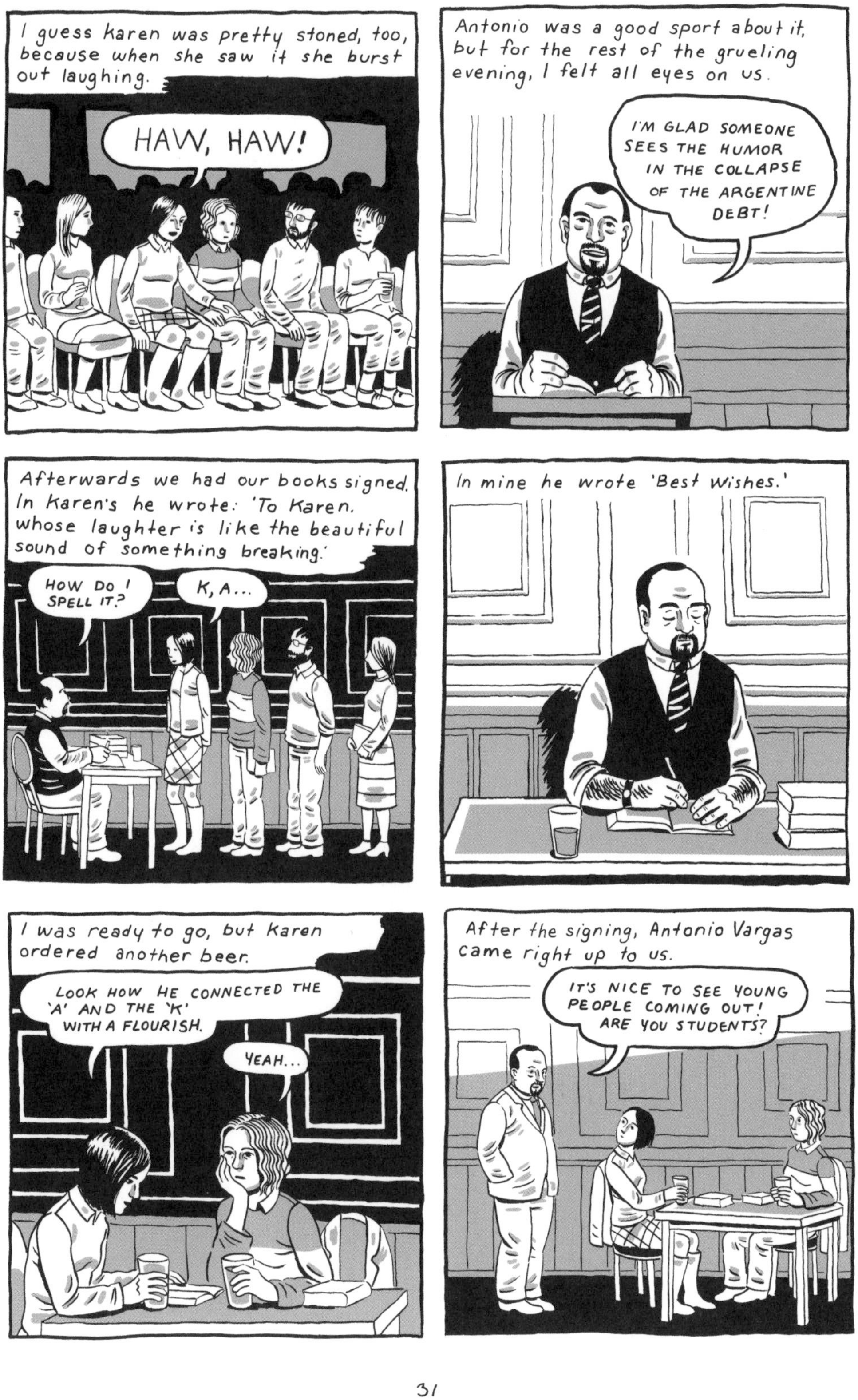
I guess Karen was pretty stoned, too, because when she saw it she burst out laughing.
HAW, HAW!
Antonio was a good sport about it, but for the rest of the grueling evening, I felt all eyes on us.
I'M GLAD SOMEONE SEES THE HUMOR IN THE COLLAPSE OF THE ARGENTINE DEBT!
Afterwards we had our books signed. In Karen's he wrote: 'To Karen, whose laughter is like the beautiful sound of something breaking.'
HOW DO I SPELL IT?
K, A...
In mine he wrote 'Best Wishes.'
I was ready to go, but Karen ordered another beer.
LOOK HOW HE CONNECTED THE 'A' AND THE 'K' WITH A FLOURISH.
YEAH...
After the signing, Antonio Vargas came right up to us.
IT'S NICE TO SEE YOUNG PEOPLE COMING OUT! ARE YOU STUDENTS?

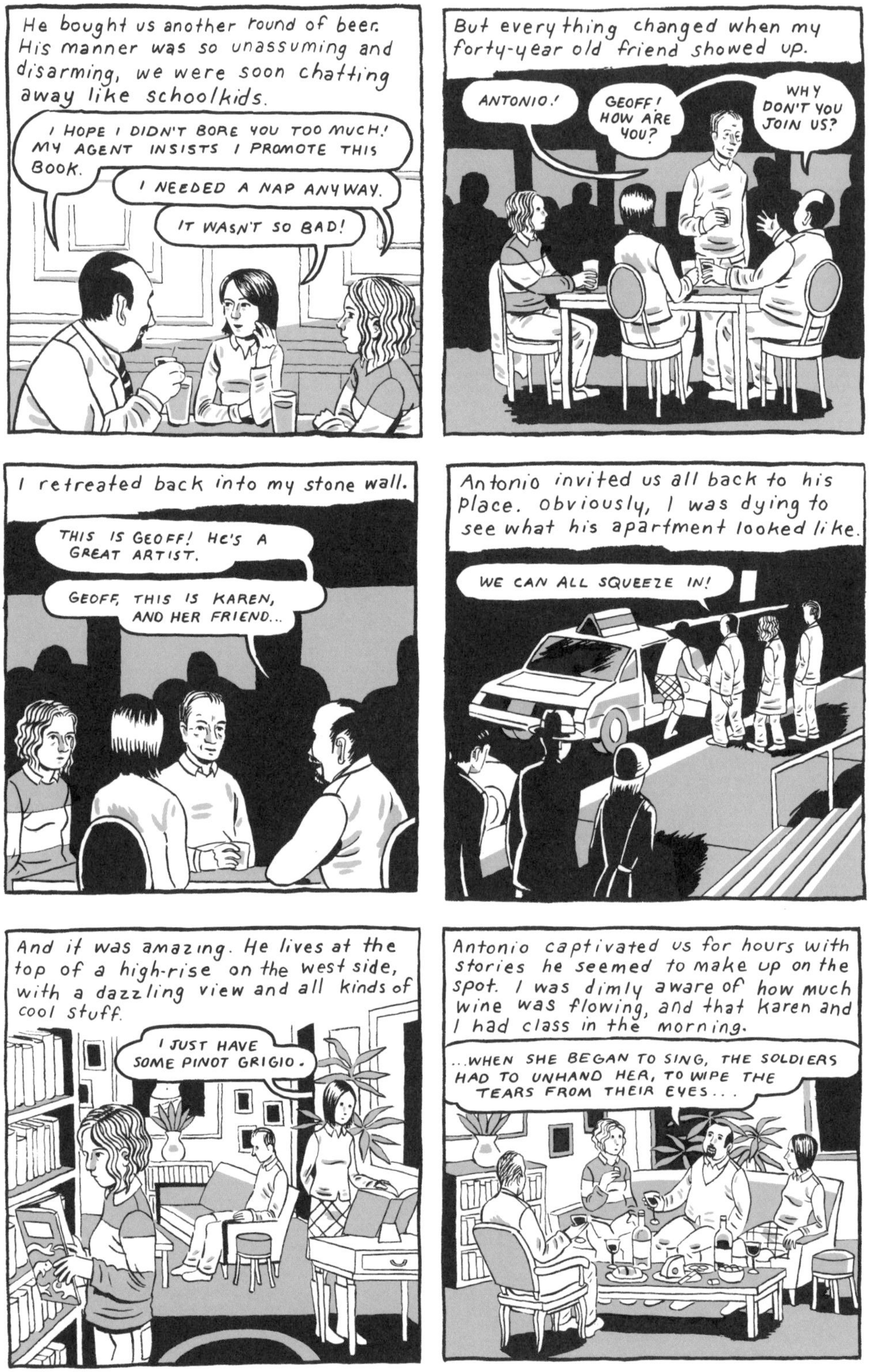
He bought us another round of beer. His manner was so unassuming and disarming, we were soon chatting away like schoolkids.
I HOPE I DIDN'T BORE YOU TOO MUCH! MY AGENT INSISTS I PROMOTE THIS BOOK.
I NEEDED A NAP ANYWAY.
IT WASN'T SO BAD!
But everything changed when my forty-year old friend showed up.
ANTONIO!
GEOFF! HOW ARE YOU?
WHY DON'T YOU JOIN US?
I retreated back into my stone wall.
THIS IS GEOFF! HE'S A GREAT ARTIST.
GEOFF, THIS IS KAREN, AND HER FRIEND...
Antonio invited us all back to his place. Obviously, I was dying to see what his apartment looked like.
WE CAN ALL SQUEEZE IN!
And it was amazing. He lives at the top of a high-rise on the west side, with a dazzling view and all kinds of cool stuff.
I JUST HAVE SOME PINOT GRIGIO.
Antonio captivated us for hours with stories he seemed to make up on the spot. I was dimly aware of how much wine was flowing, and that Karen and I had class in the morning.
...WHEN SHE BEGAN TO SING, THE SOLDIERS HAD TO UNHAND HER, TO WIPE THE TEARS FROM THEIR EYES...

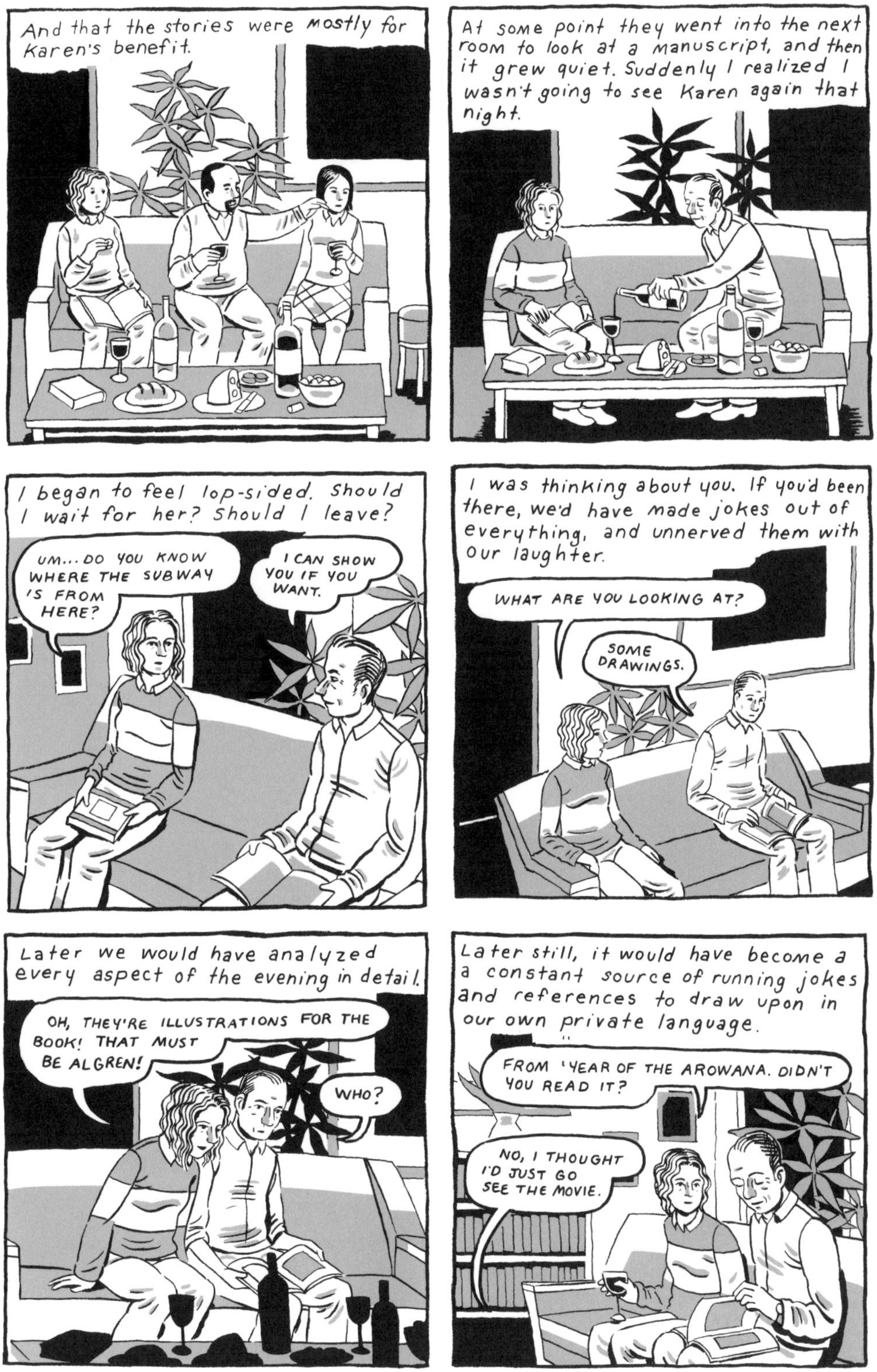
And that the stories were mostly for Karen's benefit.
At some point they went into the next room to look at a manuscript, and then it grew quiet. Suddenly I realized I wasn't going to see Karen again that night.
I began to feel lop-sided. Should I wait for her? Should I leave?
UM... DO YOU KNOW WHERE THE SUBWAY IS FROM HERE?
I CAN SHOW YOU IF YOU WANT.
I was thinking about you. If you'd been there, we'd have made jokes out of everything, and unnerved them with our laughter.
WHAT ARE YOU LOOKING AT?
SOME DRAWINGS.
Later we would have analyzed every aspect of the evening in detail.
OH, THEY'RE ILLUSTRATIONS FOR THE BOOK! THAT MUST BE ALGREN!
WHO?
Later still, it would have become a a constant source of running jokes and references to draw upon in our own private language.
FROM 'YEAR OF THE AROWANA. DIDN'T YOU READ IT?
NO, I THOUGHT I'D JUST GO SEE THE MOVIE.

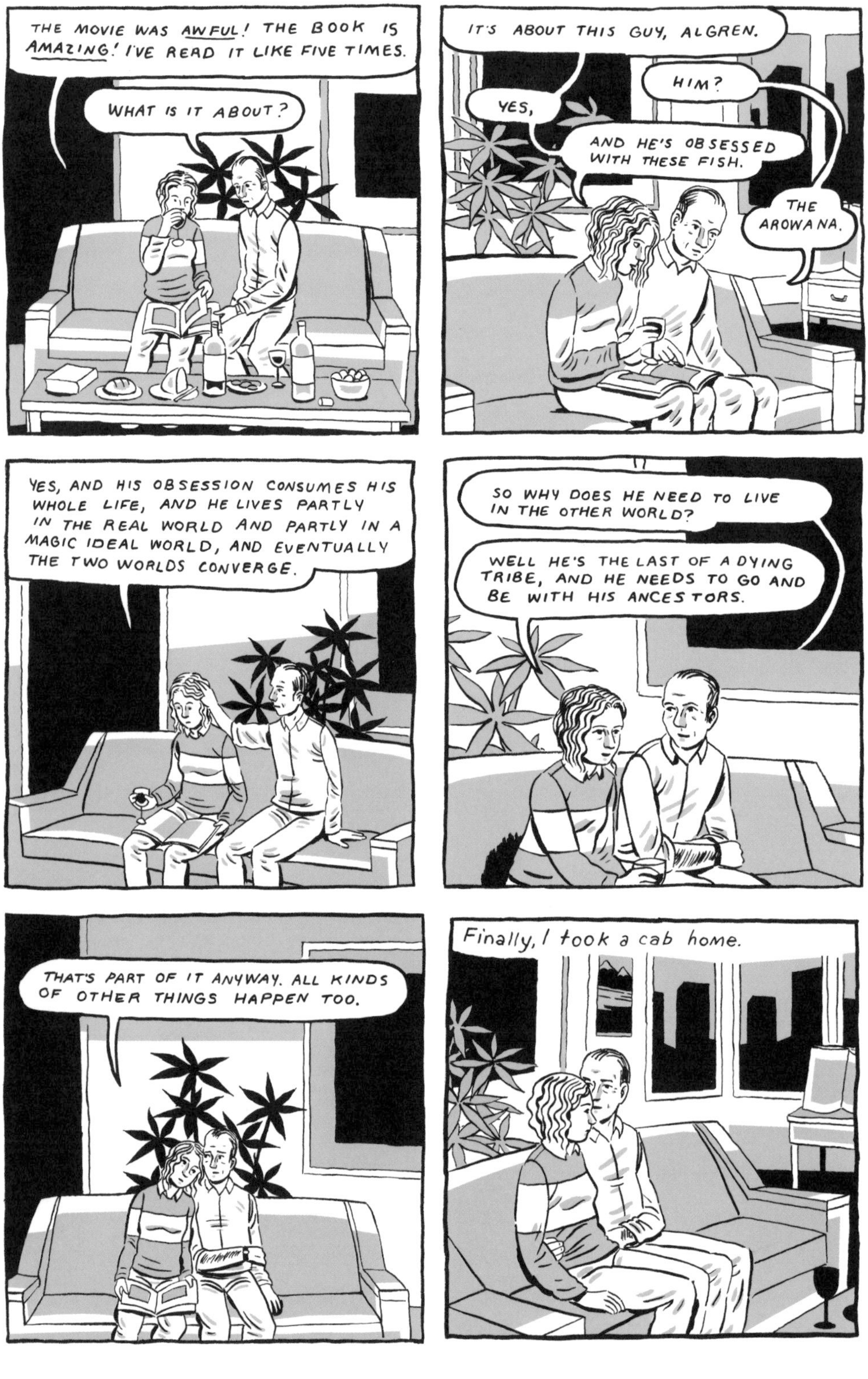
THE MOVIE WAS AWFUL! THE BOOK IS AMAZING! I'VE READ IT LIKE FIVE TIMES.
WHAT IS IT ABOUT?
IT'S ABOUT THIS GUY, ALGREN.
HIM?
YES,
AND HE'S OBSESSED WITH THESE FISH.
THE AROWANA.
YES, AND HIS OBSESSION CONSUMES HIS WHOLE LIFE, AND HE LIVES PARTLY IN THE REAL WORLD AND PARTLY IN A MAGIC IDEAL WORLD, AND EVENTUALLY THE TWO WORLDS CONVERGE.
SO WHY DOES HE NEED TO LIVE IN THE OTHER WORLD?
WELL HE'S THE LAST OF A DYING TRIBE, AND HE NEEDS TO GO AND BE WITH HIS ANCESTORS.
THAT'S PART OF IT ANYWAY. ALL KINDS OF OTHER THINGS HAPPEN TOO.
Finally, I took a cab home.

One Afternoon

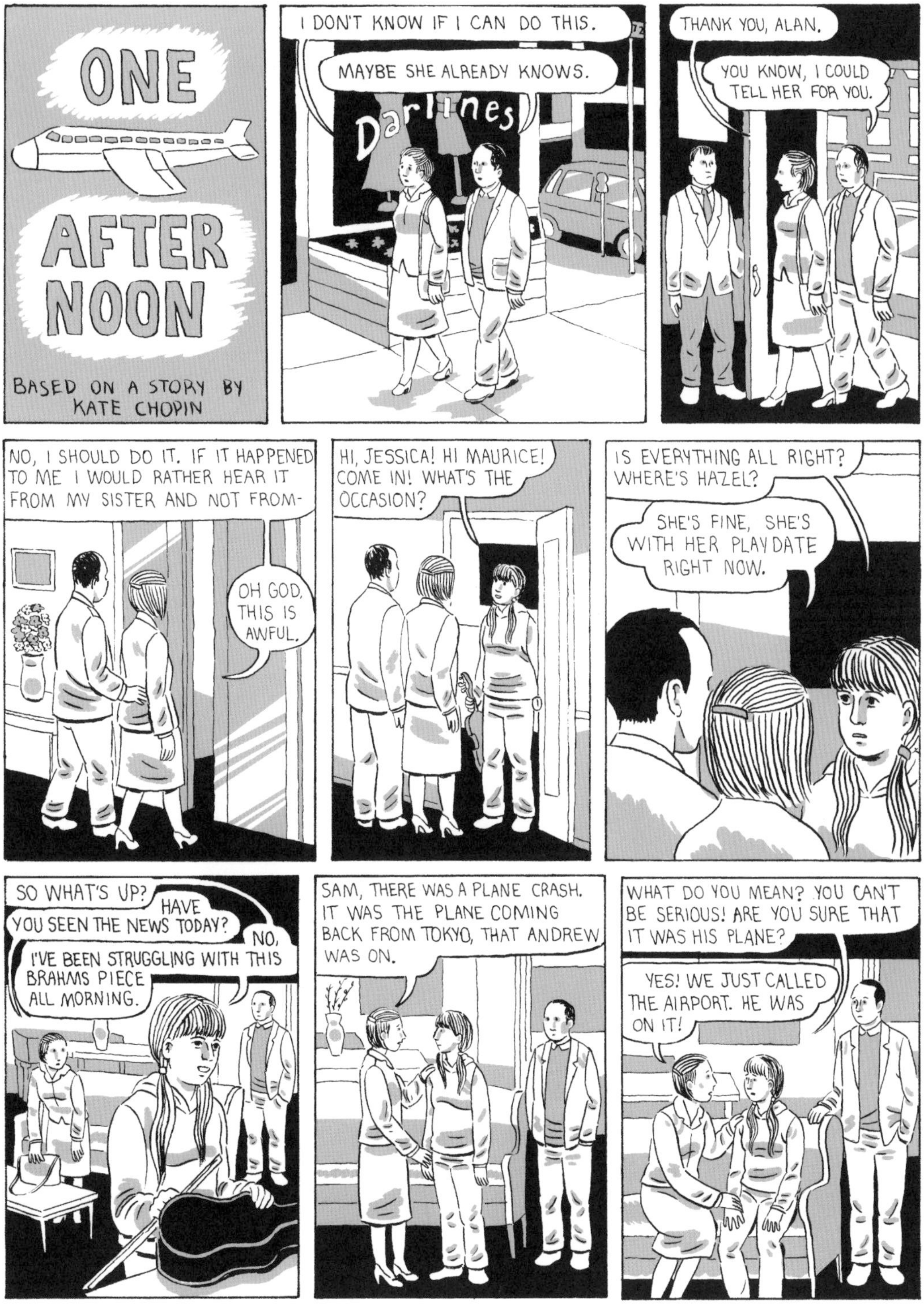
ONE
AFTER NOON
BASED ON A STORY BY KATE CHOPIN
I DON'T KNOW IF I CAN DO THIS.
MAYBE SHE ALREADY KNOWS.
Darlines
THANK YOU, ALAN.
YOU KNOW, I COULD TELL HER FOR YOU.
NO, I SHOULD DO IT. IF IT HAPPENED TO ME I WOULD RATHER HEAR IT FROM MY SISTER AND NOT FROM-
OH GOD, THIS IS AWFUL.
HI, JESSICA! HI MAURICE! COME IN! WHAT'S THE OCCASION?
IS EVERYTHING ALL RIGHT? WHERE'S HAZEL?
SHE'S FINE, SHE'S WITH HER PLAYDATE RIGHT NOW.
SO WHAT'S UP?
HAVE YOU SEEN THE NEWS TODAY?
NO, I'VE BEEN STRUGGLING WITH THIS BRAHMS PIECE ALL MORNING.
SAM, THERE WAS A PLANE CRASH. IT WAS THE PLANE COMING BACK FROM TOKYO, THAT ANDREW WAS ON.
WHAT DO YOU MEAN? YOU CAN'T BE SERIOUS! ARE YOU SURE THAT IT WAS HIS PLANE?
YES! WE JUST CALLED THE AIRPORT. HE WAS ON IT!

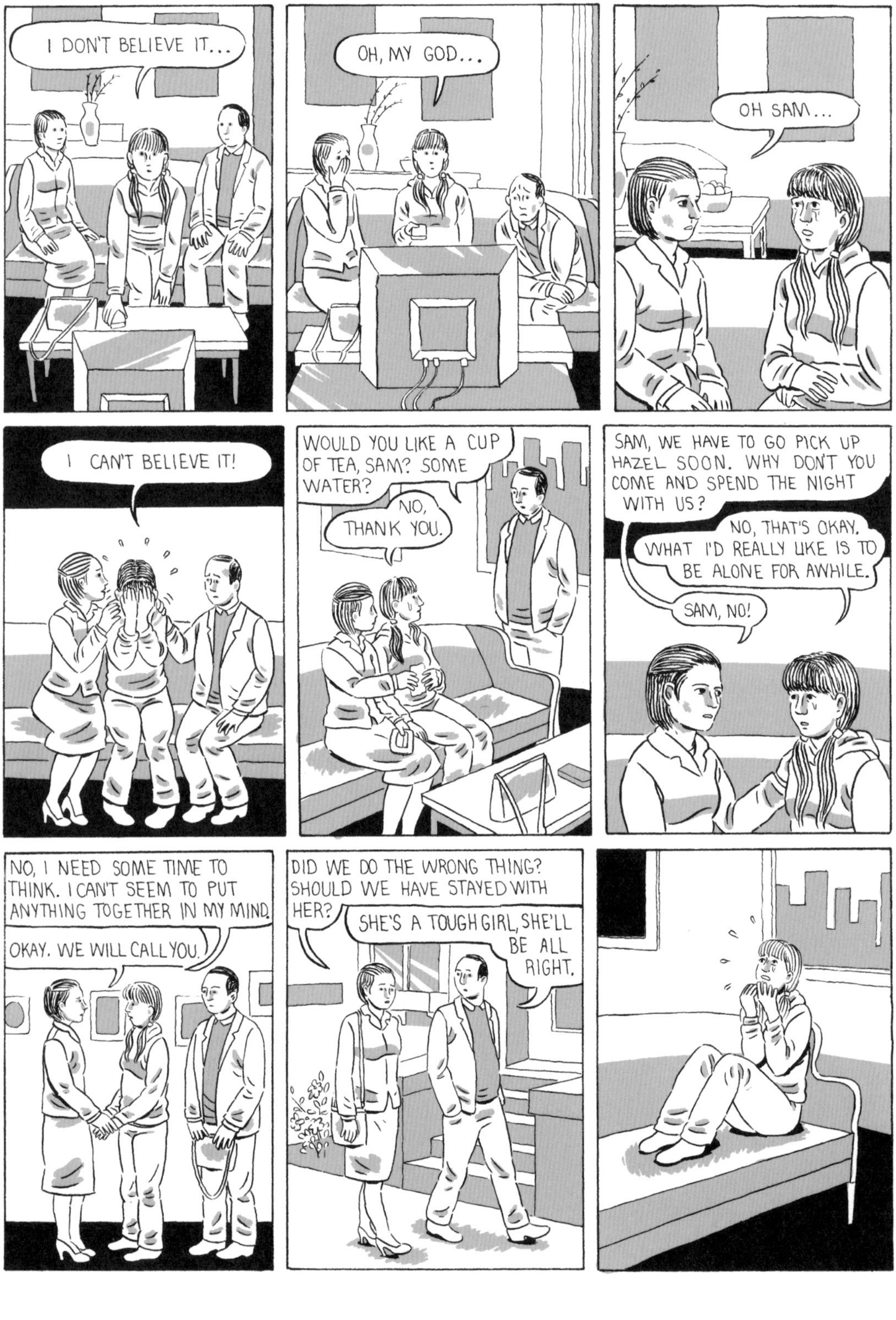
I DON'T BELIEVE IT...
OH, MY GOD...
OH SAM...
I CAN'T BELIEVE IT!
WOULD YOU LIKE A CUP OF TEA, SAM? SOME WATER?
NO, THANK YOU.
SAM, WE HAVE TO GO PICK UP HAZEL SOON. WHY DON'T YOU COME AND SPEND THE NIGHT WITH US?
NO, THAT'S OKAY. WHAT I'D REALLY LIKE IS TO BE ALONE FOR AWHILE.
SAM, NO!
NO, I NEED SOME TIME TO THINK. I CAN'T SEEM TO PUT ANYTHING TOGETHER IN MY MIND.
OKAY. WE WILL CALL YOU.
DID WE DO THE WRONG THING? SHOULD WE HAVE STAYED WITH HER?
SHE'S A TOUGH GIRL, SHE'LL BE ALL RIGHT.

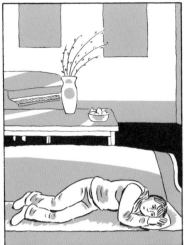

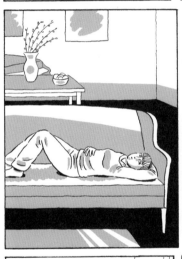

I'M FREE.

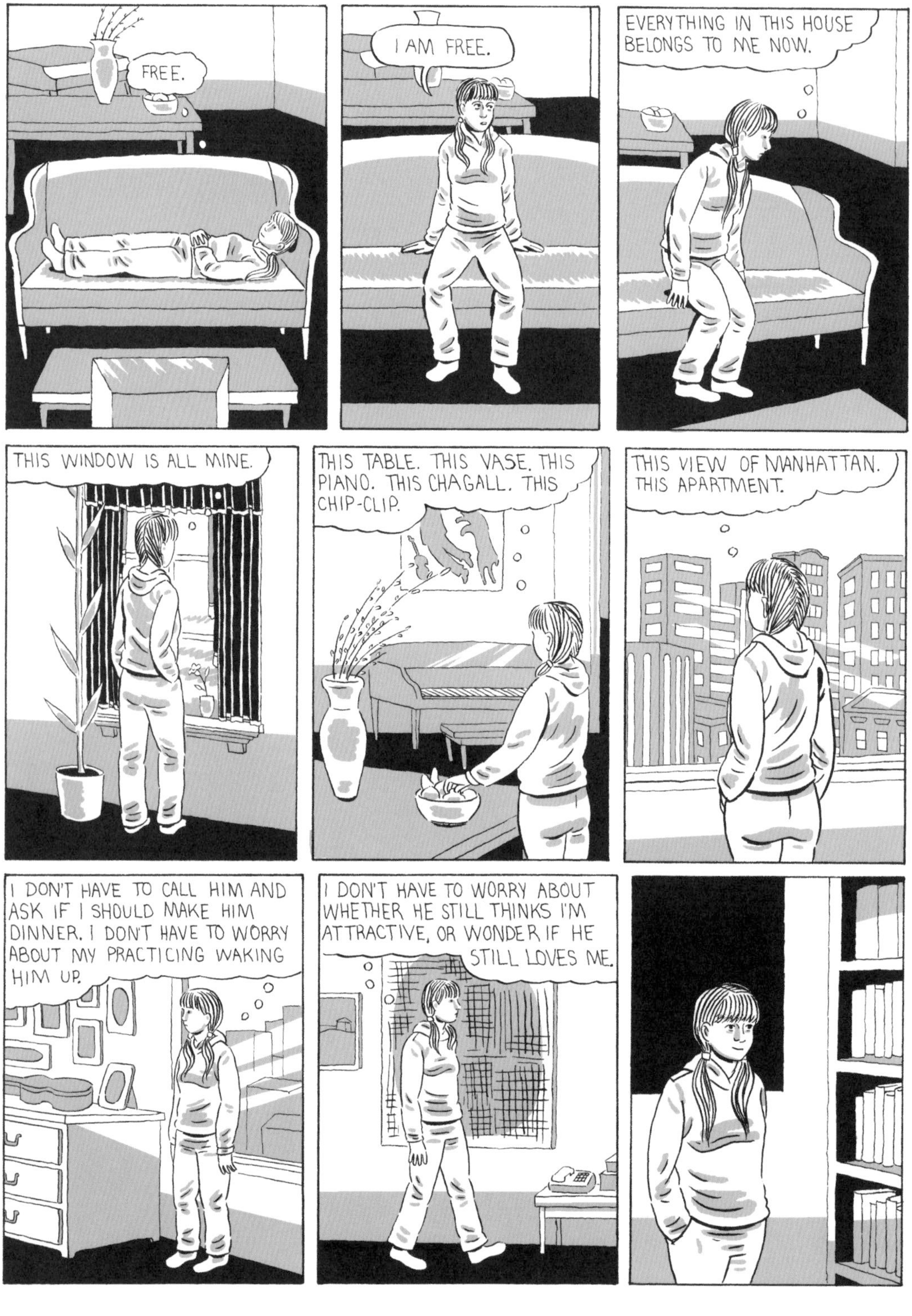
FREE.
I AM FREE.
EVERYTHING IN THIS HOUSE BELONGS TO ME NOW.
THIS WINDOW IS ALL MINE.
THIS TABLE. THIS VASE. THIS PIANO. THIS CHAGALL. THIS CHIP-CLIP.
THIS VIEW OF MANHATTAN. THIS APARTMENT.
I DON'T HAVE TO CALL HIM AND ASK IF I SHOULD MAKE HIM DINNER. I DON'T HAVE TO WORRY ABOUT MY PRACTICING WAKING HIM UP.
I DON'T HAVE TO WORRY ABOUT WHETHER HE STILL THINKS I'M ATTRACTIVE, OR WONDER IF HE STILL LOVES ME.

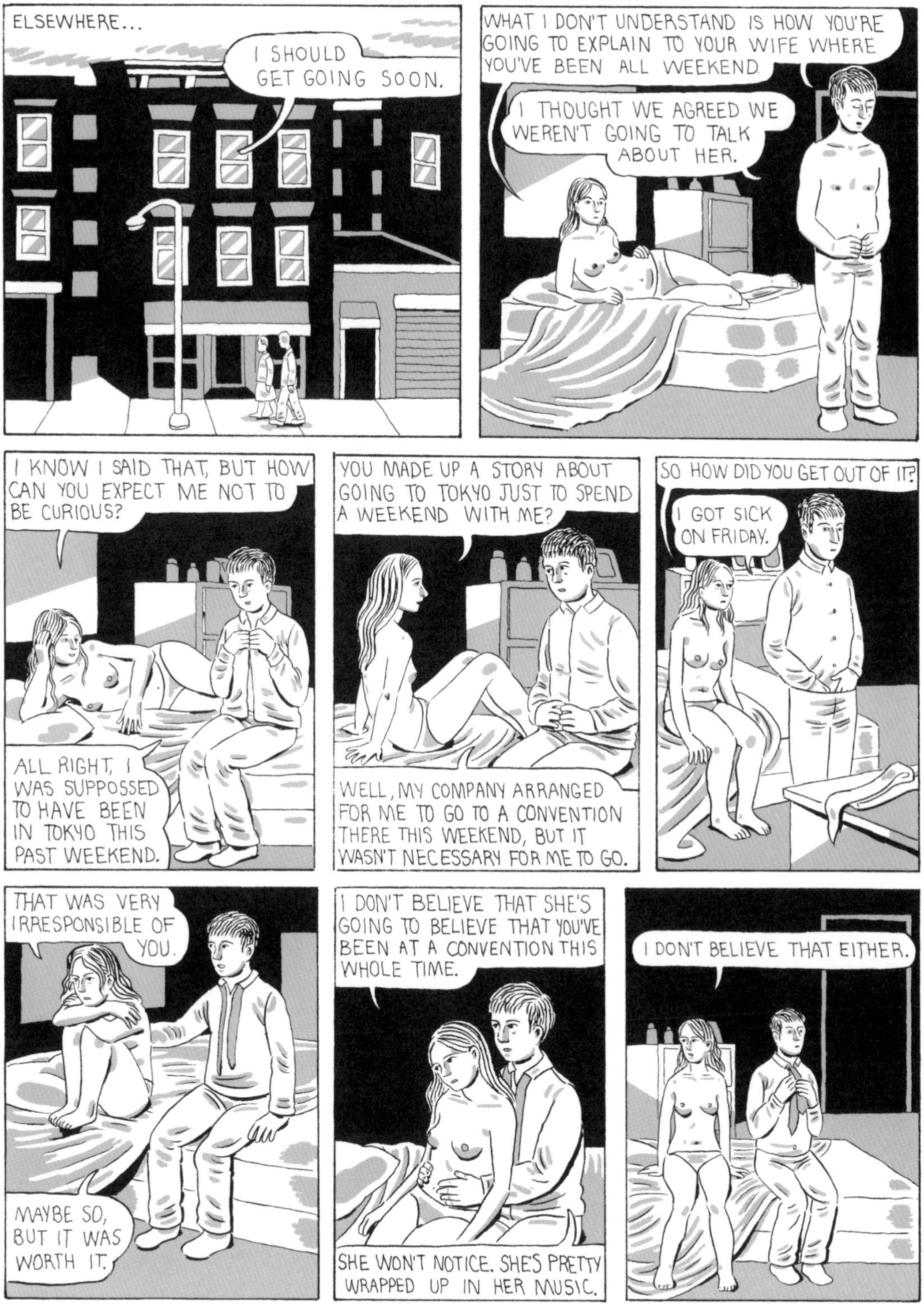
ELSEWHERE...
I SHOULD GET GOING SOON.
WHAT I DON'T UNDERSTAND IS HOW YOU'RE GOING TO EXPLAIN TO YOUR WIFE WHERE YOU'VE BEEN ALL WEEKEND.
I THOUGHT WE AGREED WE WEREN'T GOING TO TALK ABOUT HER.
I KNOW I SAID THAT, BUT HOW CAN YOU EXPECT ME NOT TO BE CURIOUS?
ALL RIGHT, I WAS SUPPOSSED TO HAVE BEEN IN TOKYO THIS PAST WEEKEND.
YOU MADE UP A STORY ABOUT GOING TO TOKYO JUST TO SPEND A WEEKEND WITH ME?
WELL, MY COMPANY ARRANGED FOR ME TO GO TO A CONVENTION THERE THIS WEEKEND, BUT IT WASN'T NECESSARY FOR ME TO GO.
SO HOW DID YOU GET OUT OF IT?
I GOT SICK ON FRIDAY.
THAT WAS VERY IRRESPONSIBLE OF YOU.
MAYBE SO, BUT IT WAS WORTH IT.
I DON'T BELIEVE THAT SHE'S GOING TO BELIEVE THAT YOU'VE BEEN AT A CONVENTION THIS WHOLE TIME.
SHE WON'T NOTICE. SHE'S PRETTY WRAPPED UP IN HER MUSIC.
I DON'T BELIEVE THAT EITHER.

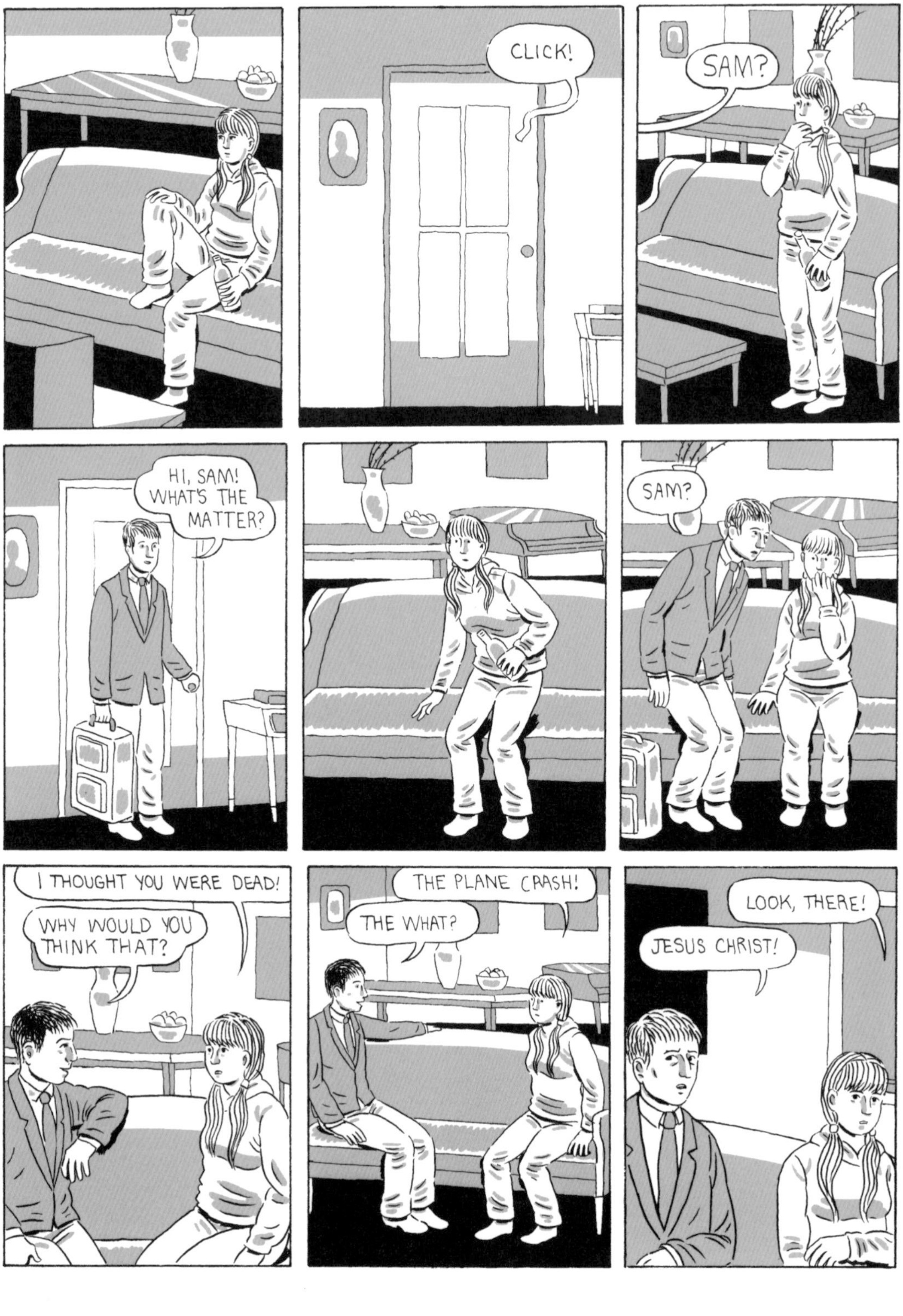
CLICK!
SAM?
HI, SAM! WHAT'S THE MATTER?
SAM?
I THOUGHT YOU WERE DEAD!
WHY WOULD YOU THINK THAT?
THE PLANE CRASH!
THE WHAT?
LOOK, THERE!
JESUS CHRIST!

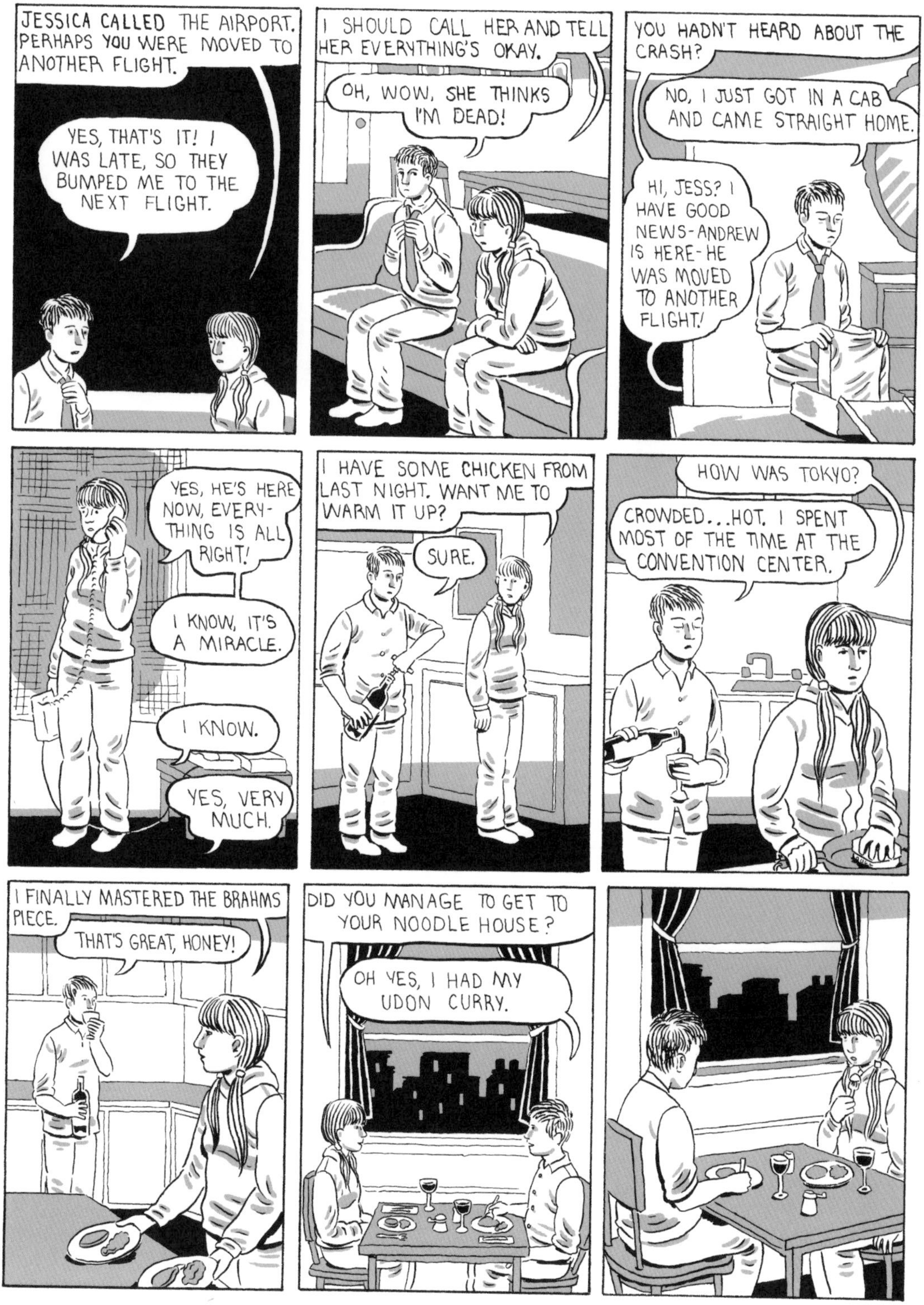

JESSICA CALLED THE AIRPORT. PERHAPS YOU WERE MOVED TO ANOTHER FLIGHT.
YES, THAT'S IT! I WAS LATE, SO THEY BUMPED ME TO THE NEXT FLIGHT.
I SHOULD CALL HER AND TELL HER EVERYTHING'S OKAY.
OH, WOW, SHE THINKS I'M DEAD!
YOU HADN'T HEARD ABOUT THE CRASH?
NO, I JUST GOT IN A CAB AND CAME STRAIGHT HOME.
HI, JESS? I HAVE GOOD NEWS-ANDREW IS HERE-HE WAS MOVED TO ANOTHER FLIGHT!
YES, HE'S HERE NOW, EVERY-THING IS ALL RIGHT!
I KNOW, IT'S A MIRACLE.
I KNOW.
YES, VERY MUCH.
I HAVE SOME CHICKEN FROM LAST NIGHT. WANT ME TO WARM IT UP?
SURE.
HOW WAS TOKYO?
CROWDED...HOT. I SPENT MOST OF THE TIME AT THE CONVENTION CENTER.
I FINALLY MASTERED THE BRAHMS PIECE.
THAT'S GREAT, HONEY!
DID YOU MANAGE TO GET TO YOUR NOODLE HOUSE?
OH YES, I HAD MY UDON CURRY.

Felix

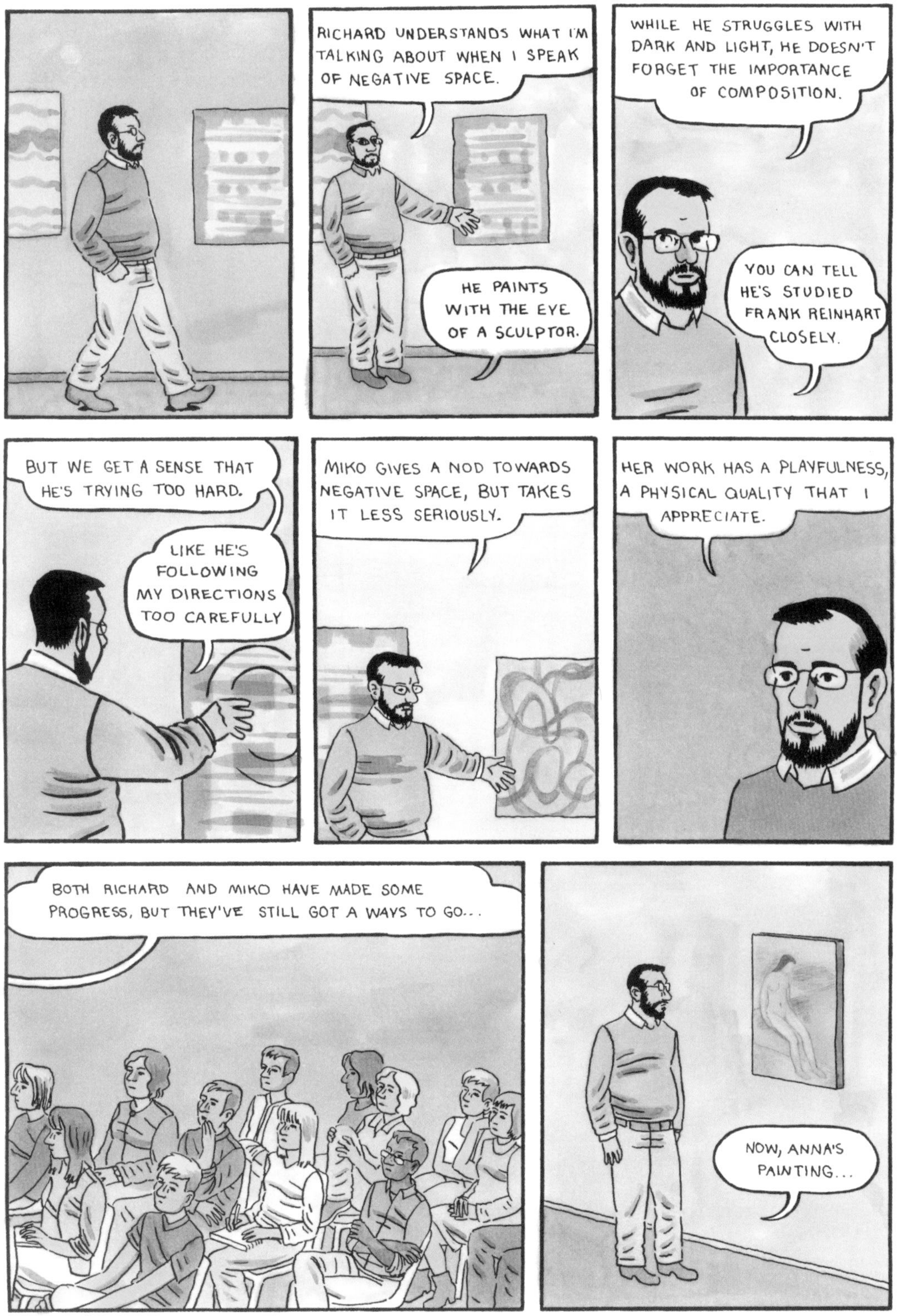
RICHARD UNDERSTANDS WHAT I'M TALKING ABOUT WHEN I SPEAK OF NEGATIVE SPACE.
HE PAINTS WITH THE EYE OF A SCULPTOR.
WHILE HE STRUGGLES WITH DARK AND LIGHT, HE DOESN'T FORGET THE IMPORTANCE OF COMPOSITION.
YOU CAN TELL HE'S STUDIED FRANK REINHART CLOSELY.
BUT WE GET A SENSE THAT HE'S TRYING TOO HARD.
LIKE HE'S FOLLOWING MY DIRECTIONS TOO CAREFULLY
MIKO GIVES A NOD TOWARDS NEGATIVE SPACE, BUT TAKES IT LESS SERIOUSLY.
HER WORK HAS A PLAYFULNESS, A PHYSICAL QUALITY THAT I APPRECIATE.
BOTH RICHARD AND MIKO HAVE MADE SOME PROGRESS, BUT THEY'VE STILL GOT A WAYS TO GO...
NOW, ANNA'S PAINTING...

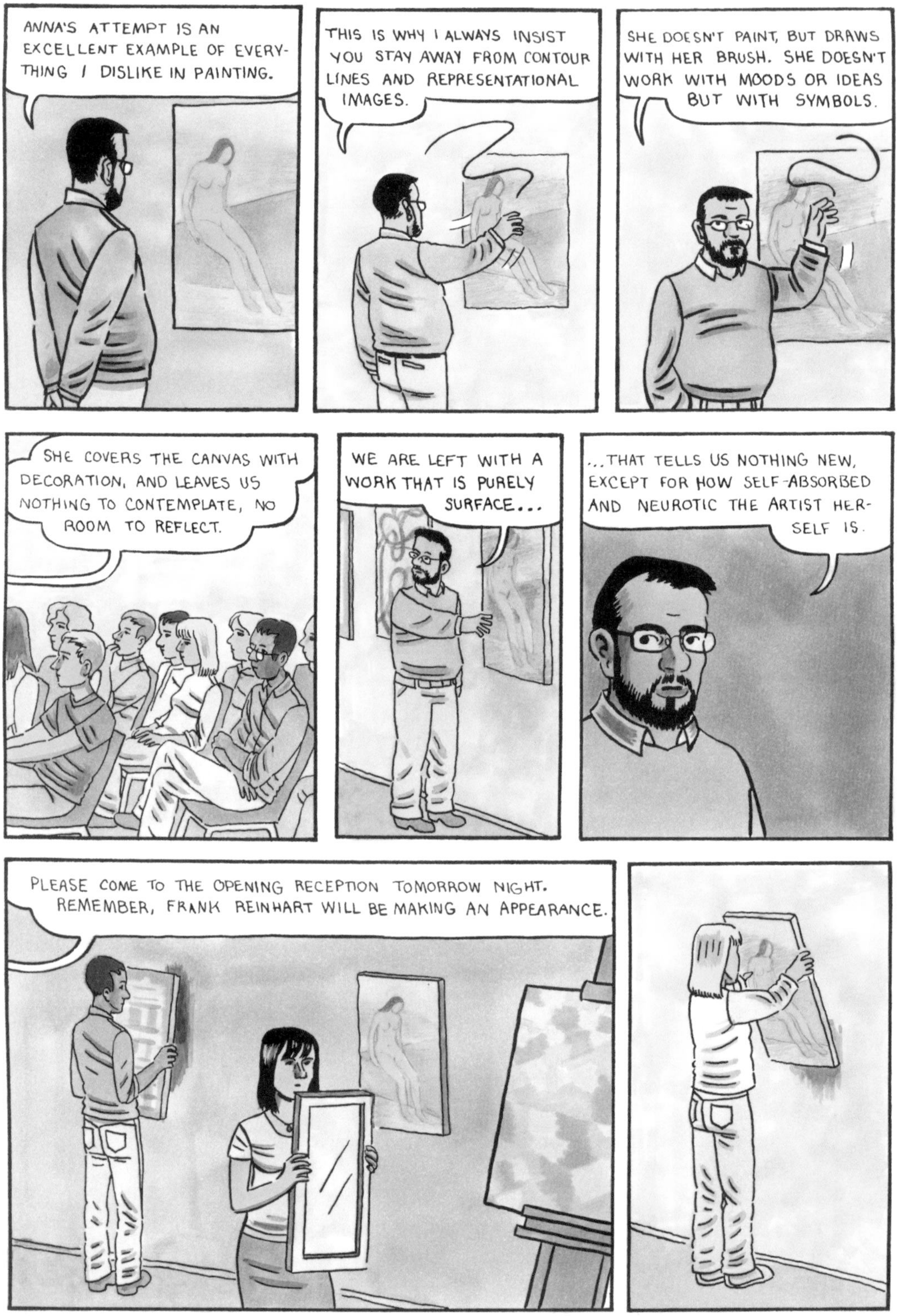
ANNA'S ATTEMPT IS AN EXCELLENT EXAMPLE OF EVERYTHING I DISLIKE IN PAINTING.
THIS IS WHY I ALWAYS INSIST YOU STAY AWAY FROM CONTOUR LINES AND REPRESENTATIONAL IMAGES.
SHE DOESN'T PAINT, BUT DRAWS WITH HER BRUSH. SHE DOESN'T WORK WITH MOODS OR IDEAS BUT WITH SYMBOLS.
SHE COVERS THE CANVAS WITH DECORATION, AND LEAVES US NOTHING TO CONTEMPLATE, NO ROOM TO REFLECT.
WE ARE LEFT WITH A WORK THAT IS PURELY SURFACE...
...THAT TELLS US NOTHING NEW, EXCEPT FOR HOW SELF-ABSORBED AND NEUROTIC THE ARTIST HERSELF IS.
PLEASE COME TO THE OPENING RECEPTION TOMORROW NIGHT. REMEMBER, FRANK REINHART WILL BE MAKING AN APPEARANCE.

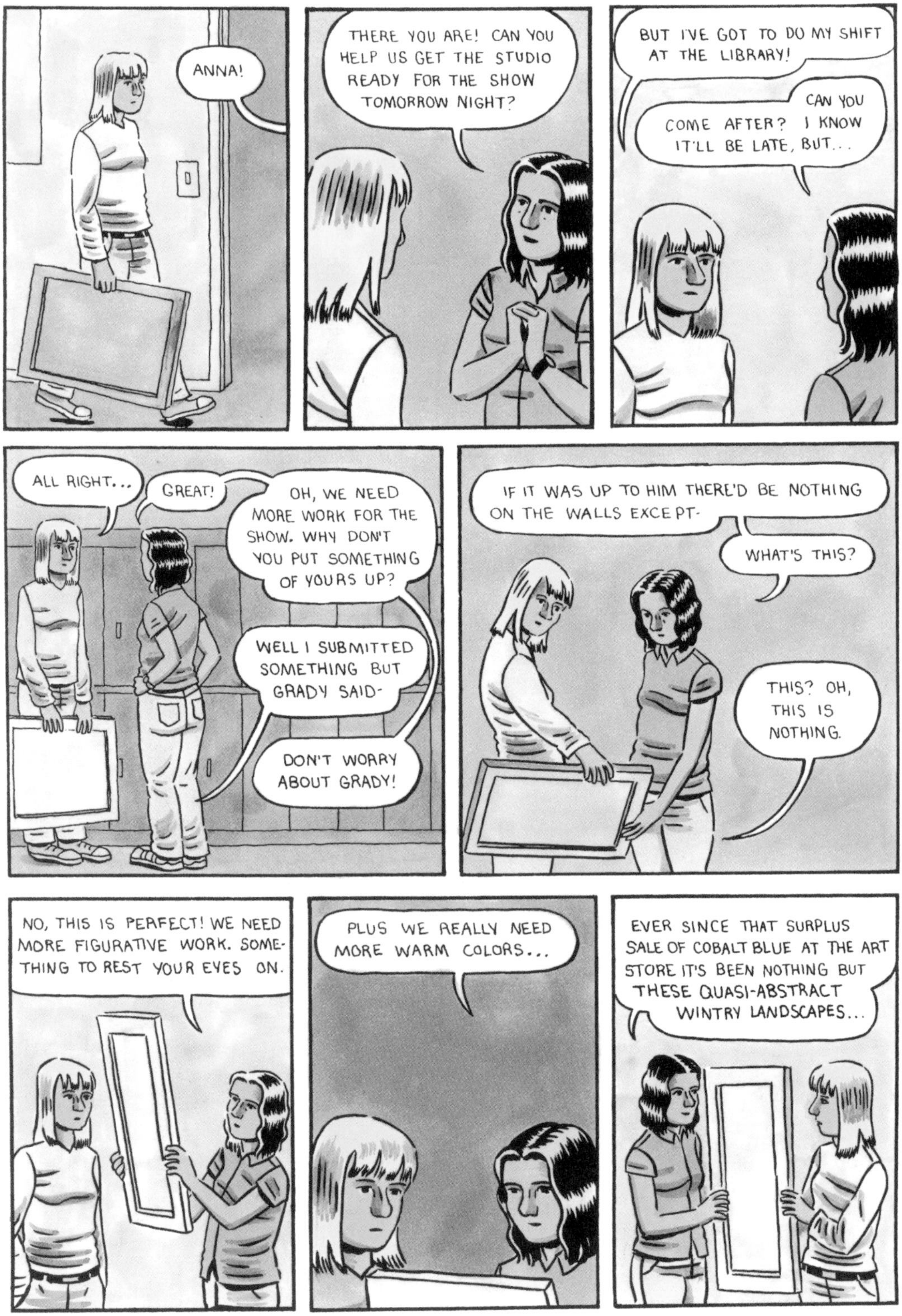
ANNA!
THERE YOU ARE! CAN YOU HELP US GET THE STUDIO READY FOR THE SHOW TOMORROW NIGHT?
BUT I'VE GOT TO DO MY SHIFT AT THE LIBRARY!
CAN YOU COME AFTER? I KNOW IT'LL BE LATE, BUT...
ALL RIGHT...
GREAT!
OH, WE NEED MORE WORK FOR THE SHOW. WHY DON'T YOU PUT SOMETHING OF YOURS UP?
WELL I SUBMITTED SOMETHING BUT GRADY SAID-
DON'T WORRY ABOUT GRADY!
IF IT WAS UP TO HIM THERE'D BE NOTHING ON THE WALLS EXCEPT-
WHAT'S THIS?
THIS? OH, THIS IS NOTHING.
NO, THIS IS PERFECT! WE NEED MORE FIGURATIVE WORK. SOMETHING TO REST YOUR EYES ON.
PLUS WE REALLY NEED MORE WARM COLORS...
EVER SINCE THAT SURPLUS SALE OF COBALT BLUE AT THE ART STORE IT'S BEEN NOTHING BUT THESE QUASI-ABSTRACT WINTRY LANDSCAPES...

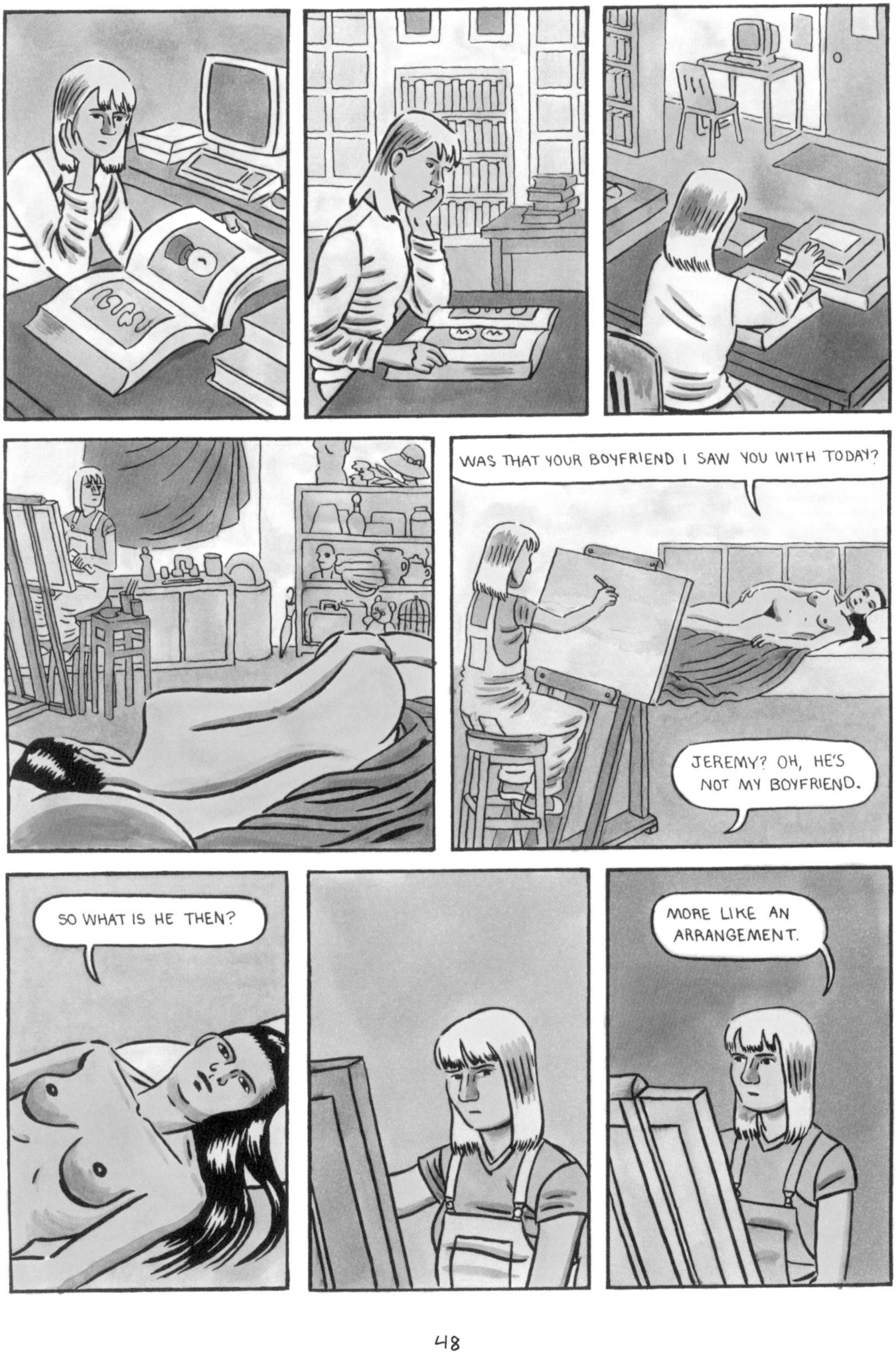

WAS THAT YOUR BOYFRIEND I SAW YOU WITH TODAY?
JEREMY? OH, HE'S NOT MY BOYFRIEND.
SO WHAT IS HE THEN?
MORE LIKE AN ARRANGEMENT.

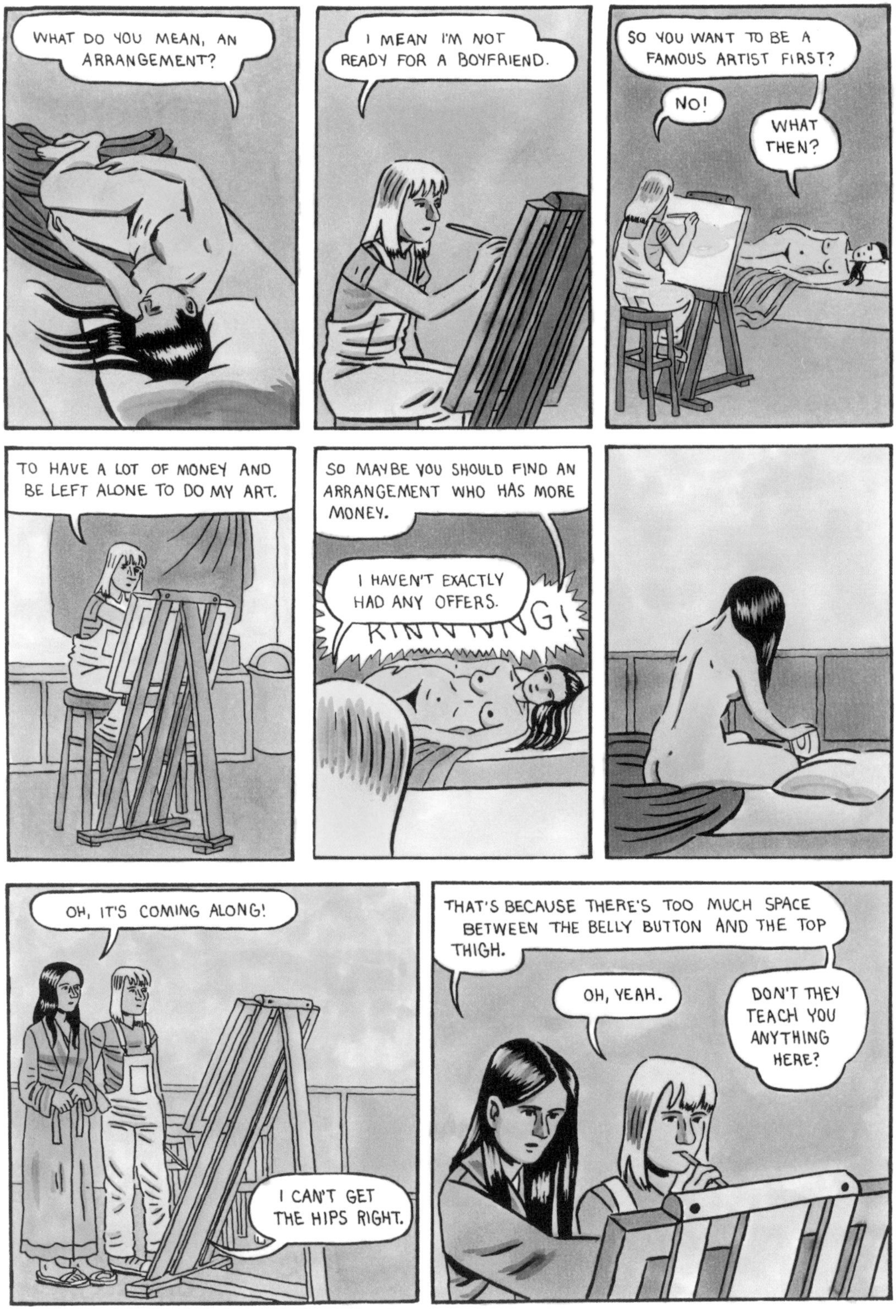
WHAT DO YOU MEAN, AN ARRANGEMENT?
I MEAN I'M NOT READY FOR A BOYFRIEND.
SO YOU WANT TO BE A FAMOUS ARTIST FIRST?
NO!
WHAT THEN?
TO HAVE A LOT OF MONEY AND BE LEFT ALONE TO DO MY ART.
SO MAYBE YOU SHOULD FIND AN ARRANGEMENT WHO HAS MORE MONEY.
I HAVEN'T EXACTLY HAD ANY OFFERS.
RINNNNNG!
OH, IT'S COMING ALONG!
I CAN'T GET THE HIPS RIGHT.
THAT'S BECAUSE THERE'S TOO MUCH SPACE BETWEEN THE BELLY BUTTON AND THE TOP THIGH.
OH, YEAH.
DON'T THEY TEACH YOU ANYTHING HERE?

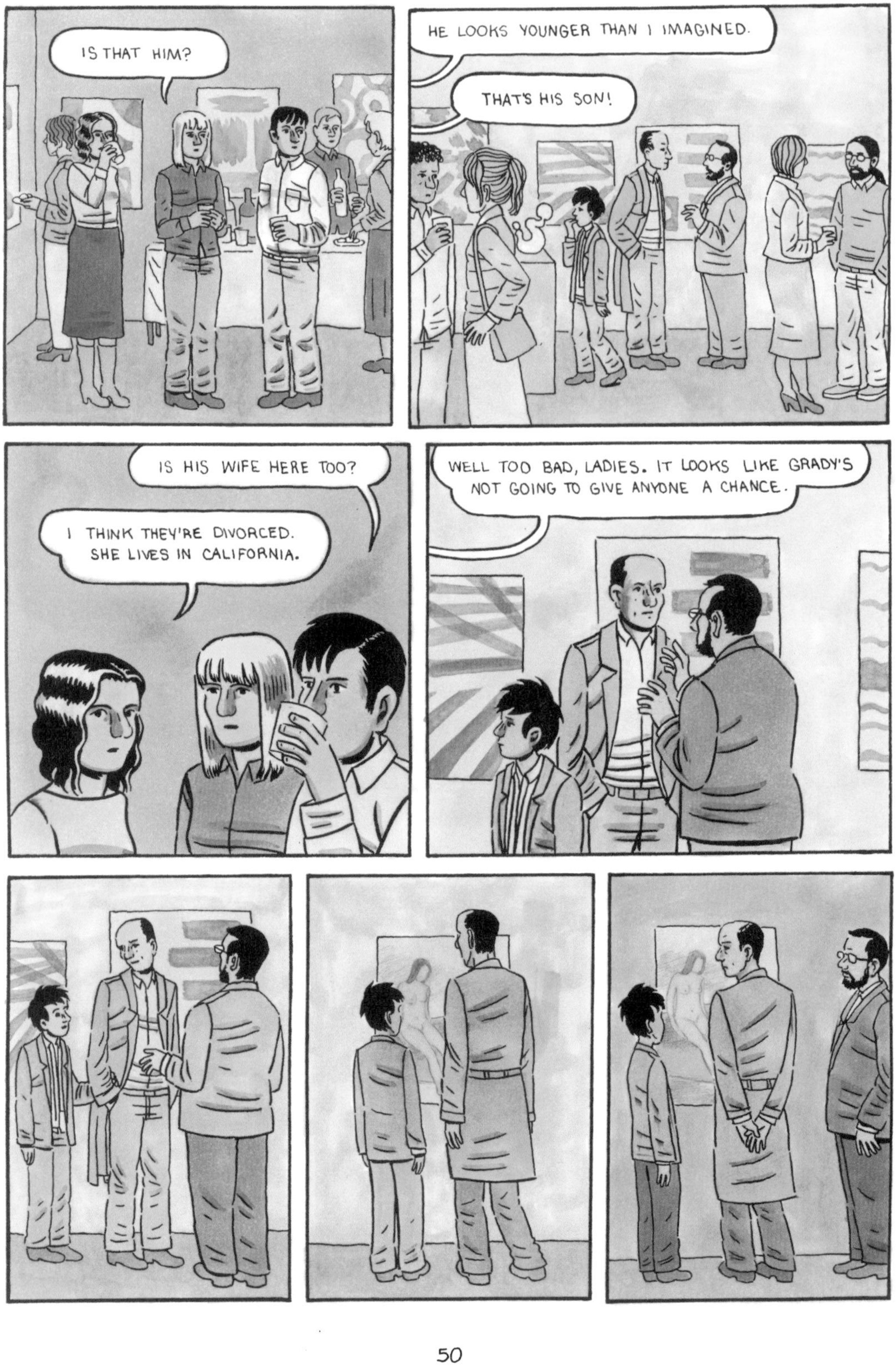
IS THAT HIM?
HE LOOKS YOUNGER THAN I IMAGINED.
THAT'S HIS SON!
IS HIS WIFE HERE TOO?
I THINK THEY'RE DIVORCED. SHE LIVES IN CALIFORNIA.
WELL TOO BAD, LADIES. IT LOOKS LIKE GRADY'S NOT GOING TO GIVE ANYONE A CHANCE.

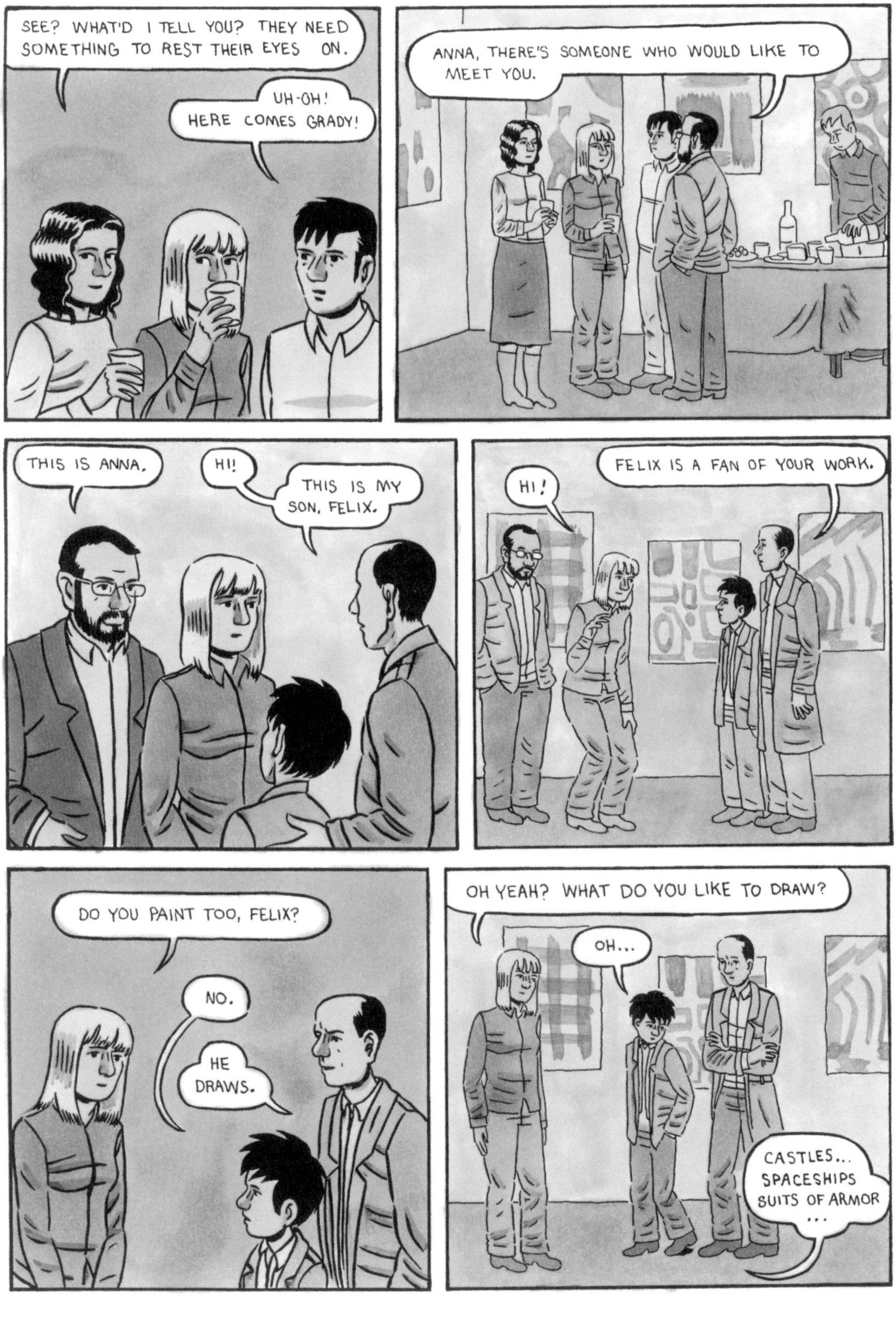
SEE? WHAT'D I TELL YOU? THEY NEED SOMETHING TO REST THEIR EYES ON.
UH-OH! HERE COMES GRADY!
ANNA, THERE'S SOMEONE WHO WOULD LIKE TO MEET YOU.
THIS IS ANNA.
HI!
THIS IS MY SON, FELIX.
FELIX IS A FAN OF YOUR WORK.
HI!
DO YOU PAINT TOO, FELIX?
NO.
HE DRAWS.
OH YEAH? WHAT DO YOU LIKE TO DRAW?
OH...
CASTLES... SPACESHIPS SUITS OF ARMOR ...

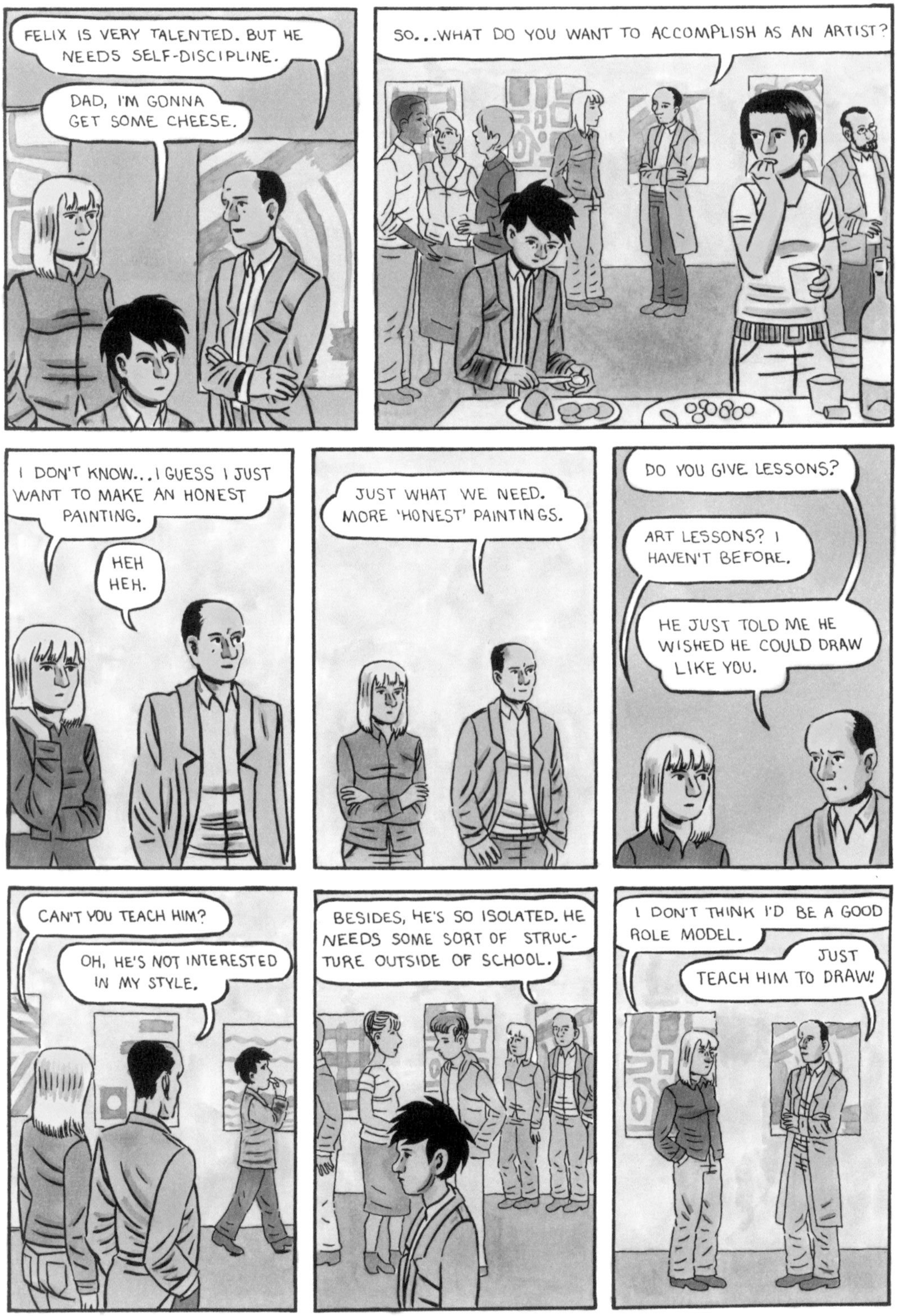
FELIX IS VERY TALENTED. BUT HE NEEDS SELF-DISCIPLINE.
DAD, I'M GONNA GET SOME CHEESE.
SO...WHAT DO YOU WANT TO ACCOMPLISH AS AN ARTIST?
I DON'T KNOW...I GUESS I JUST WANT TO MAKE AN HONEST PAINTING.
HEH HEH.
JUST WHAT WE NEED. MORE 'HONEST' PAINTINGS.
DO YOU GIVE LESSONS?
ART LESSONS? I HAVEN'T BEFORE.
HE JUST TOLD ME HE WISHED HE COULD DRAW LIKE YOU.
CAN'T YOU TEACH HIM?
OH, HE'S NOT INTERESTED IN MY STYLE.
BESIDES, HE'S SO ISOLATED. HE NEEDS SOME SORT OF STRUCTURE OUTSIDE OF SCHOOL.
I DON'T THINK I'D BE A GOOD ROLE MODEL.
JUST TEACH HIM TO DRAW!

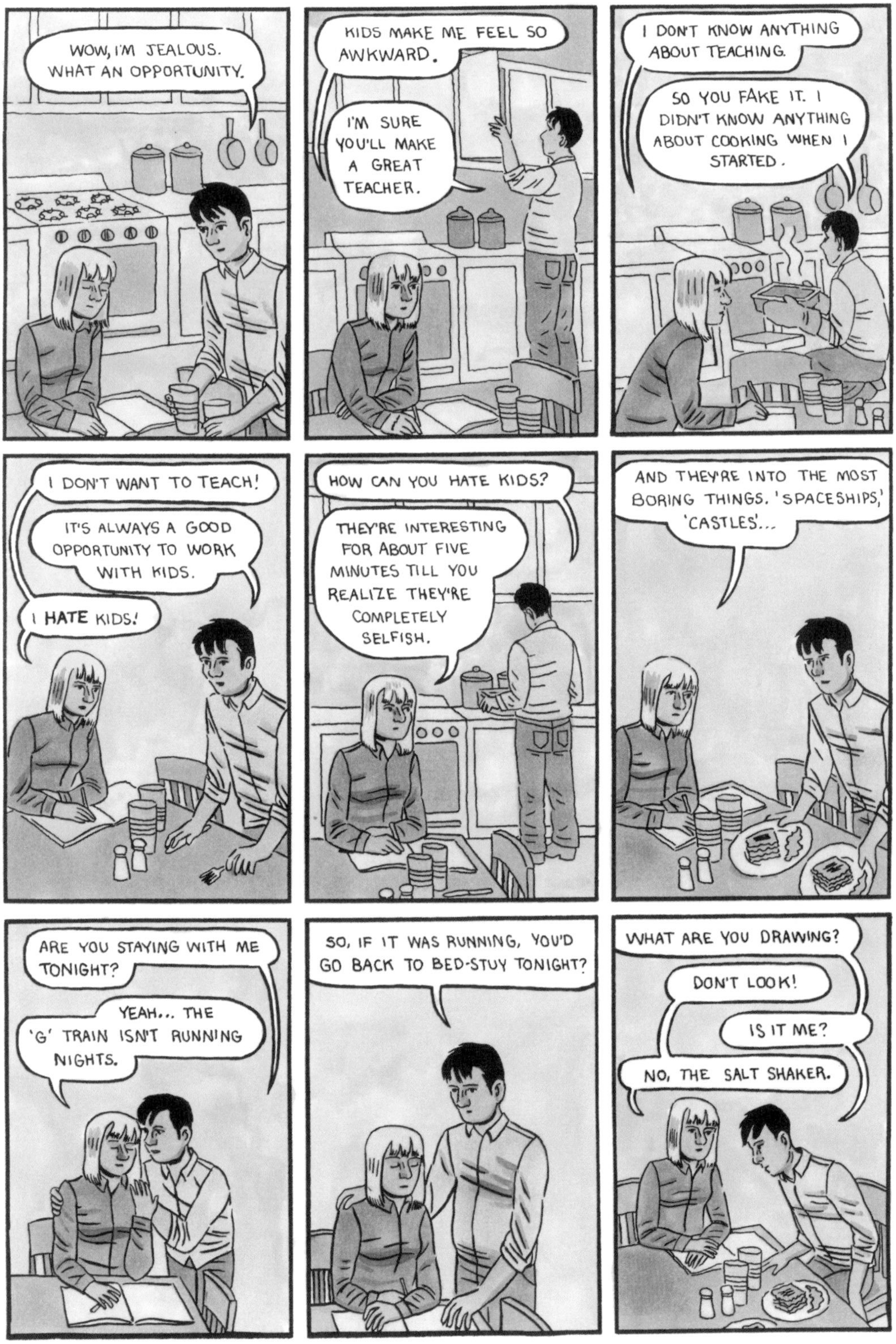
WOW, I'M JEALOUS. WHAT AN OPPORTUNITY.
KIDS MAKE ME FEEL SO AWKWARD.
I'M SURE YOU'LL MAKE A GREAT TEACHER.
I DON'T KNOW ANYTHING ABOUT TEACHING.
SO YOU FAKE IT. I DIDN'T KNOW ANYTHING ABOUT COOKING WHEN I STARTED.
I DON'T WANT TO TEACH!
IT'S ALWAYS A GOOD OPPORTUNITY TO WORK WITH KIDS.
I HATE KIDS!
HOW CAN YOU HATE KIDS?
THEY'RE INTERESTING FOR ABOUT FIVE MINUTES TILL YOU REALIZE THEY'RE COMPLETELY SELFISH.
AND THEY'RE INTO THE MOST BORING THINGS. 'SPACESHIPS,' 'CASTLES'...
ARE YOU STAYING WITH ME TONIGHT?
YEAH... THE 'G' TRAIN ISN'T RUNNING NIGHTS.
SO, IF IT WAS RUNNING, YOU'D GO BACK TO BED-STUY TONIGHT?
WHAT ARE YOU DRAWING?
DON'T LOOK!
IS IT ME?
NO, THE SALT SHAKER.

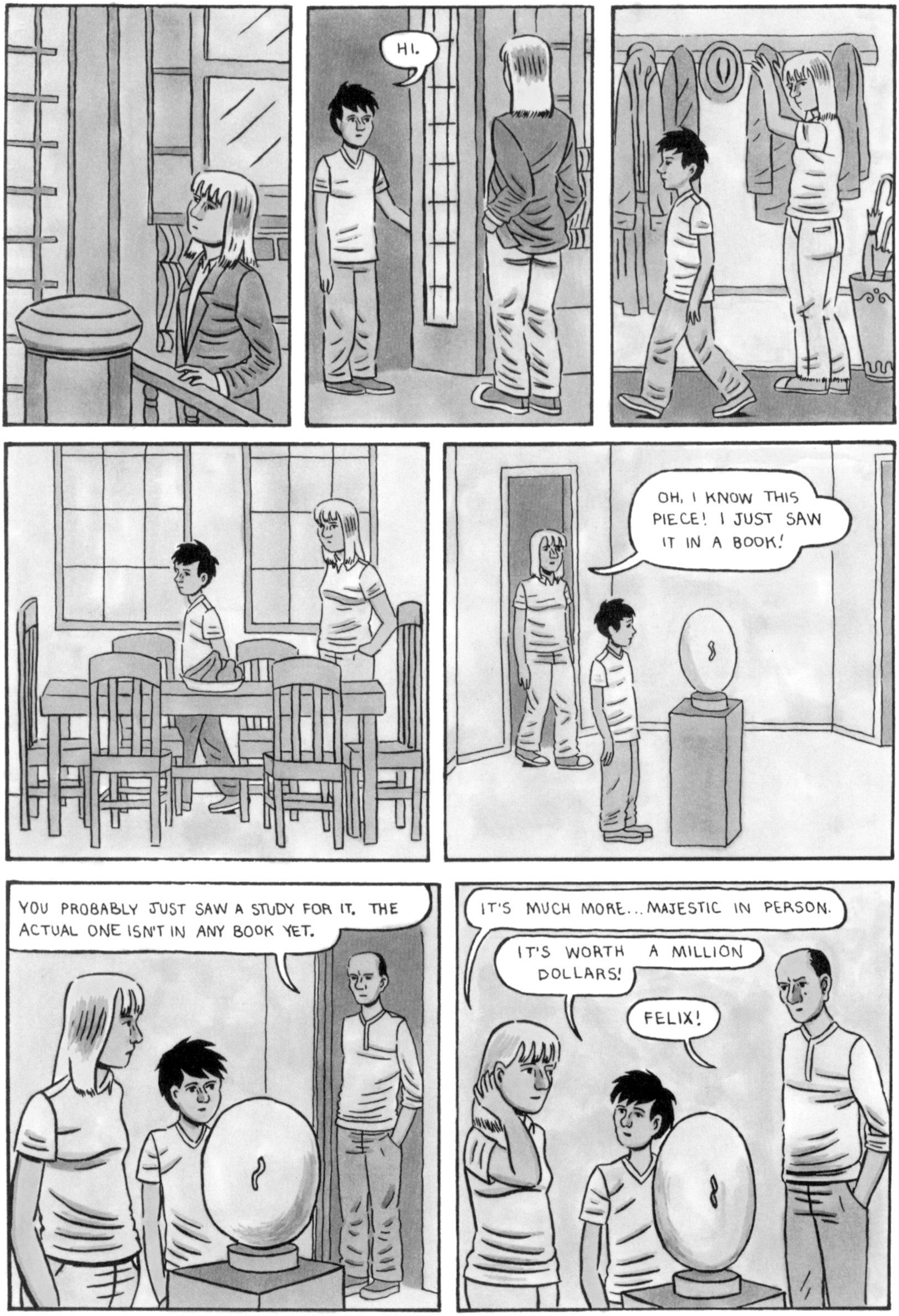
HI.
OH, I KNOW THIS PIECE! I JUST SAW IT IN A BOOK!
YOU PROBABLY JUST SAW A STUDY FOR IT. THE ACTUAL ONE ISN'T IN ANY BOOK YET.
IT'S MUCH MORE... MAJESTIC IN PERSON.
IT'S WORTH A MILLION DOLLARS!
FELIX!

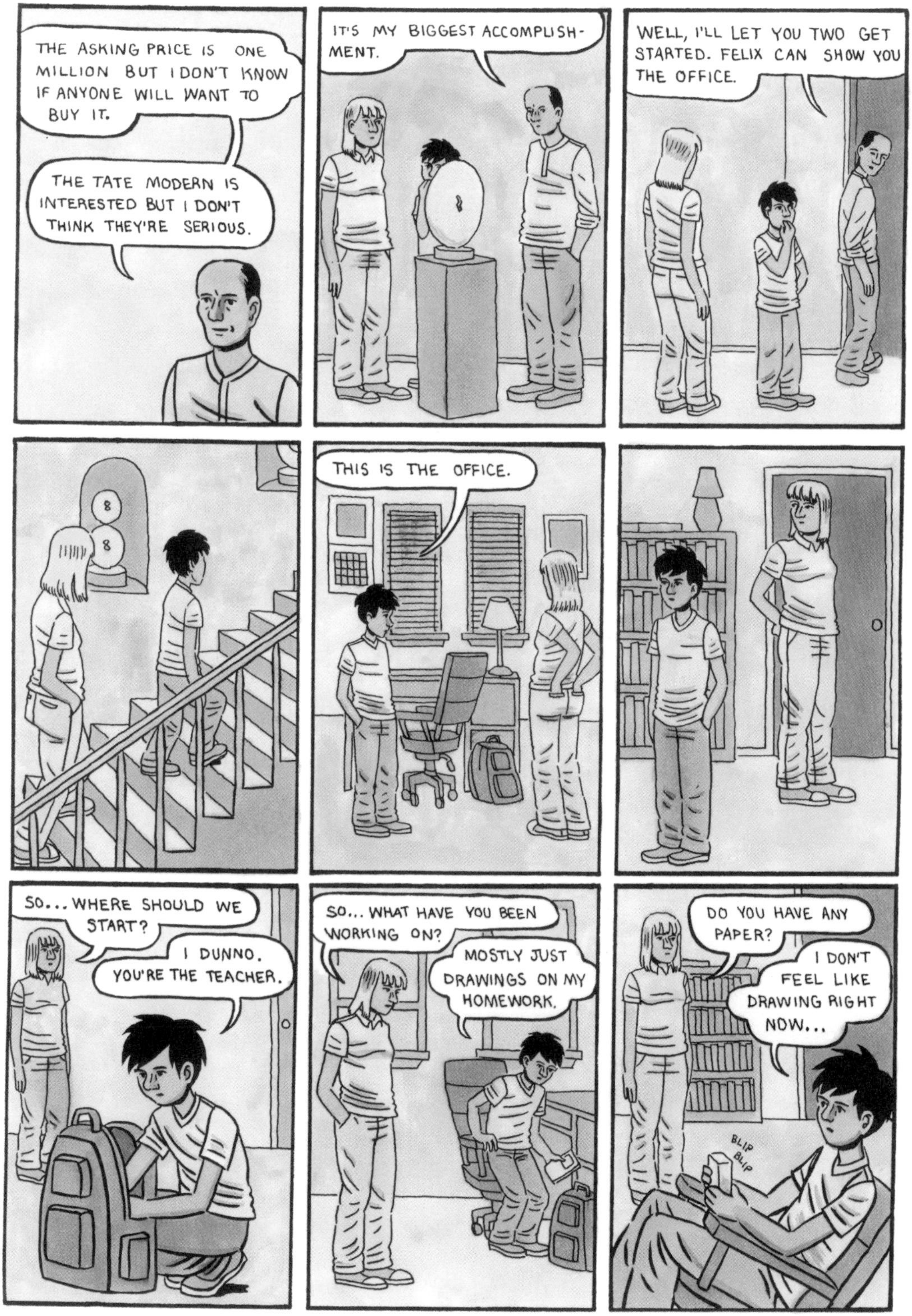
THE ASKING PRICE IS ONE MILLION BUT I DON'T KNOW IF ANYONE WILL WANT TO BUY IT.
THE TATE MODERN IS INTERESTED BUT I DON'T THINK THEY'RE SERIOUS.
IT'S MY BIGGEST ACCOMPLISH-MENT.
WELL, I'LL LET YOU TWO GET STARTED. FELIX CAN SHOW YOU THE OFFICE.
8
8
THIS IS THE OFFICE.
SO... WHERE SHOULD WE START?
I DUNNO. YOU'RE THE TEACHER.
SO... WHAT HAVE YOU BEEN WORKING ON?
MOSTLY JUST DRAWINGS ON MY HOMEWORK.
DO YOU HAVE ANY PAPER?
I DON'T FEEL LIKE DRAWING RIGHT NOW...
BLIP BLIP

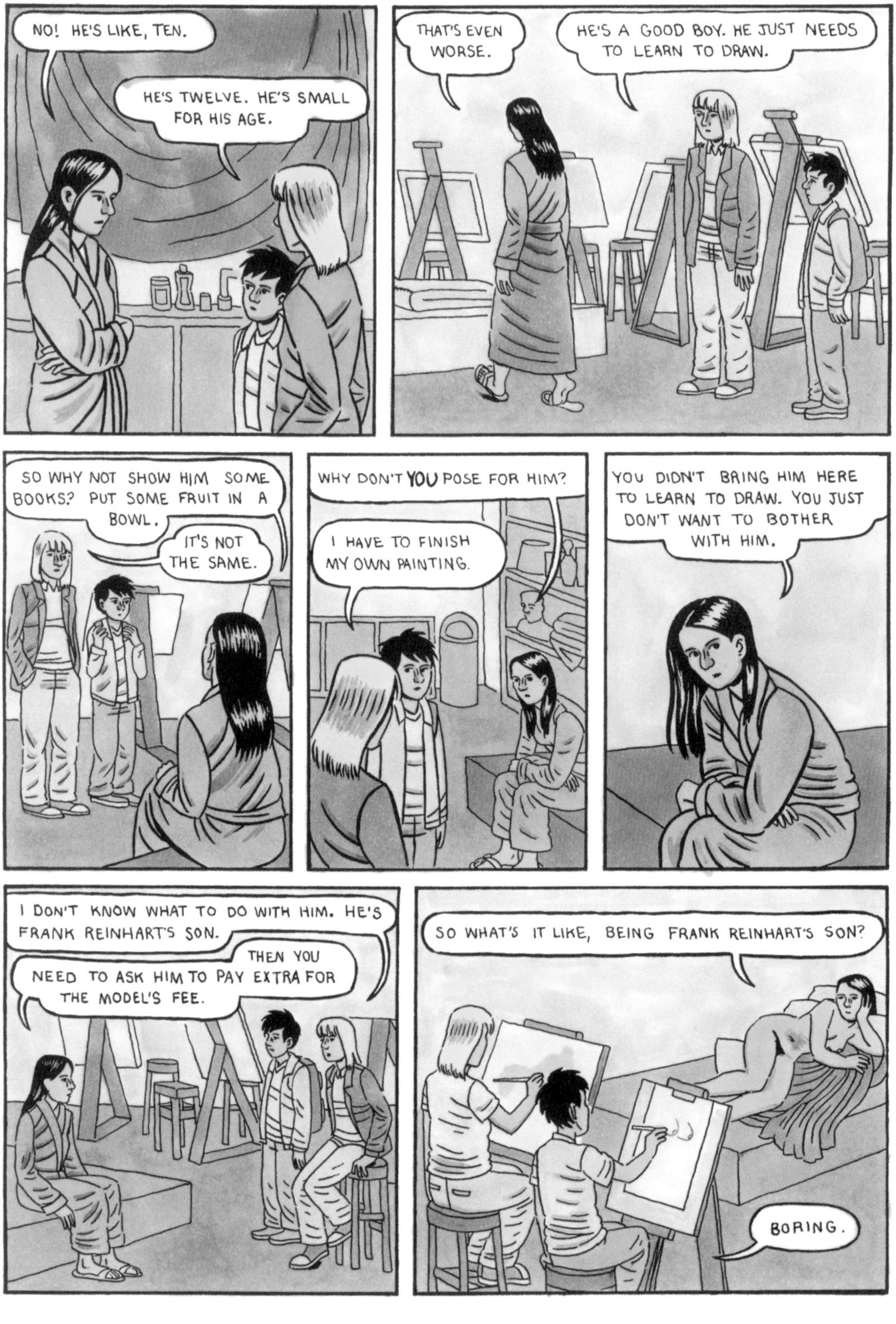

NO! HE'S LIKE, TEN.
HE'S TWELVE. HE'S SMALL FOR HIS AGE.
THAT'S EVEN WORSE.
HE'S A GOOD BOY. HE JUST NEEDS TO LEARN TO DRAW.
SO WHY NOT SHOW HIM SOME BOOKS? PUT SOME FRUIT IN A BOWL.
IT'S NOT THE SAME.
WHY DON'T YOU POSE FOR HIM?
I HAVE TO FINISH MY OWN PAINTING.
YOU DIDN'T BRING HIM HERE TO LEARN TO DRAW. YOU JUST DON'T WANT TO BOTHER WITH HIM.
I DON'T KNOW WHAT TO DO WITH HIM. HE'S FRANK REINHART'S SON.
THEN YOU NEED TO ASK HIM TO PAY EXTRA FOR THE MODEL'S FEE.
SO WHAT'S IT LIKE, BEING FRANK REINHART'S SON?
BORING.

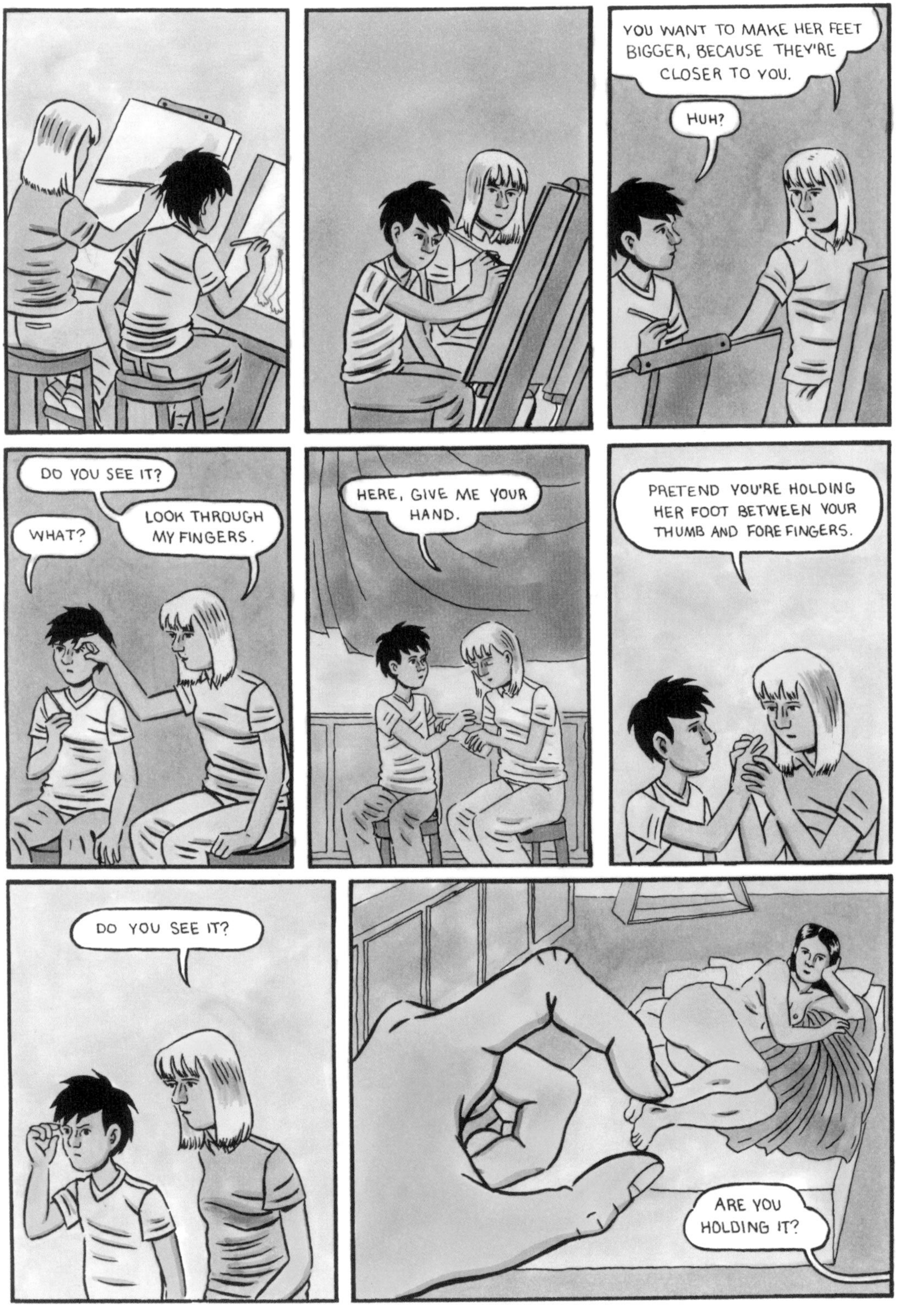
YOU WANT TO MAKE HER FEET BIGGER, BECAUSE THEY'RE CLOSER TO YOU.
HUH?
DO YOU SEE IT?
WHAT?
LOOK THROUGH MY FINGERS.
HERE, GIVE ME YOUR HAND.
PRETEND YOU'RE HOLDING HER FOOT BETWEEN YOUR THUMB AND FORE FINGERS.
DO YOU SEE IT?
ARE YOU HOLDING IT?

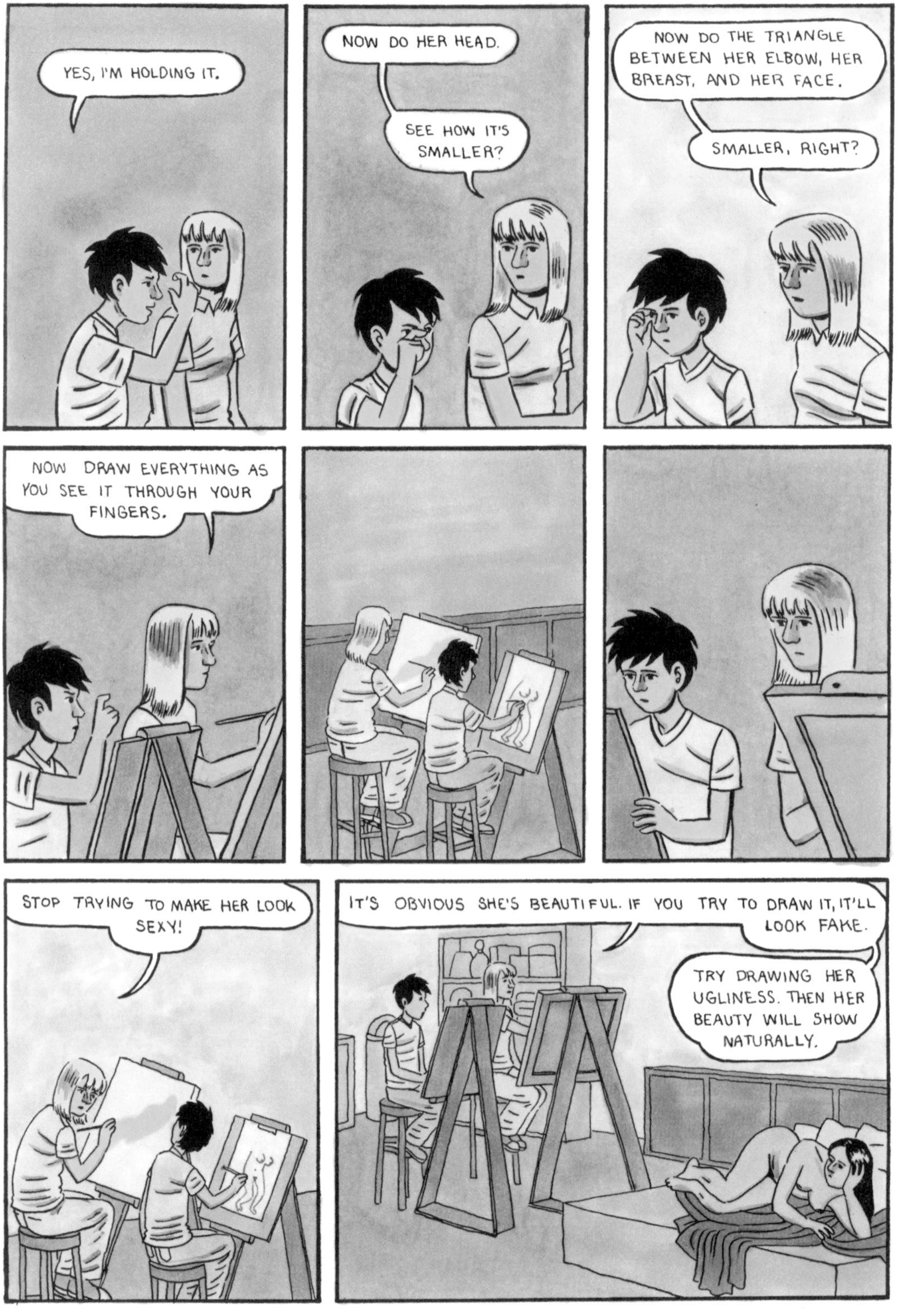
YES, I'M HOLDING IT.
NOW DO HER HEAD.
SEE HOW IT'S SMALLER?
NOW DO THE TRIANGLE BETWEEN HER ELBOW, HER BREAST, AND HER FACE.
SMALLER, RIGHT?
NOW DRAW EVERYTHING AS YOU SEE IT THROUGH YOUR FINGERS.
STOP TRYING TO MAKE HER LOOK SEXY!
IT'S OBVIOUS SHE'S BEAUTIFUL. IF YOU TRY TO DRAW IT, IT'LL LOOK FAKE.
TRY DRAWING HER UGLINESS. THEN HER BEAUTY WILL SHOW NATURALLY.

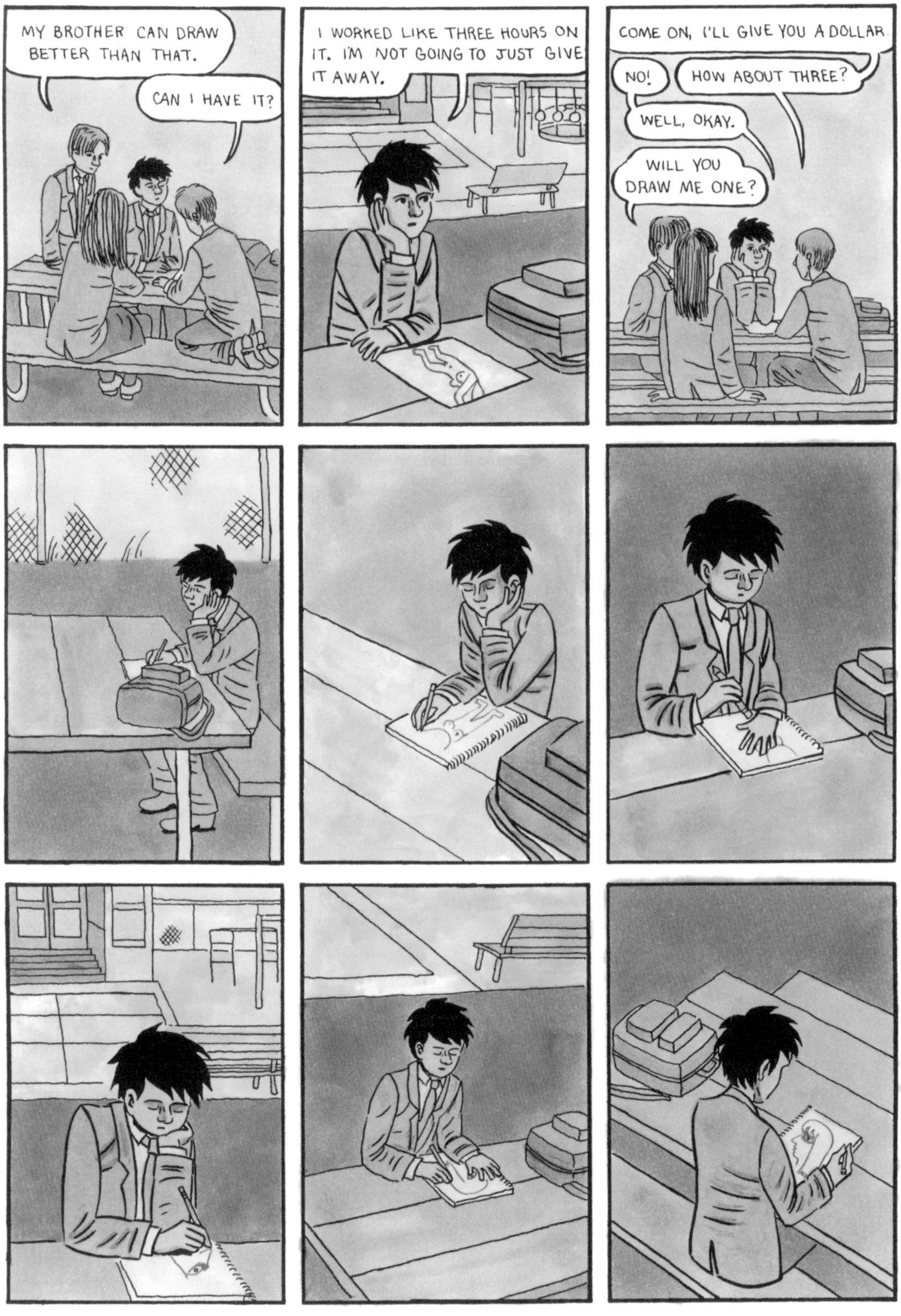
MY BROTHER CAN DRAW BETTER THAN THAT.
CAN I HAVE IT?
I WORKED LIKE THREE HOURS ON IT. I'M NOT GOING TO JUST GIVE IT AWAY.
COME ON, I'LL GIVE YOU A DOLLAR.
NO!
HOW ABOUT THREE?
WELL, OKAY.
WILL YOU DRAW ME ONE?

DO YOU THINK WE COULD START A DIFFERENT POSE TODAY?

I HAVE TO FINISH MY OWN PAINTING. WHY DON'T YOU SIT IN A DIFFERENT SPOT?

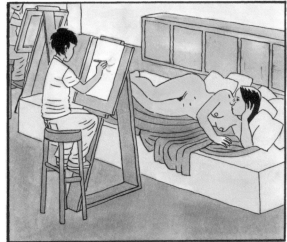

DO YOU SELL YOUR PAINTINGS, ANNA?

I ONCE SOLD ONE OF SARA FOR FIFTY BUCKS.

REALLY? YOU DIDN'T TELL ME THAT! TO WHO?

ONE OF MY MOM'S FRIENDS.

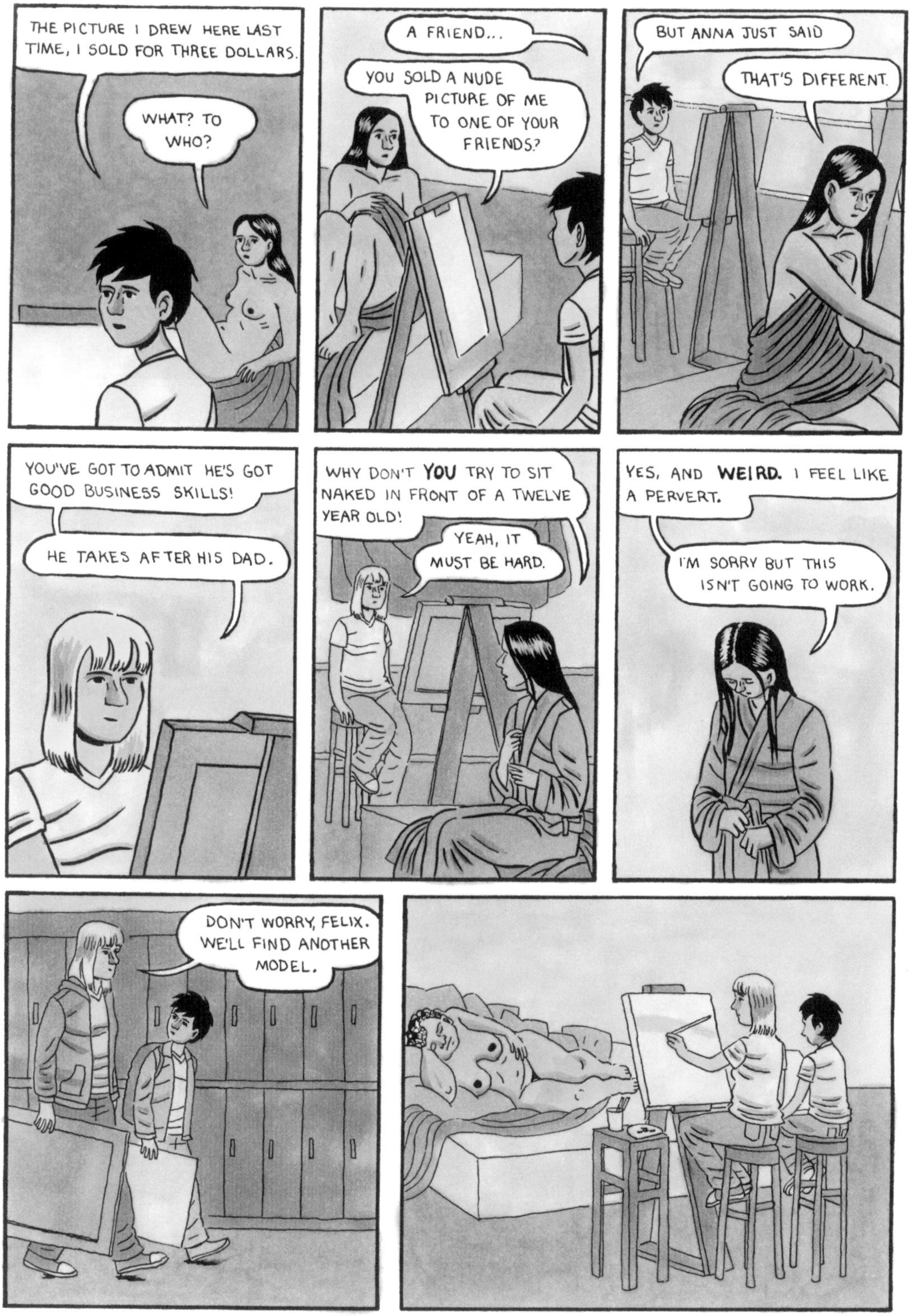
THE PICTURE I DREW HERE LAST TIME, I SOLD FOR THREE DOLLARS.
WHAT? TO WHO?
A FRIEND...
YOU SOLD A NUDE PICTURE OF ME TO ONE OF YOUR FRIENDS?
BUT ANNA JUST SAID
THAT'S DIFFERENT.
YOU'VE GOT TO ADMIT HE'S GOT GOOD BUSINESS SKILLS!
HE TAKES AFTER HIS DAD.
WHY DON'T **YOU** TRY TO SIT NAKED IN FRONT OF A TWELVE YEAR OLD!
YEAH, IT MUST BE HARD.
YES, AND **WEIRD.** I FEEL LIKE A PERVERT.
I'M SORRY BUT THIS ISN'T GOING TO WORK.
DON'T WORRY, FELIX. WE'LL FIND ANOTHER MODEL.

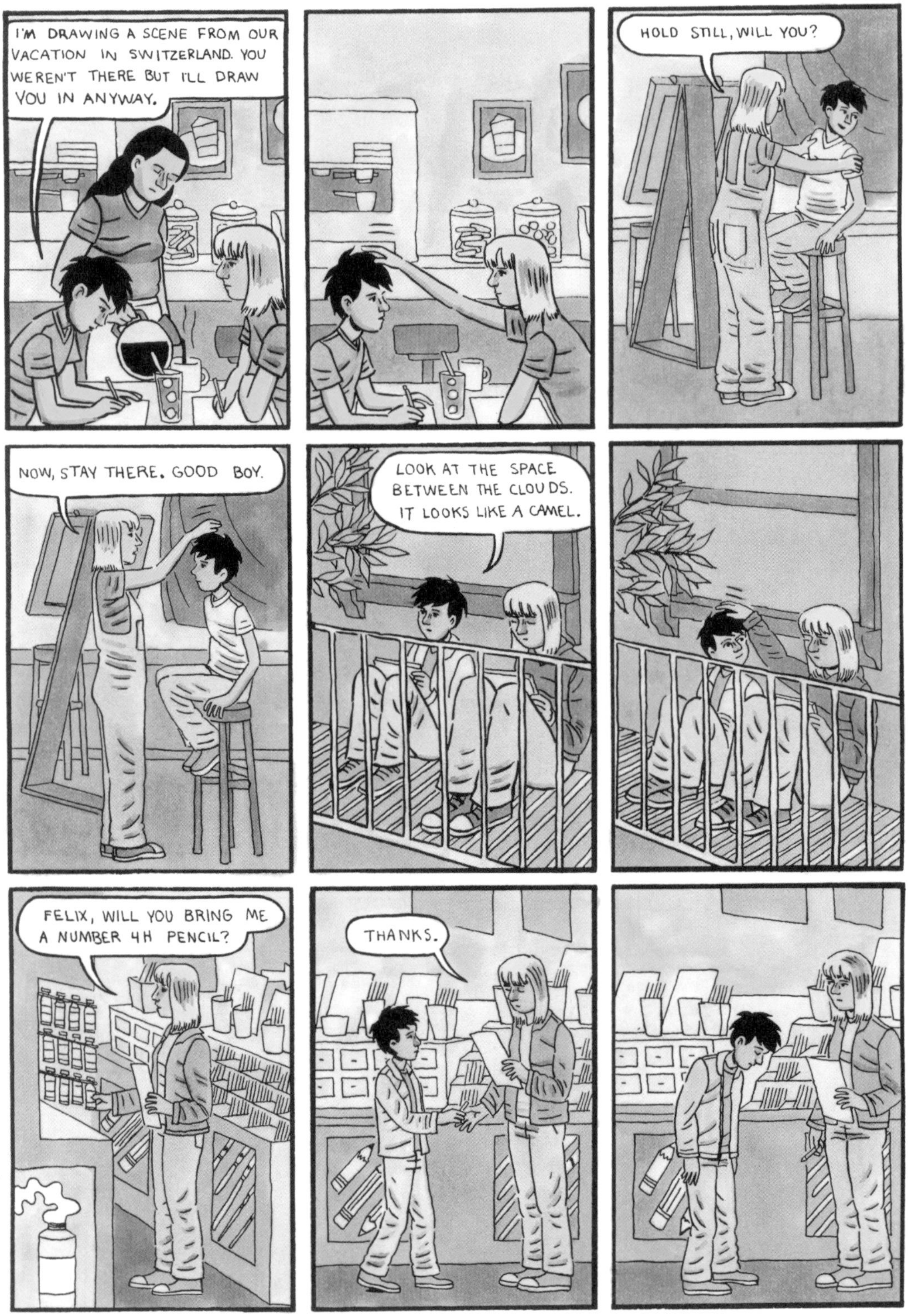
I'M DRAWING A SCENE FROM OUR VACATION IN SWITZERLAND. YOU WEREN'T THERE BUT I'LL DRAW YOU IN ANYWAY.
HOLD STILL, WILL YOU?
NOW, STAY THERE. GOOD BOY.
LOOK AT THE SPACE BETWEEN THE CLOUDS. IT LOOKS LIKE A CAMEL.
FELIX, WILL YOU BRING ME A NUMBER 4H PENCIL?
THANKS.

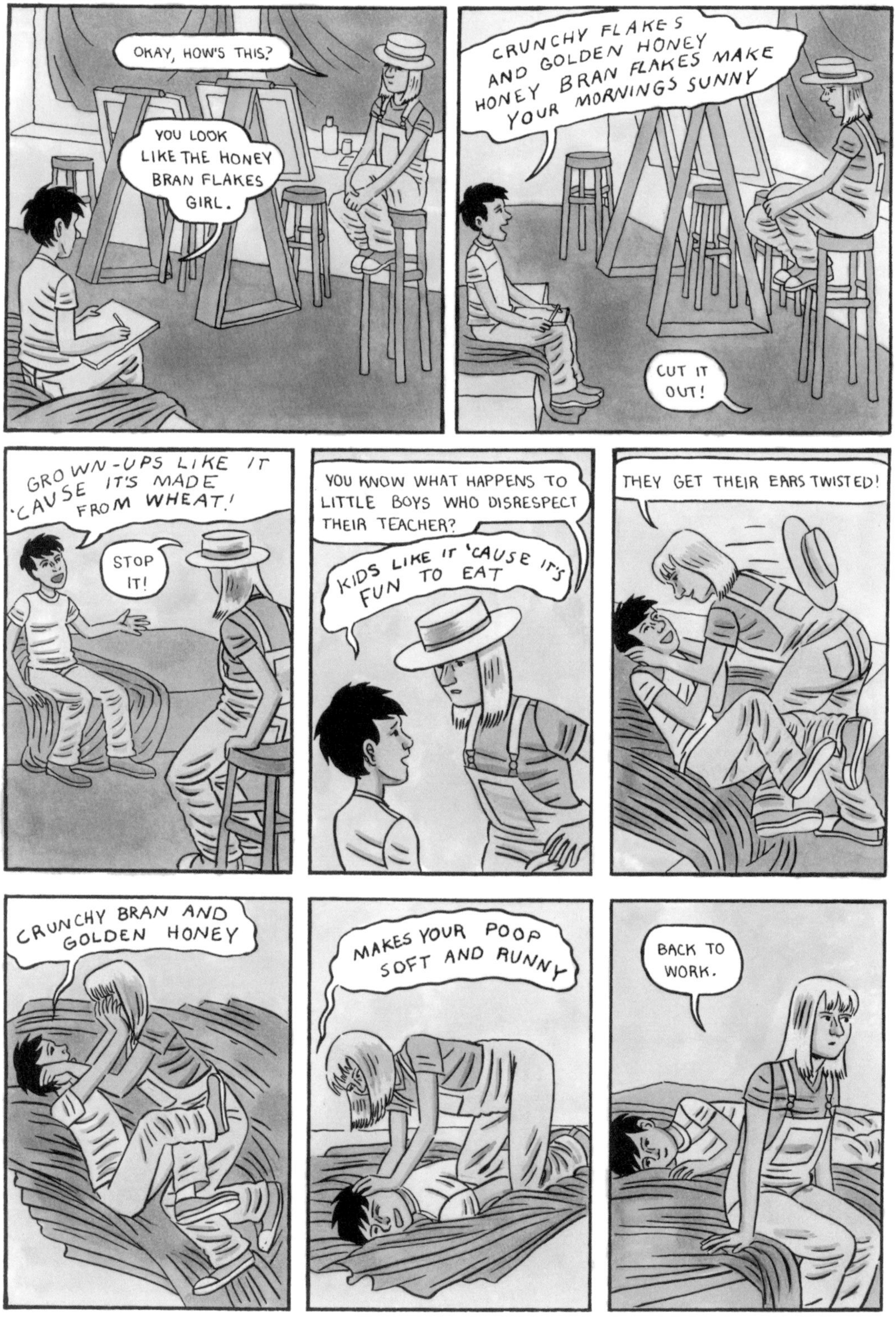
OKAY, HOW'S THIS?
YOU LOOK LIKE THE HONEY BRAN FLAKES GIRL.
CRUNCHY FLAKES AND GOLDEN HONEY HONEY BRAN FLAKES MAKE YOUR MORNINGS SUNNY
CUT IT OUT!
GROWN-UPS LIKE IT 'CAUSE IT'S MADE FROM WHEAT!
STOP IT!
YOU KNOW WHAT HAPPENS TO LITTLE BOYS WHO DISRESPECT THEIR TEACHER?
KIDS LIKE IT 'CAUSE IT'S FUN TO EAT
THEY GET THEIR EARS TWISTED!
CRUNCHY BRAN AND GOLDEN HONEY
MAKES YOUR POOP SOFT AND RUNNY
BACK TO WORK.

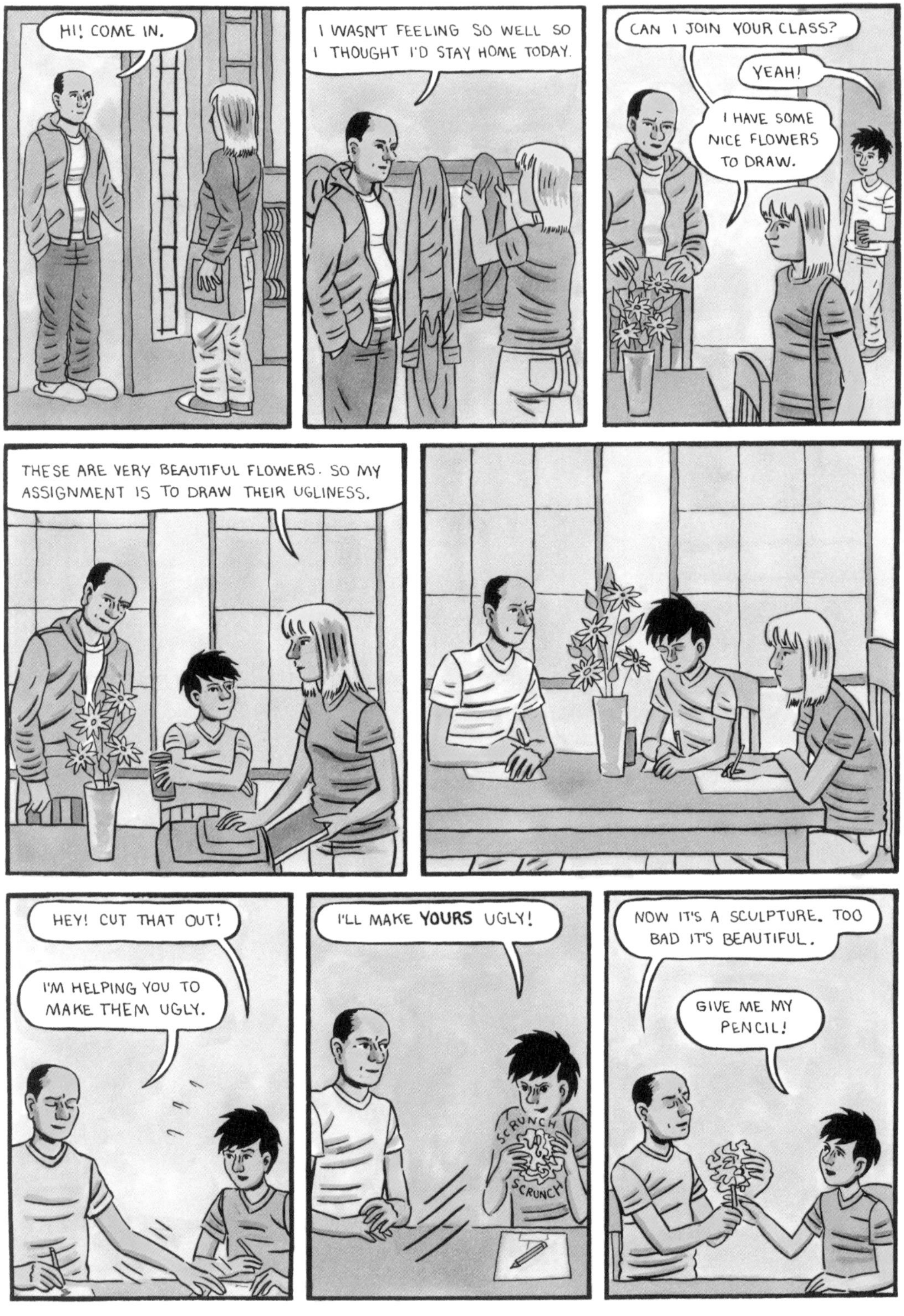
HI! COME IN.
I WASN'T FEELING SO WELL SO I THOUGHT I'D STAY HOME TODAY.
CAN I JOIN YOUR CLASS?
YEAH!
I HAVE SOME NICE FLOWERS TO DRAW.
THESE ARE VERY BEAUTIFUL FLOWERS. SO MY ASSIGNMENT IS TO DRAW THEIR UGLINESS.
HEY! CUT THAT OUT!
I'M HELPING YOU TO MAKE THEM UGLY.
I'LL MAKE **YOURS** UGLY!
SCRUNCH
SCRUNCH
NOW IT'S A SCULPTURE. TOO BAD IT'S BEAUTIFUL.
GIVE ME MY PENCIL!

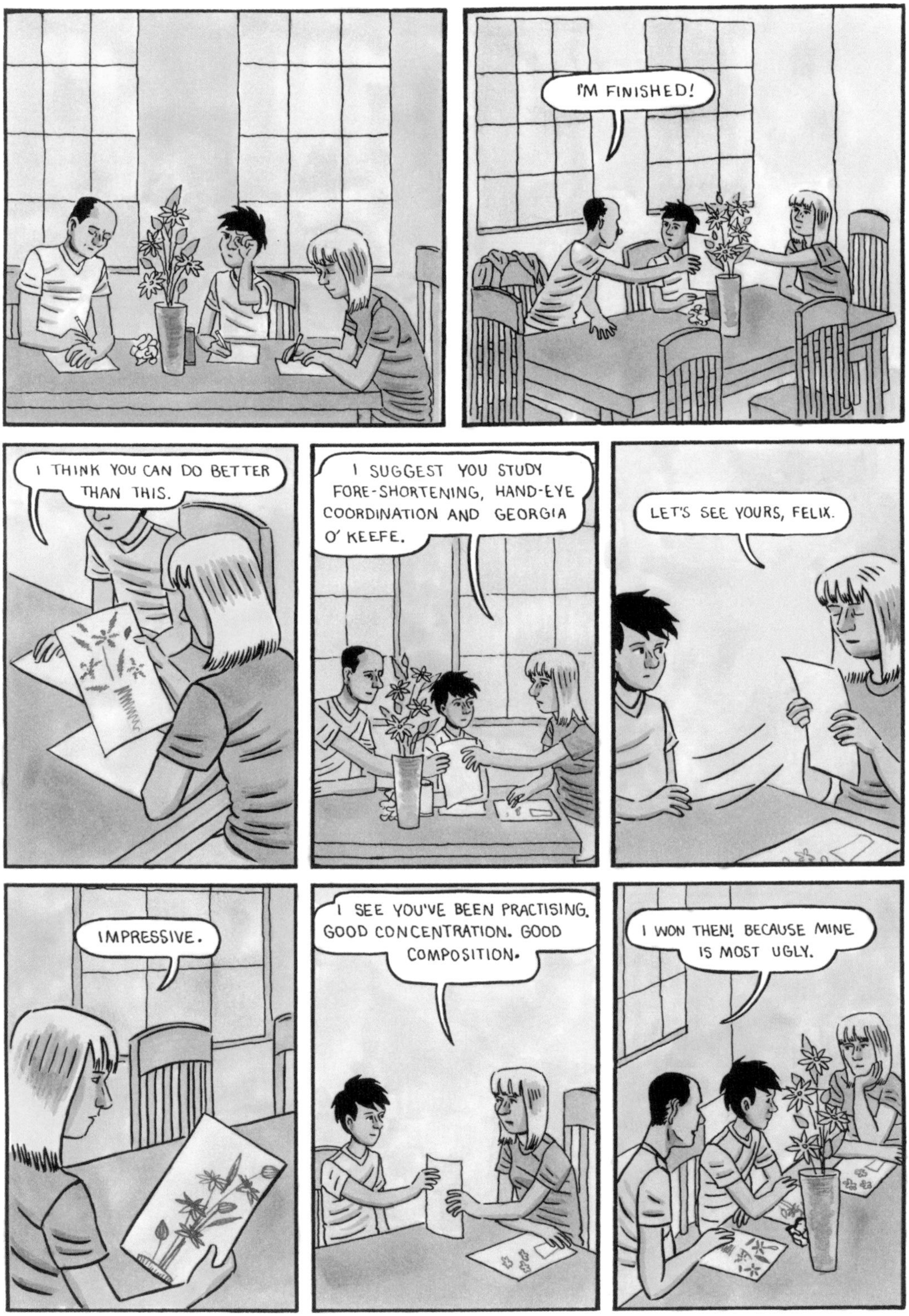
I'M FINISHED!
I THINK YOU CAN DO BETTER THAN THIS.
I SUGGEST YOU STUDY FORE-SHORTENING, HAND-EYE COORDINATION AND GEORGIA O' KEEFE.
LET'S SEE YOURS, FELIX.
IMPRESSIVE.
I SEE YOU'VE BEEN PRACTISING. GOOD CONCENTRATION. GOOD COMPOSITION.
I WON THEN! BECAUSE MINE IS MOST UGLY.

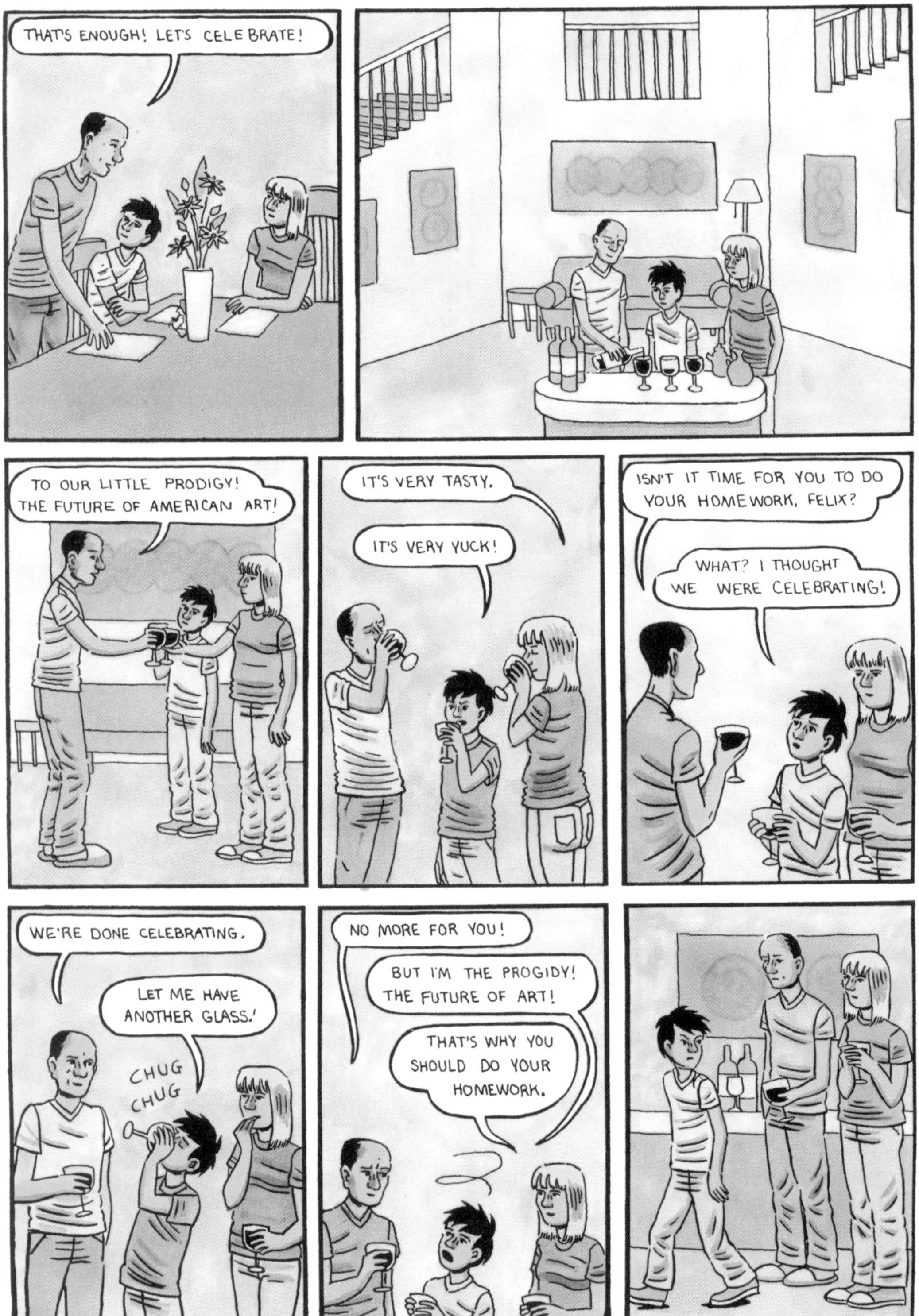
THAT'S ENOUGH! LET'S CELEBRATE!
TO OUR LITTLE PRODIGY! THE FUTURE OF AMERICAN ART!
IT'S VERY TASTY.
IT'S VERY YUCK!
ISN'T IT TIME FOR YOU TO DO YOUR HOMEWORK, FELIX?
WHAT? I THOUGHT WE WERE CELEBRATING!
WE'RE DONE CELEBRATING.
LET ME HAVE ANOTHER GLASS.'
CHUG CHUG
NO MORE FOR YOU!
BUT I'M THE PROGIDY! THE FUTURE OF ART!
THAT'S WHY YOU SHOULD DO YOUR HOMEWORK.

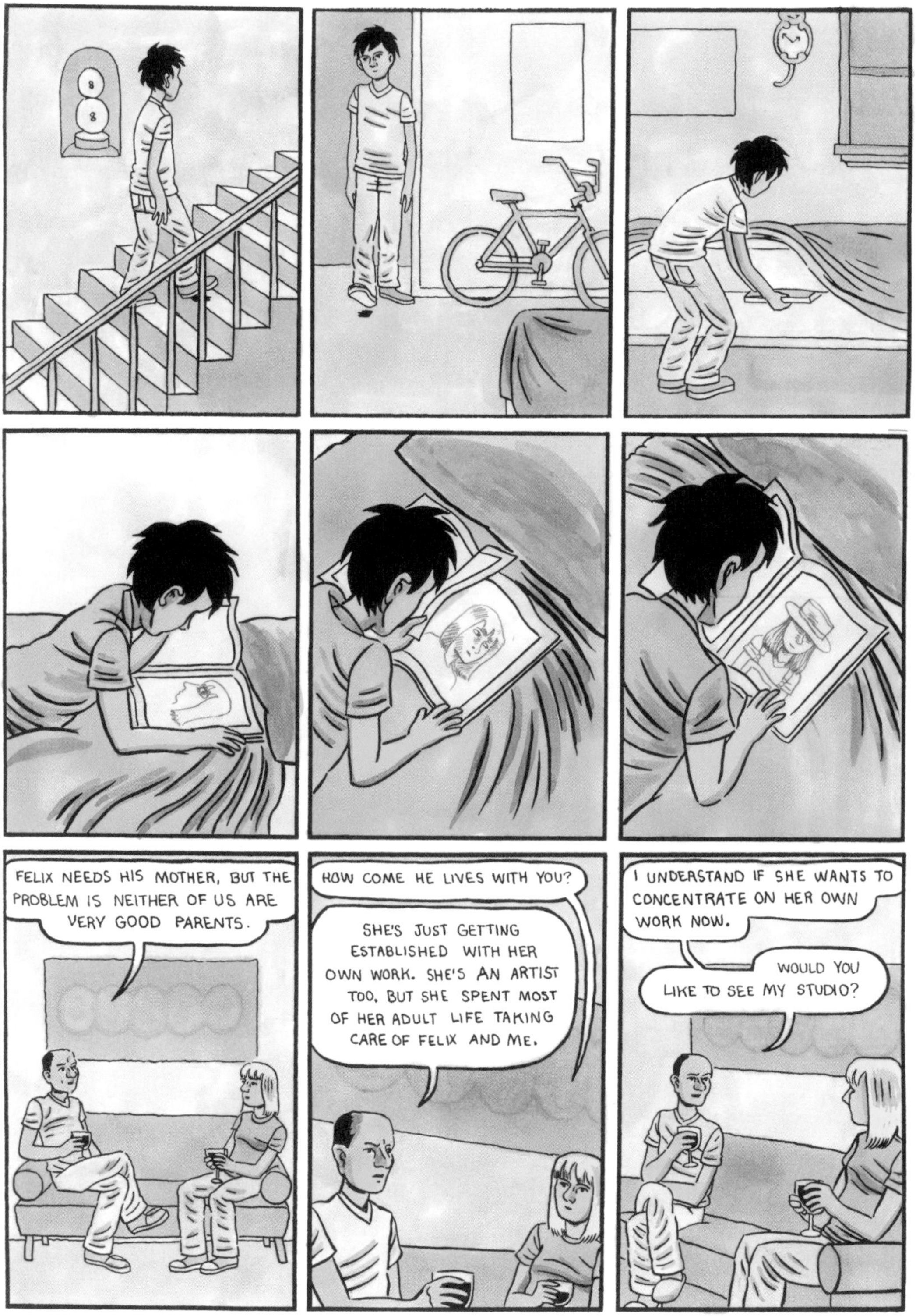
FELIX NEEDS HIS MOTHER, BUT THE PROBLEM IS NEITHER OF US ARE VERY GOOD PARENTS.
HOW COME HE LIVES WITH YOU?
SHE'S JUST GETTING ESTABLISHED WITH HER OWN WORK. SHE'S AN ARTIST TOO, BUT SHE SPENT MOST OF HER ADULT LIFE TAKING CARE OF FELIX AND ME.
I UNDERSTAND IF SHE WANTS TO CONCENTRATE ON HER OWN WORK NOW.
WOULD YOU LIKE TO SEE MY STUDIO?

WHAT WAS HIS STUDIO LIKE?

FASCINATING.

IT WASN'T WHERE THE ACTUAL STRUCTURES WERE MADE BUT IT WAS FULL OF LITTLE DIAGRAMS AND SKETCHES AND MODELS.

YOU KNOW, I'VE NEVER UNDERSTOOD HIS SCULPTURE BEFORE, BUT SUDDENLY I SAW HOW HIS MIND WORKED.

ALL THAT STUFF GRADY SAYS ABOUT NEGATIVE SPACE, I THOUGHT I UNDERSTOOD IT, BUT I HAD NO CLUE!

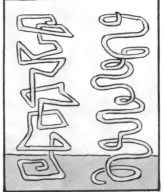

IT WAS LIKE I'D DISCOVERED A WHOLE NEW WAY TO COMMUNICATE, AND WAS INSTINCTIVELY FLUENT IN IT.

I WAS SO INSPIRED! I LEARNED MORE IN ONE EVENING THAN WHAT THIS SCHOOL HAS BEEN TRYING TO DRUM INTO MY HEAD FOR THE PAST THREE YEARS!

THEN WHAT HAPPENED?

NOTHING.

EXCEPT THAT HE'S TAKING ME TO DINNER TOMORROW NIGHT!

OH HO!

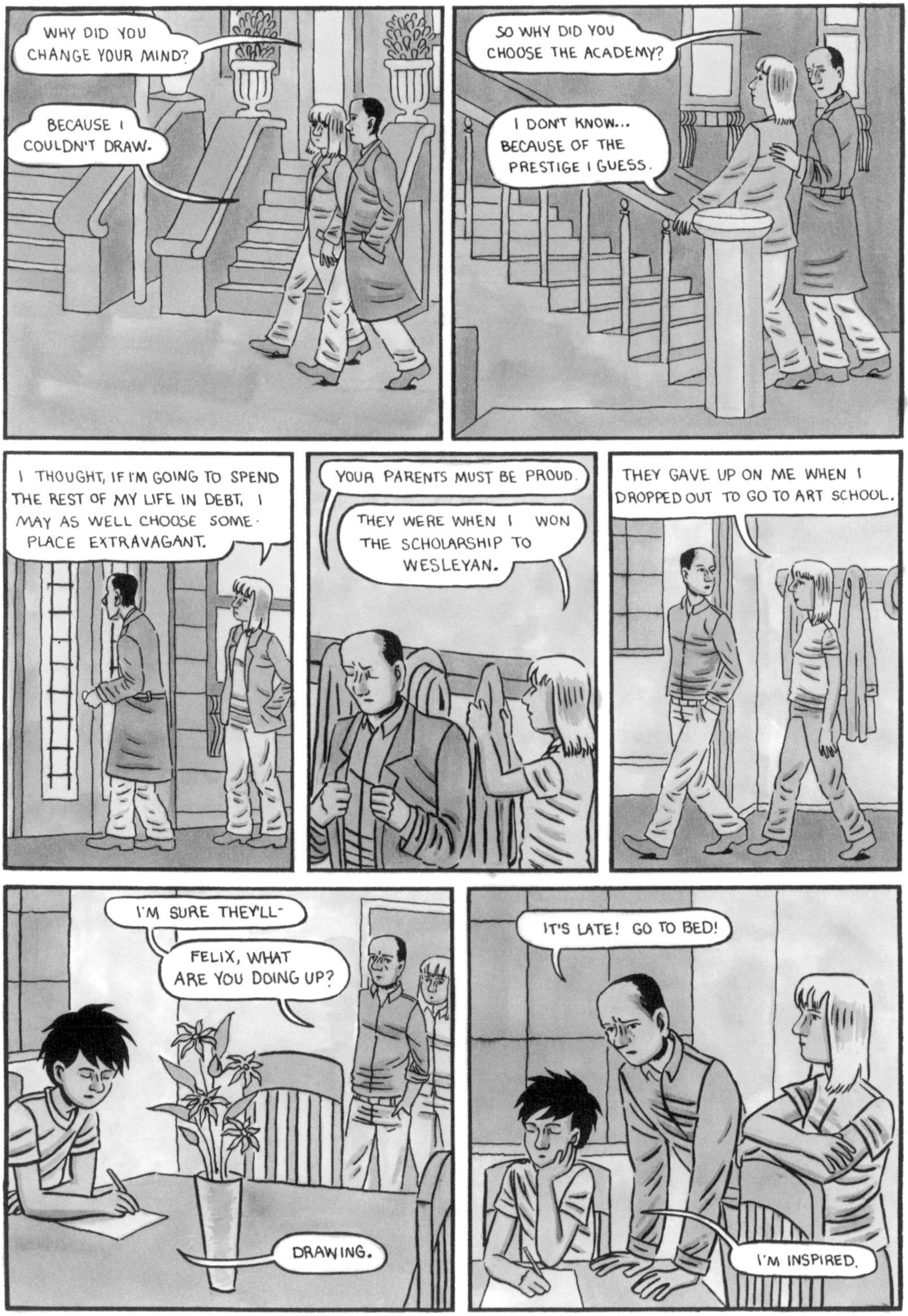
WHY DID YOU CHANGE YOUR MIND?
BECAUSE I COULDN'T DRAW.
SO WHY DID YOU CHOOSE THE ACADEMY?
I DON'T KNOW... BECAUSE OF THE PRESTIGE I GUESS.
I THOUGHT, IF I'M GOING TO SPEND THE REST OF MY LIFE IN DEBT, I MAY AS WELL CHOOSE SOME-PLACE EXTRAVAGANT.
YOUR PARENTS MUST BE PROUD.
THEY WERE WHEN I WON THE SCHOLARSHIP TO WESLEYAN.
THEY GAVE UP ON ME WHEN I DROPPED OUT TO GO TO ART SCHOOL.
I'M SURE THEY'LL-
FELIX, WHAT ARE YOU DOING UP?
DRAWING.
IT'S LATE! GO TO BED!
I'M INSPIRED.

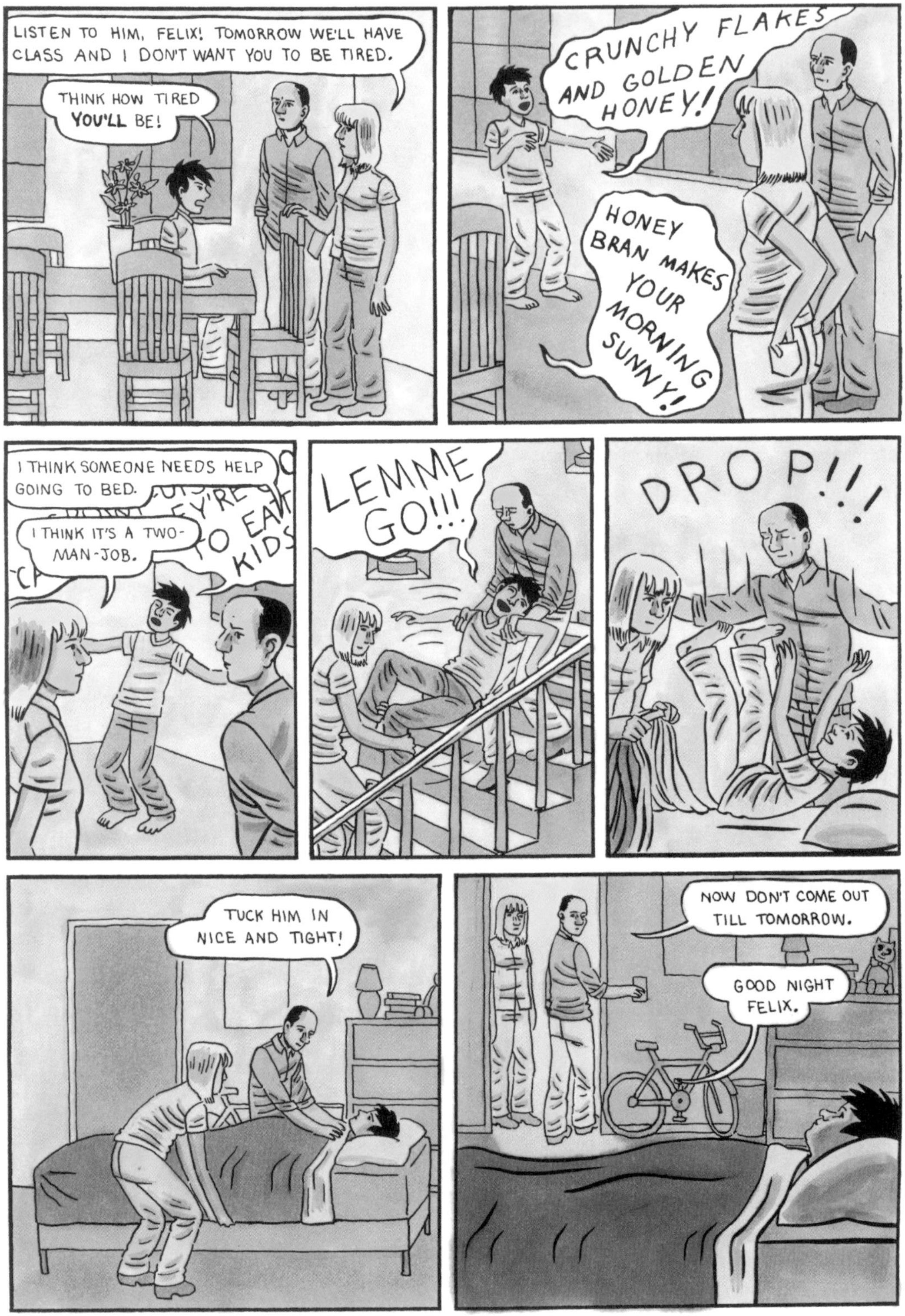
LISTEN TO HIM, FELIX! TOMORROW WE'LL HAVE CLASS AND I DON'T WANT YOU TO BE TIRED.
THINK HOW TIRED **YOU'LL** BE!
CRUNCHY FLAKES AND GOLDEN HONEY!
HONEY BRAN MAKES YOUR MORNING SUNNY!
I THINK SOMEONE NEEDS HELP GOING TO BED.
I THINK IT'S A TWO-MAN-JOB.
LEMME GO!!!
DROP!!!
TUCK HIM IN NICE AND TIGHT!
NOW DON'T COME OUT TILL TOMORROW.
GOOD NIGHT FELIX.

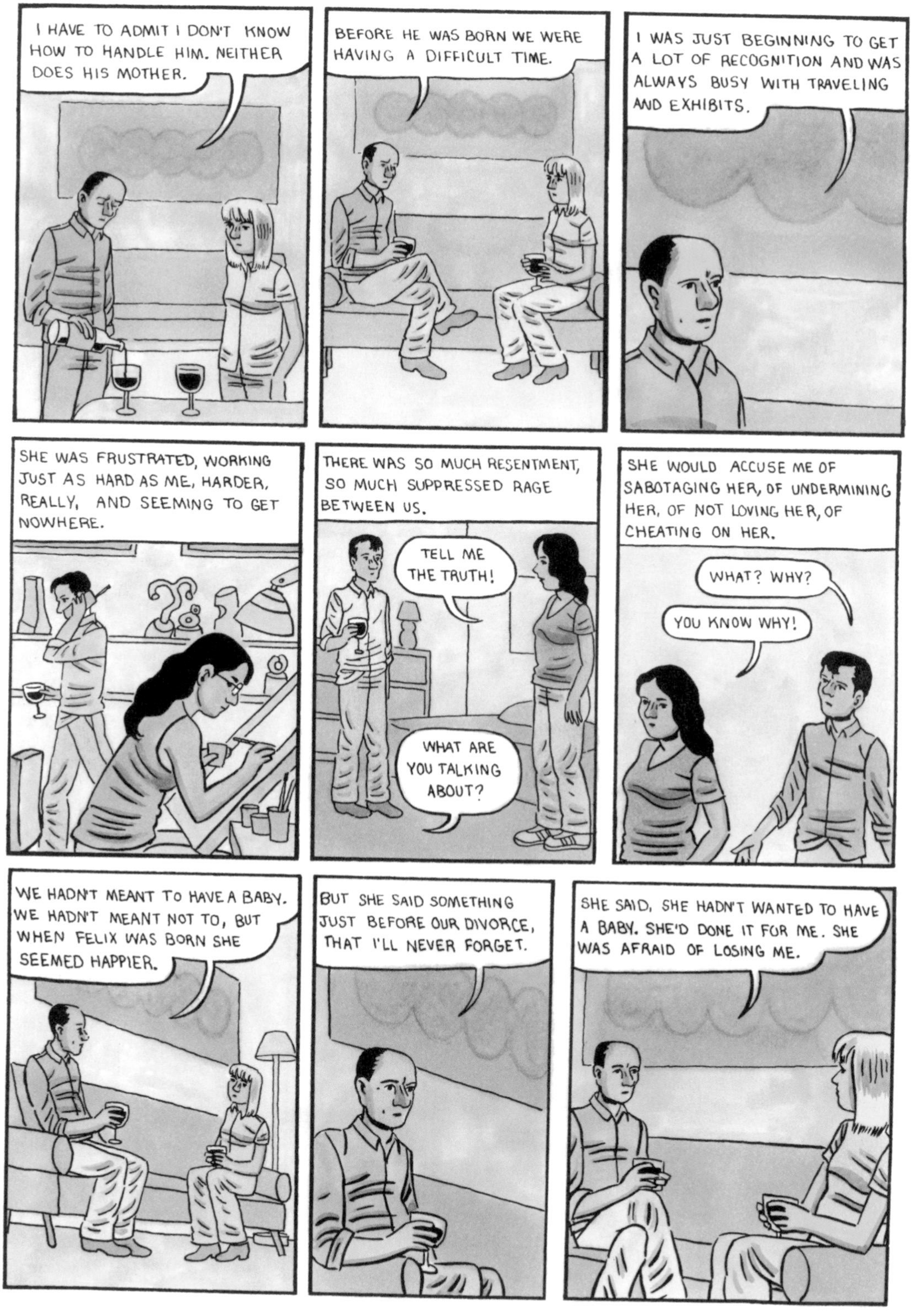
I HAVE TO ADMIT I DON'T KNOW HOW TO HANDLE HIM. NEITHER DOES HIS MOTHER.
BEFORE HE WAS BORN WE WERE HAVING A DIFFICULT TIME.
I WAS JUST BEGINNING TO GET A LOT OF RECOGNITION AND WAS ALWAYS BUSY WITH TRAVELING AND EXHIBITS.
SHE WAS FRUSTRATED, WORKING JUST AS HARD AS ME, HARDER, REALLY, AND SEEMING TO GET NOWHERE.
THERE WAS SO MUCH RESENTMENT, SO MUCH SUPPRESSED RAGE BETWEEN US.
TELL ME THE TRUTH!
WHAT ARE YOU TALKING ABOUT?
SHE WOULD ACCUSE ME OF SABOTAGING HER, OF UNDERMINING HER, OF NOT LOVING HER, OF CHEATING ON HER.
WHAT? WHY?
YOU KNOW WHY!
WE HADN'T MEANT TO HAVE A BABY. WE HADN'T MEANT NOT TO, BUT WHEN FELIX WAS BORN SHE SEEMED HAPPIER.
BUT SHE SAID SOMETHING JUST BEFORE OUR DIVORCE, THAT I'LL NEVER FORGET.
SHE SAID, SHE HADN'T WANTED TO HAVE A BABY. SHE'D DONE IT FOR ME. SHE WAS AFRAID OF LOSING ME.

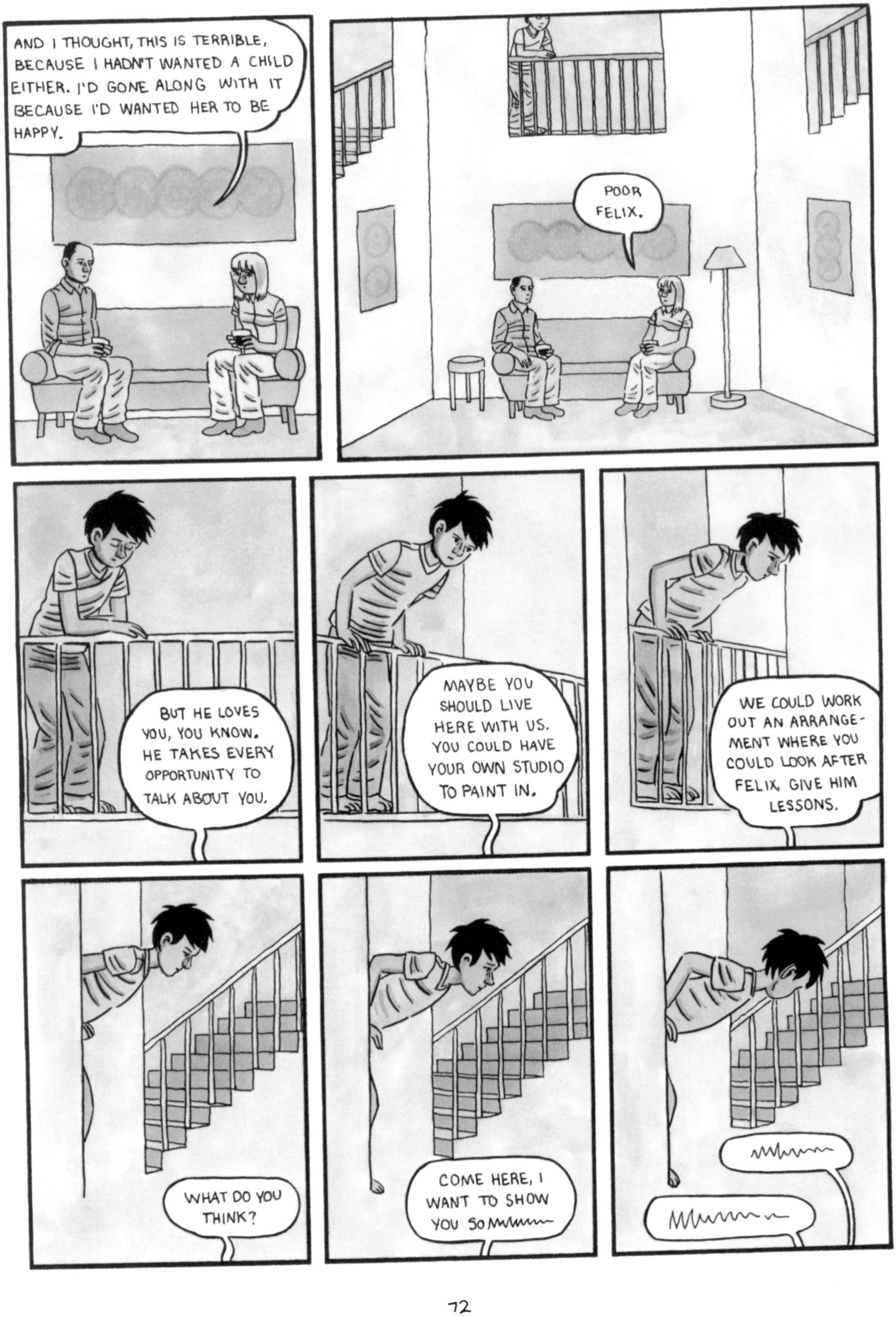
AND I THOUGHT, THIS IS TERRIBLE, BECAUSE I HADN'T WANTED A CHILD EITHER. I'D GONE ALONG WITH IT BECAUSE I'D WANTED HER TO BE HAPPY.
POOR FELIX.
BUT HE LOVES YOU, YOU KNOW. HE TAKES EVERY OPPORTUNITY TO TALK ABOUT YOU.
MAYBE YOU SHOULD LIVE HERE WITH US. YOU COULD HAVE YOUR OWN STUDIO TO PAINT IN.
WE COULD WORK OUT AN ARRANGE-MENT WHERE YOU COULD LOOK AFTER FELIX, GIVE HIM LESSONS.
WHAT DO YOU THINK?
COME HERE, I WANT TO SHOW YOU SO

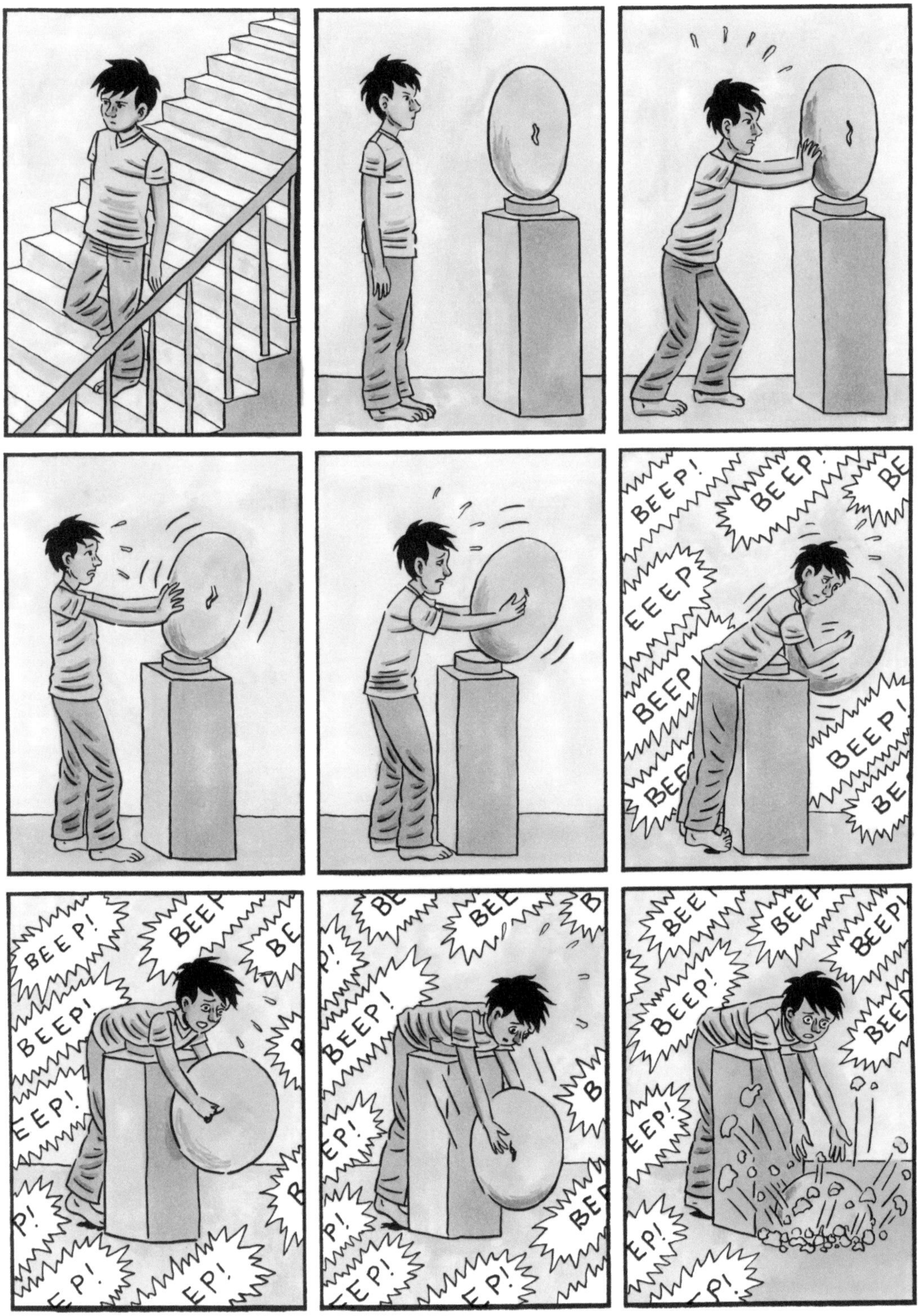
BEEP!
BEEP!
BEEP!
BEEP!
BEEP!
BEEP!
BEEP!
BEEP!
BEEP!
BEEP!
BEEP!

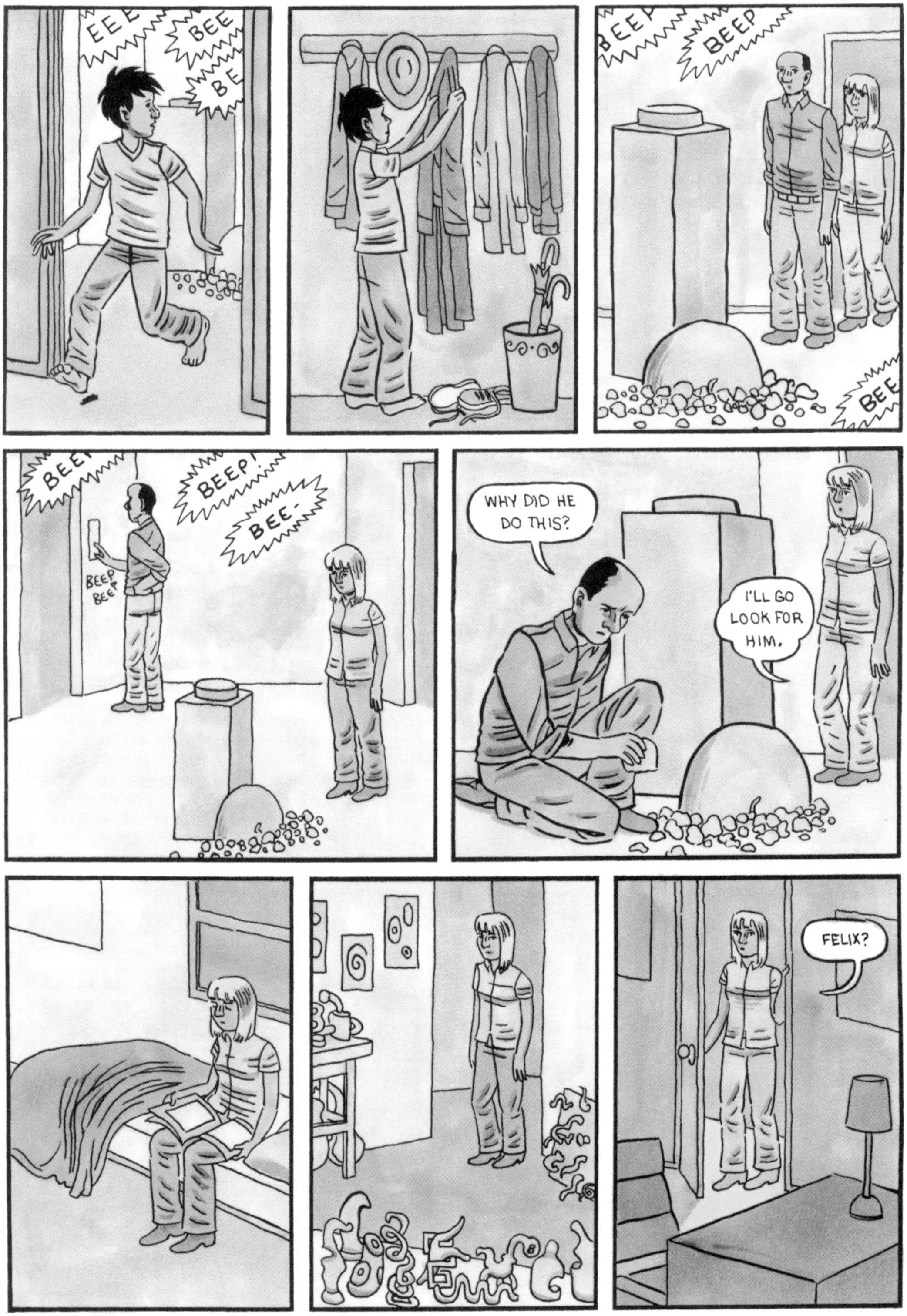
EEE
BEE
BE
BEEP
BEEP
BEE
BEEP
BEEP!
BEE-
BEEP BEEP
WHY DID HE DO THIS?
I'LL GO LOOK FOR HIM.
FELIX?

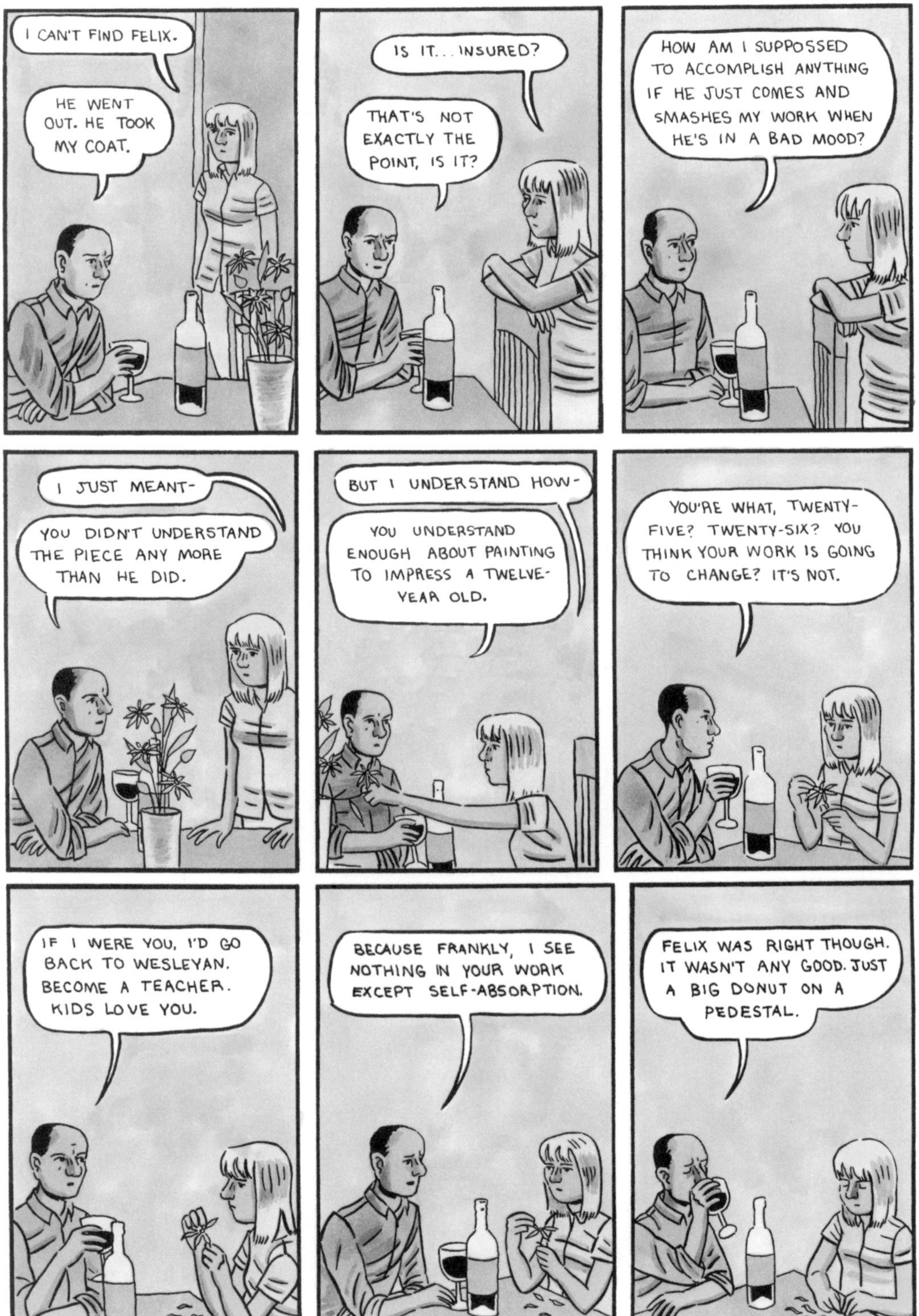
I CAN'T FIND FELIX.
HE WENT OUT. HE TOOK MY COAT.
IS IT... INSURED?
THAT'S NOT EXACTLY THE POINT, IS IT?
HOW AM I SUPPOSSED TO ACCOMPLISH ANYTHING IF HE JUST COMES AND SMASHES MY WORK WHEN HE'S IN A BAD MOOD?
I JUST MEANT-
YOU DIDN'T UNDERSTAND THE PIECE ANY MORE THAN HE DID.
BUT I UNDERSTAND HOW-
YOU UNDERSTAND ENOUGH ABOUT PAINTING TO IMPRESS A TWELVE-YEAR OLD.
YOU'RE WHAT, TWENTY-FIVE? TWENTY-SIX? YOU THINK YOUR WORK IS GOING TO CHANGE? IT'S NOT.
IF I WERE YOU, I'D GO BACK TO WESLEYAN. BECOME A TEACHER. KIDS LOVE YOU.
BECAUSE FRANKLY, I SEE NOTHING IN YOUR WORK EXCEPT SELF-ABSORPTION.
FELIX WAS RIGHT THOUGH. IT WASN'T ANY GOOD. JUST A BIG DONUT ON A PEDESTAL.

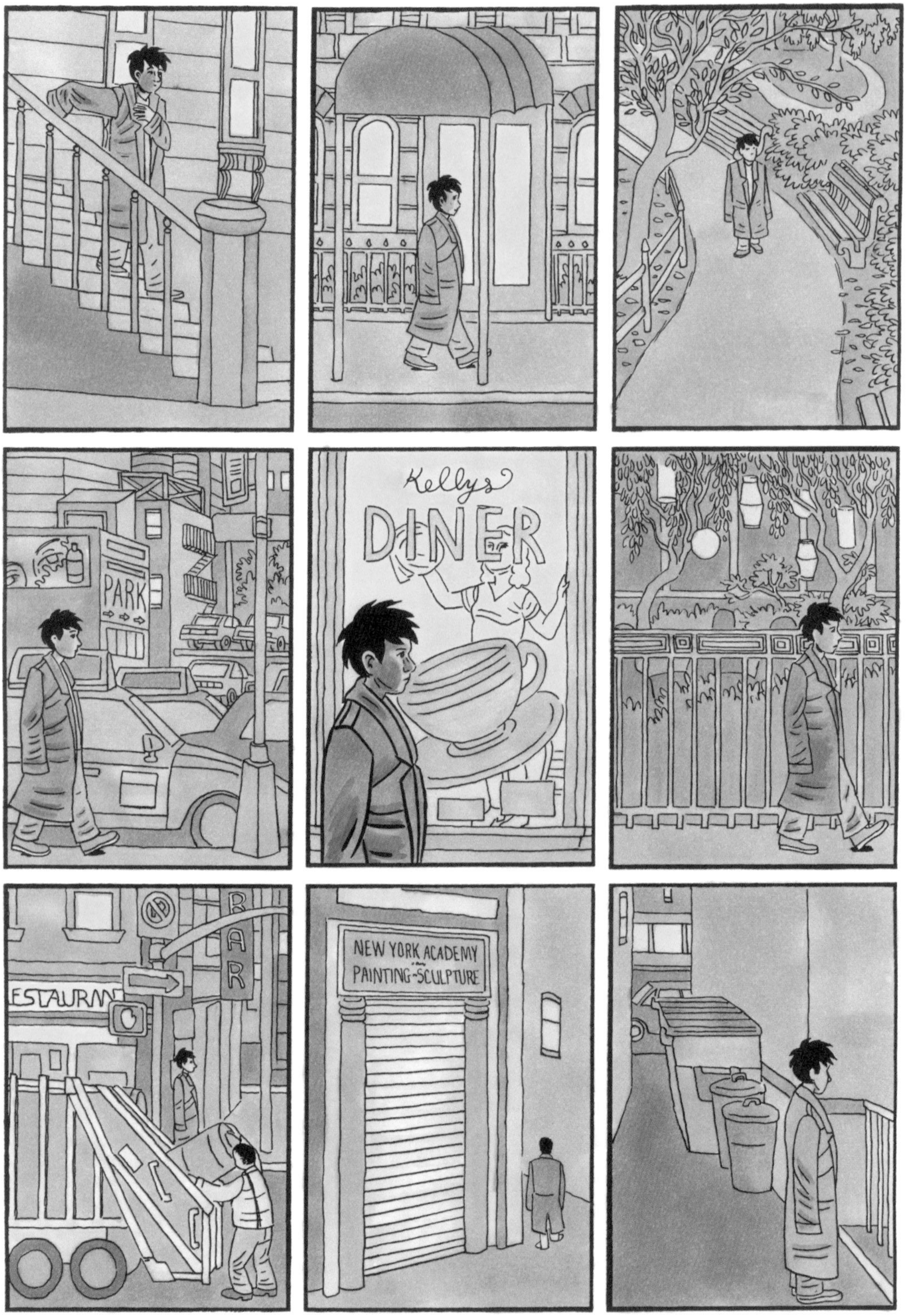
Kelly's
DINER
PARK
ESTAURAN
BAR
NEW YORK ACADEMY
PAINTING - SCULPTURE

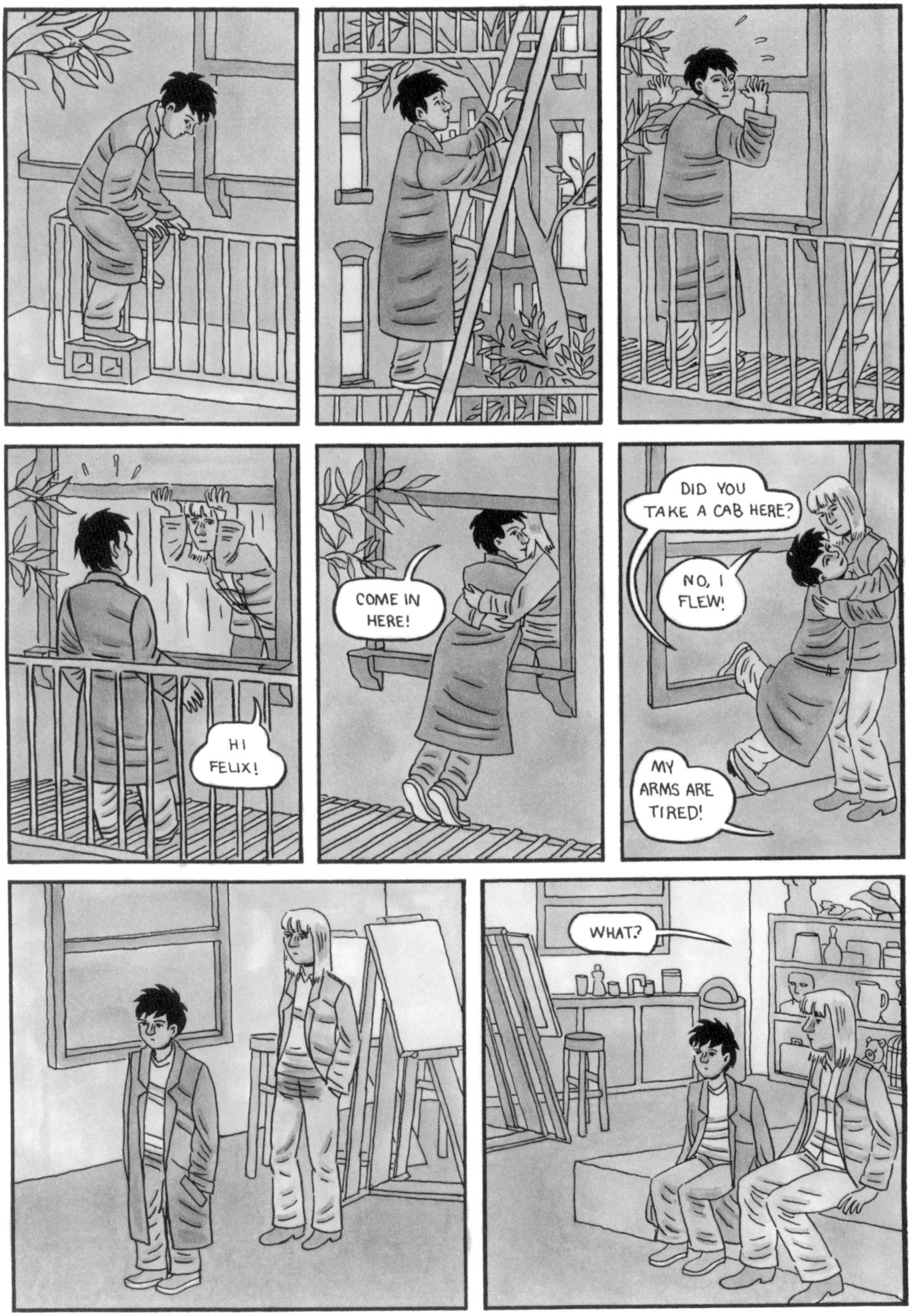
HI FELIX!
COME IN HERE!
DID YOU TAKE A CAB HERE?
NO, I FLEW!
MY ARMS ARE TIRED!
WHAT?

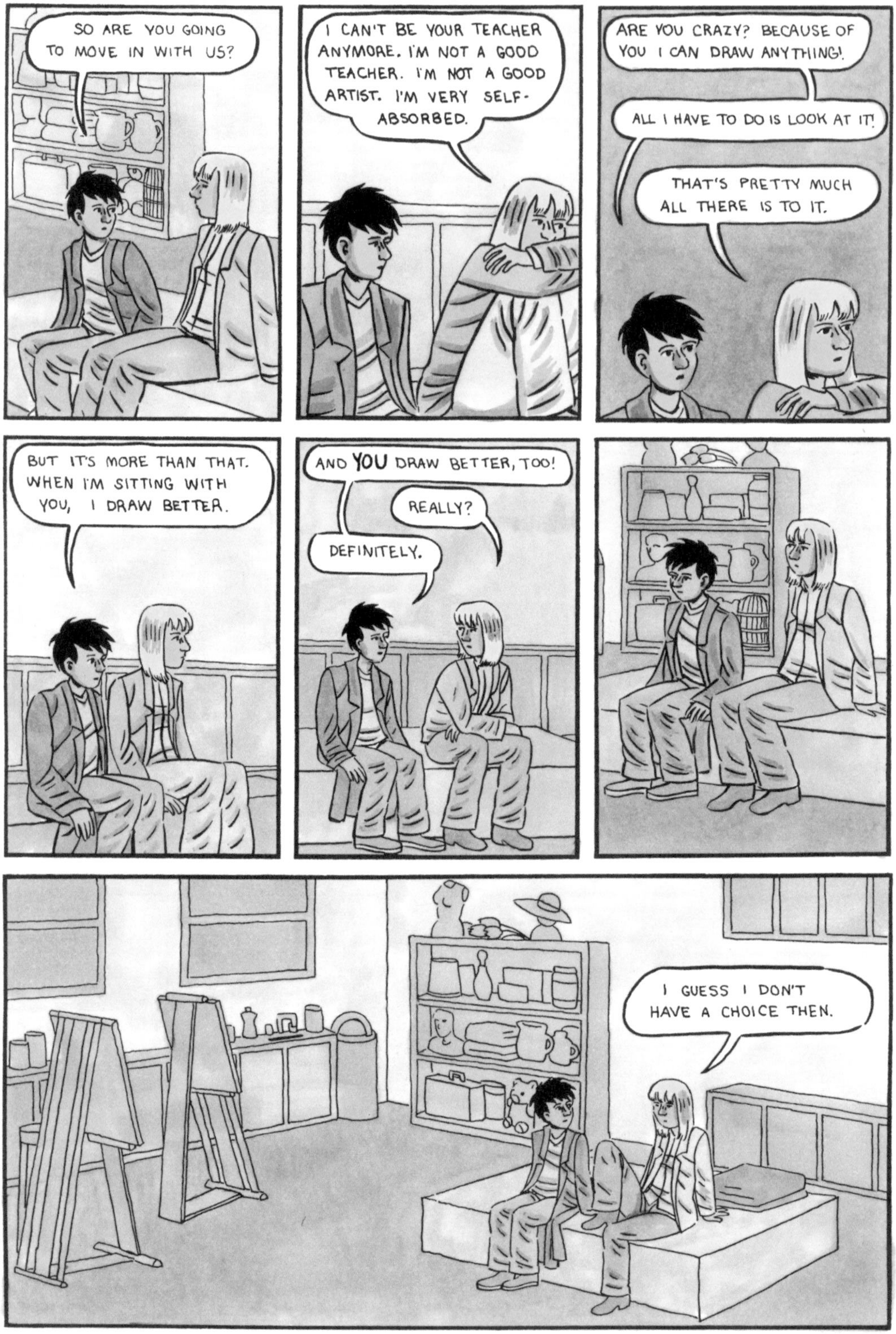
SO ARE YOU GOING TO MOVE IN WITH US?
I CAN'T BE YOUR TEACHER ANYMORE. I'M NOT A GOOD TEACHER. I'M NOT A GOOD ARTIST. I'M VERY SELF-ABSORBED.
ARE YOU CRAZY? BECAUSE OF YOU I CAN DRAW ANYTHING!
ALL I HAVE TO DO IS LOOK AT IT!
THAT'S PRETTY MUCH ALL THERE IS TO IT.
BUT IT'S MORE THAN THAT. WHEN I'M SITTING WITH YOU, I DRAW BETTER.
AND YOU DRAW BETTER, TOO!
REALLY?
DEFINITELY.
I GUESS I DON'T HAVE A CHOICE THEN.

Robot DJ

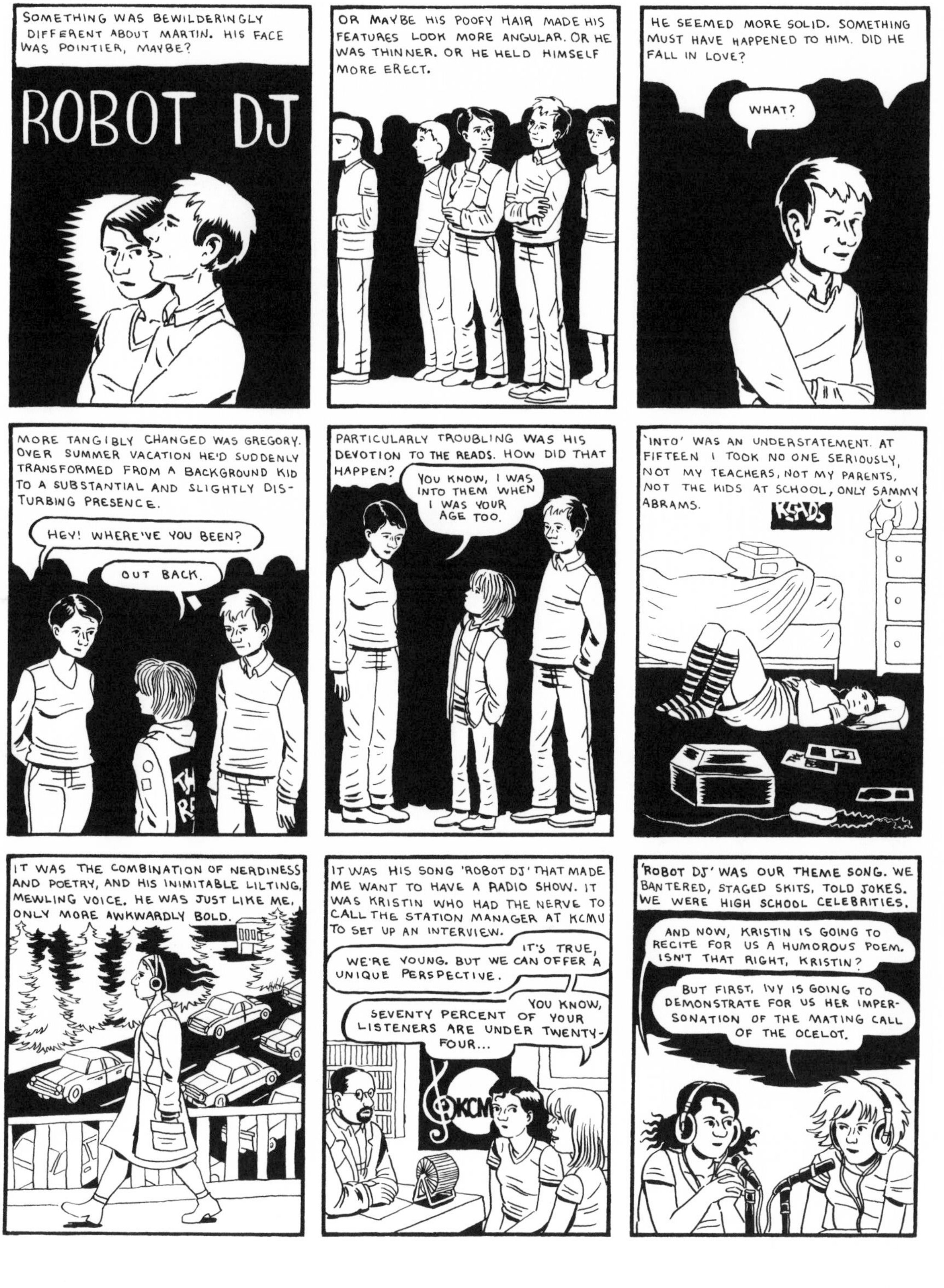
SOMETHING WAS BEWILDERINGLY DIFFERENT ABOUT MARTIN. HIS FACE WAS POINTIER, MAYBE?
ROBOT DJ
OR MAYBE HIS POOFY HAIR MADE HIS FEATURES LOOK MORE ANGULAR. OR HE WAS THINNER. OR HE HELD HIMSELF MORE ERECT.
HE SEEMED MORE SOLID. SOMETHING MUST HAVE HAPPENED TO HIM. DID HE FALL IN LOVE?
WHAT?
MORE TANGIBLY CHANGED WAS GREGORY. OVER SUMMER VACATION HE'D SUDDENLY TRANSFORMED FROM A BACKGROUND KID TO A SUBSTANTIAL AND SLIGHTLY DIS-TURBING PRESENCE.
HEY! WHERE'VE YOU BEEN?
OUT BACK.
PARTICULARLY TROUBLING WAS HIS DEVOTION TO THE READS. HOW DID THAT HAPPEN?
YOU KNOW, I WAS INTO THEM WHEN I WAS YOUR AGE TOO.
'INTO' WAS AN UNDERSTATEMENT. AT FIFTEEN I TOOK NO ONE SERIOUSLY, NOT MY TEACHERS, NOT MY PARENTS, NOT THE KIDS AT SCHOOL, ONLY SAMMY ABRAMS.
READS
IT WAS THE COMBINATION OF NERDINESS AND POETRY, AND HIS INIMITABLE LILTING, MEWLING VOICE. HE WAS JUST LIKE ME, ONLY MORE AWKWARDLY BOLD.
IT WAS HIS SONG 'ROBOT DJ' THAT MADE ME WANT TO HAVE A RADIO SHOW. IT WAS KRISTIN WHO HAD THE NERVE TO CALL THE STATION MANAGER AT KCMU TO SET UP AN INTERVIEW.
IT'S TRUE, WE'RE YOUNG. BUT WE CAN OFFER A UNIQUE PERSPECTIVE.
YOU KNOW, SEVENTY PERCENT OF YOUR LISTENERS ARE UNDER TWENTY-FOUR...
KCM
'ROBOT DJ' WAS OUR THEME SONG. WE BANTERED, STAGED SKITS, TOLD JOKES. WE WERE HIGH SCHOOL CELEBRITIES.
AND NOW, KRISTIN IS GOING TO RECITE FOR US A HUMOROUS POEM. ISN'T THAT RIGHT, KRISTIN?
BUT FIRST, IVY IS GOING TO DEMONSTRATE FOR US HER IMPER-SONATION OF THE MATING CALL OF THE OCELOT.

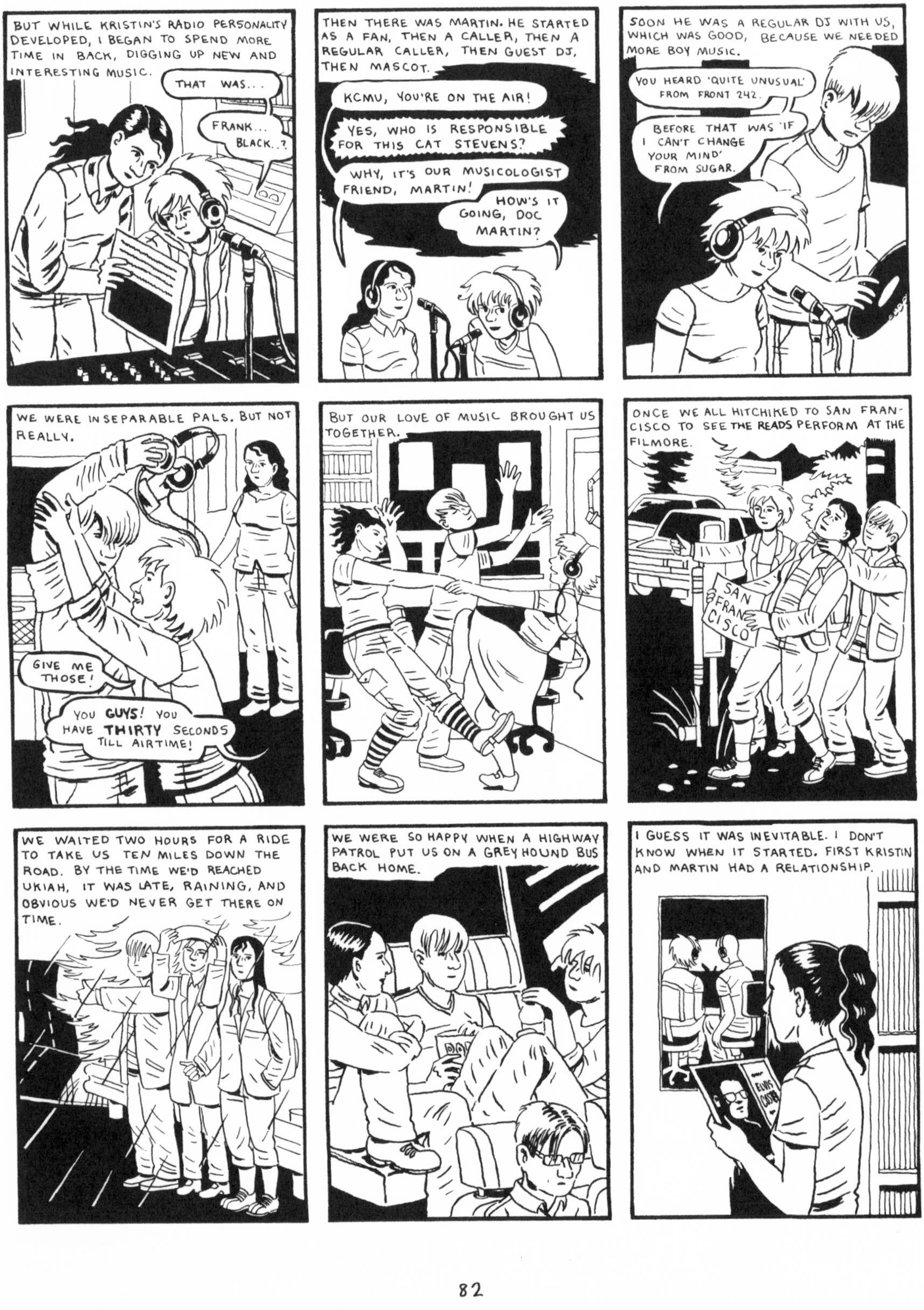

BUT WHILE KRISTIN'S RADIO PERSONALITY DEVELOPED, I BEGAN TO SPEND MORE TIME IN BACK, DIGGING UP NEW AND INTERESTING MUSIC.
THAT WAS...
FRANK... BLACK..?
THEN THERE WAS MARTIN. HE STARTED AS A FAN, THEN A CALLER, THEN A REGULAR CALLER, THEN GUEST DJ, THEN MASCOT.
KCMU, YOU'RE ON THE AIR!
YES, WHO IS RESPONSIBLE FOR THIS CAT STEVENS?
WHY, IT'S OUR MUSICOLOGIST FRIEND, MARTIN!
HOW'S IT GOING, DOC MARTIN?
SOON HE WAS A REGULAR DJ WITH US, WHICH WAS GOOD, BECAUSE WE NEEDED MORE BOY MUSIC.
YOU HEARD 'QUITE UNUSUAL' FROM FRONT 242.
BEFORE THAT WAS 'IF I CAN'T CHANGE YOUR MIND' FROM SUGAR.
WE WERE INSEPARABLE PALS. BUT NOT REALLY.
GIVE ME THOSE!
YOU GUYS! YOU HAVE THIRTY SECONDS TILL AIRTIME!
BUT OUR LOVE OF MUSIC BROUGHT US TOGETHER.
ONCE WE ALL HITCHIKED TO SAN FRANCISCO TO SEE THE READS PERFORM AT THE FILMORE.
SAN FRAN CISCO
WE WAITED TWO HOURS FOR A RIDE TO TAKE US TEN MILES DOWN THE ROAD. BY THE TIME WE'D REACHED UKIAH, IT WAS LATE, RAINING, AND OBVIOUS WE'D NEVER GET THERE ON TIME.
WE WERE SO HAPPY WHEN A HIGHWAY PATROL PUT US ON A GREYHOUND BUS BACK HOME.
I GUESS IT WAS INEVITABLE. I DON'T KNOW WHEN IT STARTED. FIRST KRISTIN AND MARTIN HAD A RELATIONSHIP.
ELVIS COSTELLO

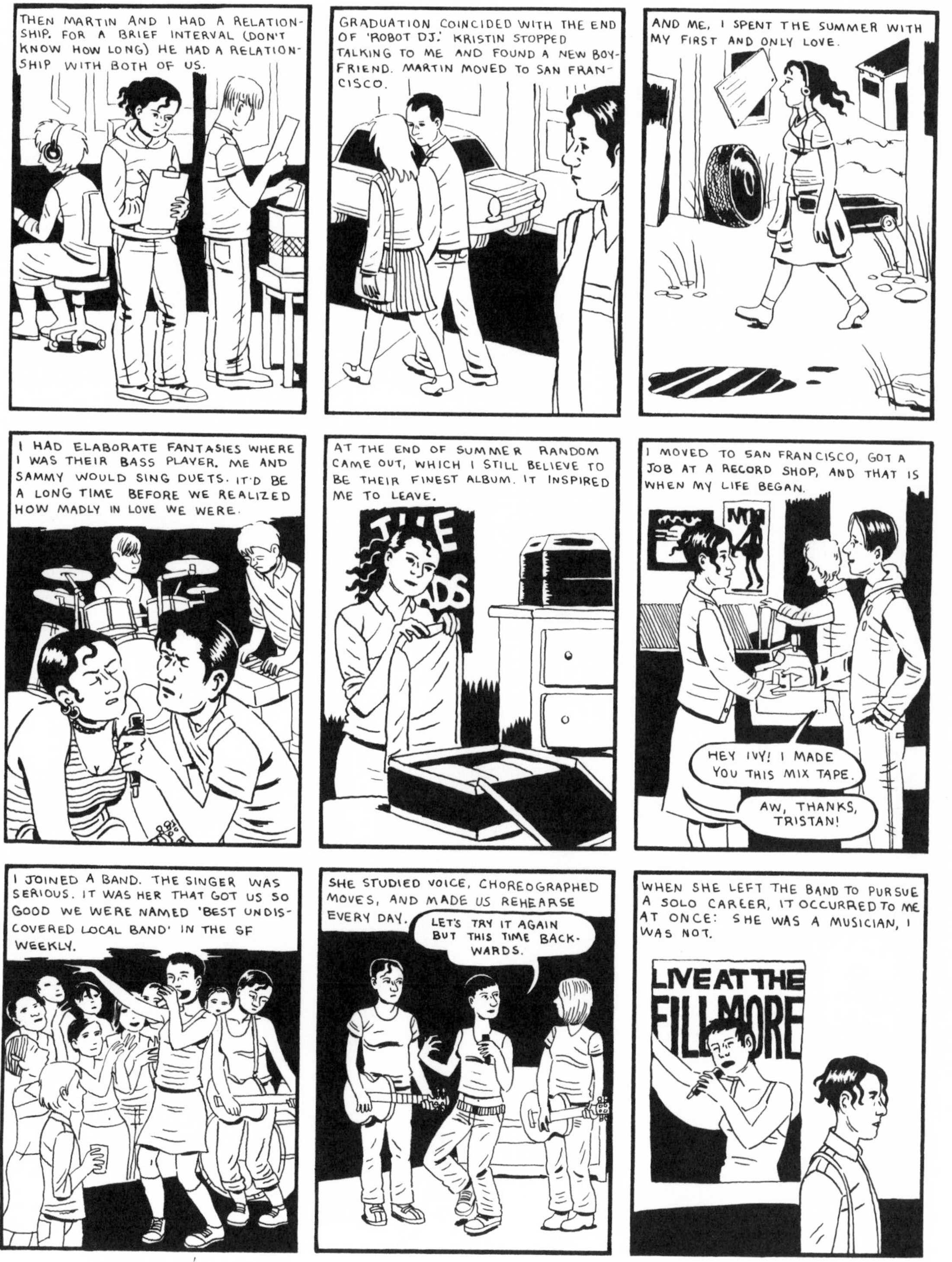
THEN MARTIN AND I HAD A RELATIONSHIP. FOR A BRIEF INTERVAL (DON'T KNOW HOW LONG) HE HAD A RELATIONSHIP WITH BOTH OF US.
GRADUATION COINCIDED WITH THE END OF 'ROBOT DJ.' KRISTIN STOPPED TALKING TO ME AND FOUND A NEW BOYFRIEND. MARTIN MOVED TO SAN FRANCISCO.
AND ME, I SPENT THE SUMMER WITH MY FIRST AND ONLY LOVE.
I HAD ELABORATE FANTASIES WHERE I WAS THEIR BASS PLAYER. ME AND SAMMY WOULD SING DUETS. IT'D BE A LONG TIME BEFORE WE REALIZED HOW MADLY IN LOVE WE WERE.
AT THE END OF SUMMER RANDOM CAME OUT, WHICH I STILL BELIEVE TO BE THEIR FINEST ALBUM. IT INSPIRED ME TO LEAVE.
I MOVED TO SAN FRANCISCO, GOT A JOB AT A RECORD SHOP, AND THAT IS WHEN MY LIFE BEGAN.
HEY IVY! I MADE YOU THIS MIX TAPE.
AW, THANKS, TRISTAN!
I JOINED A BAND. THE SINGER WAS SERIOUS. IT WAS HER THAT GOT US SO GOOD WE WERE NAMED 'BEST UNDISCOVERED LOCAL BAND' IN THE SF WEEKLY.
SHE STUDIED VOICE, CHOREOGRAPHED MOVES, AND MADE US REHEARSE EVERY DAY.
LET'S TRY IT AGAIN BUT THIS TIME BACKWARDS.
WHEN SHE LEFT THE BAND TO PURSUE A SOLO CAREER, IT OCCURRED TO ME AT ONCE: SHE WAS A MUSICIAN, I WAS NOT.
LIVE AT THE FILLMORE

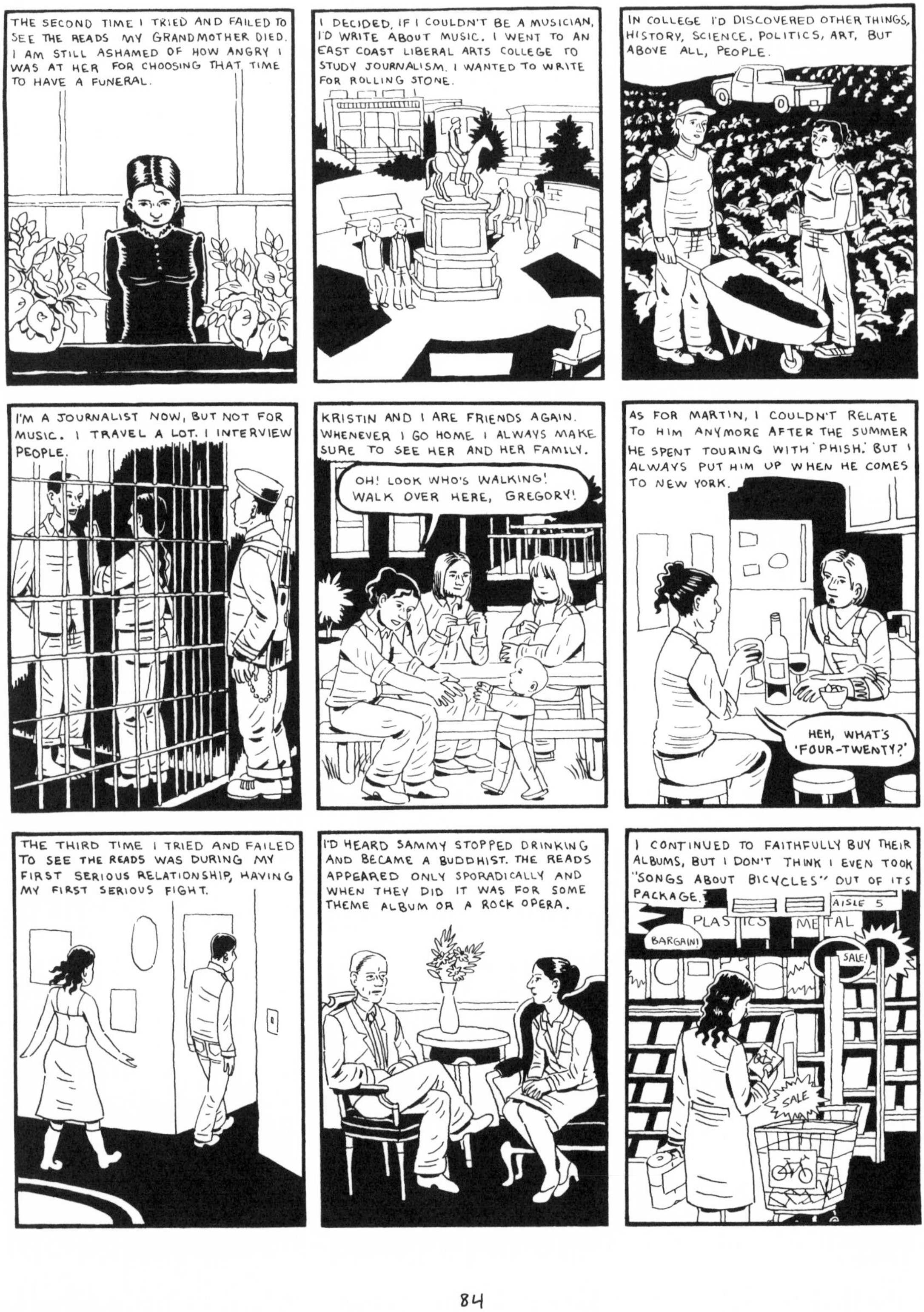
THE SECOND TIME I TRIED AND FAILED TO SEE THE READS MY GRANDMOTHER DIED. I AM STILL ASHAMED OF HOW ANGRY I WAS AT HER FOR CHOOSING THAT TIME TO HAVE A FUNERAL.
I DECIDED, IF I COULDN'T BE A MUSICIAN, I'D WRITE ABOUT MUSIC. I WENT TO AN EAST COAST LIBERAL ARTS COLLEGE TO STUDY JOURNALISM. I WANTED TO WRITE FOR ROLLING STONE.
IN COLLEGE I'D DISCOVERED OTHER THINGS, HISTORY, SCIENCE, POLITICS, ART, BUT ABOVE ALL, PEOPLE.
I'M A JOURNALIST NOW, BUT NOT FOR MUSIC. I TRAVEL A LOT. I INTERVIEW PEOPLE.
KRISTIN AND I ARE FRIENDS AGAIN. WHENEVER I GO HOME I ALWAYS MAKE SURE TO SEE HER AND HER FAMILY.
OH! LOOK WHO'S WALKING! WALK OVER HERE, GREGORY!
AS FOR MARTIN, I COULDN'T RELATE TO HIM ANYMORE AFTER THE SUMMER HE SPENT TOURING WITH "PHISH." BUT I ALWAYS PUT HIM UP WHEN HE COMES TO NEW YORK.
HEH, WHAT'S 'FOUR-TWENTY?'
THE THIRD TIME I TRIED AND FAILED TO SEE THE READS WAS DURING MY FIRST SERIOUS RELATIONSHIP, HAVING MY FIRST SERIOUS FIGHT.
I'D HEARD SAMMY STOPPED DRINKING AND BECAME A BUDDHIST. THE READS APPEARED ONLY SPORADICALLY AND WHEN THEY DID IT WAS FOR SOME THEME ALBUM OR A ROCK OPERA.
I CONTINUED TO FAITHFULLY BUY THEIR ALBUMS, BUT I DON'T THINK I EVEN TOOK "SONGS ABOUT BICYCLES" OUT OF ITS PACKAGE.
AISLE 5
PLASTICS
METAL
BARGAIN!
SALE!
SALE

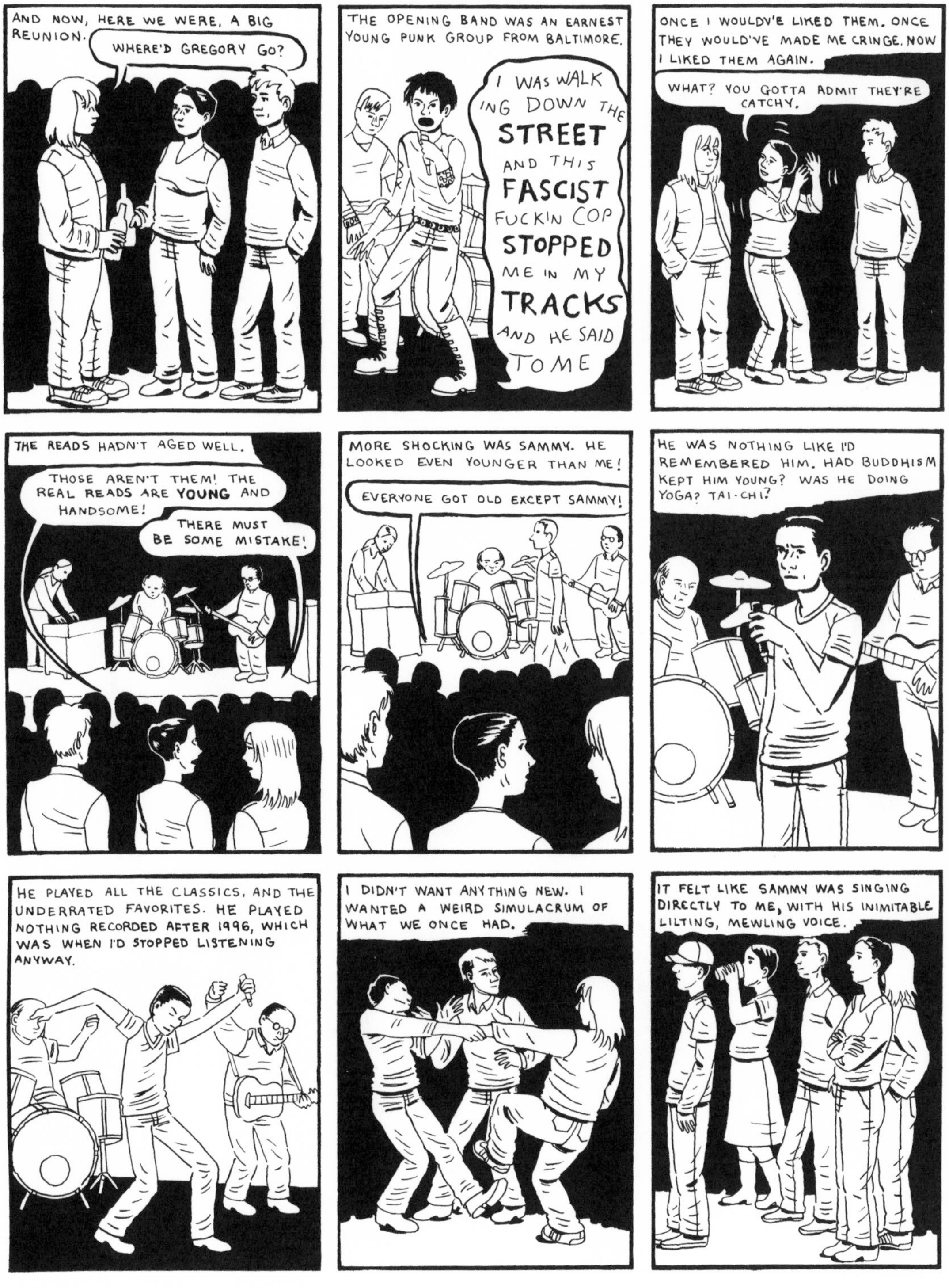
AND NOW, HERE WE WERE, A BIG REUNION.
WHERE'D GREGORY GO?
THE OPENING BAND WAS AN EARNEST YOUNG PUNK GROUP FROM BALTIMORE.
I WAS WALK ING DOWN THE STREET AND THIS FASCIST FUCKIN COP STOPPED ME IN MY TRACKS AND HE SAID TO ME
ONCE I WOULDV'E LIKED THEM. ONCE THEY WOULD'VE MADE ME CRINGE. NOW I LIKED THEM AGAIN.
WHAT? YOU GOTTA ADMIT THEY'RE CATCHY.
THE READS HADN'T AGED WELL.
THOSE AREN'T THEM! THE REAL READS ARE YOUNG AND HANDSOME!
THERE MUST BE SOME MISTAKE!
MORE SHOCKING WAS SAMMY. HE LOOKED EVEN YOUNGER THAN ME!
EVERYONE GOT OLD EXCEPT SAMMY!
HE WAS NOTHING LIKE I'D REMEMBERED HIM. HAD BUDDHISM KEPT HIM YOUNG? WAS HE DOING YOGA? TAI-CHI?
HE PLAYED ALL THE CLASSICS, AND THE UNDERRATED FAVORITES. HE PLAYED NOTHING RECORDED AFTER 1996, WHICH WAS WHEN I'D STOPPED LISTENING ANYWAY.
I DIDN'T WANT ANYTHING NEW. I WANTED A WEIRD SIMULACRUM OF WHAT WE ONCE HAD.
IT FELT LIKE SAMMY WAS SINGING DIRECTLY TO ME, WITH HIS INIMITABLE LILTING, MEWLING VOICE.

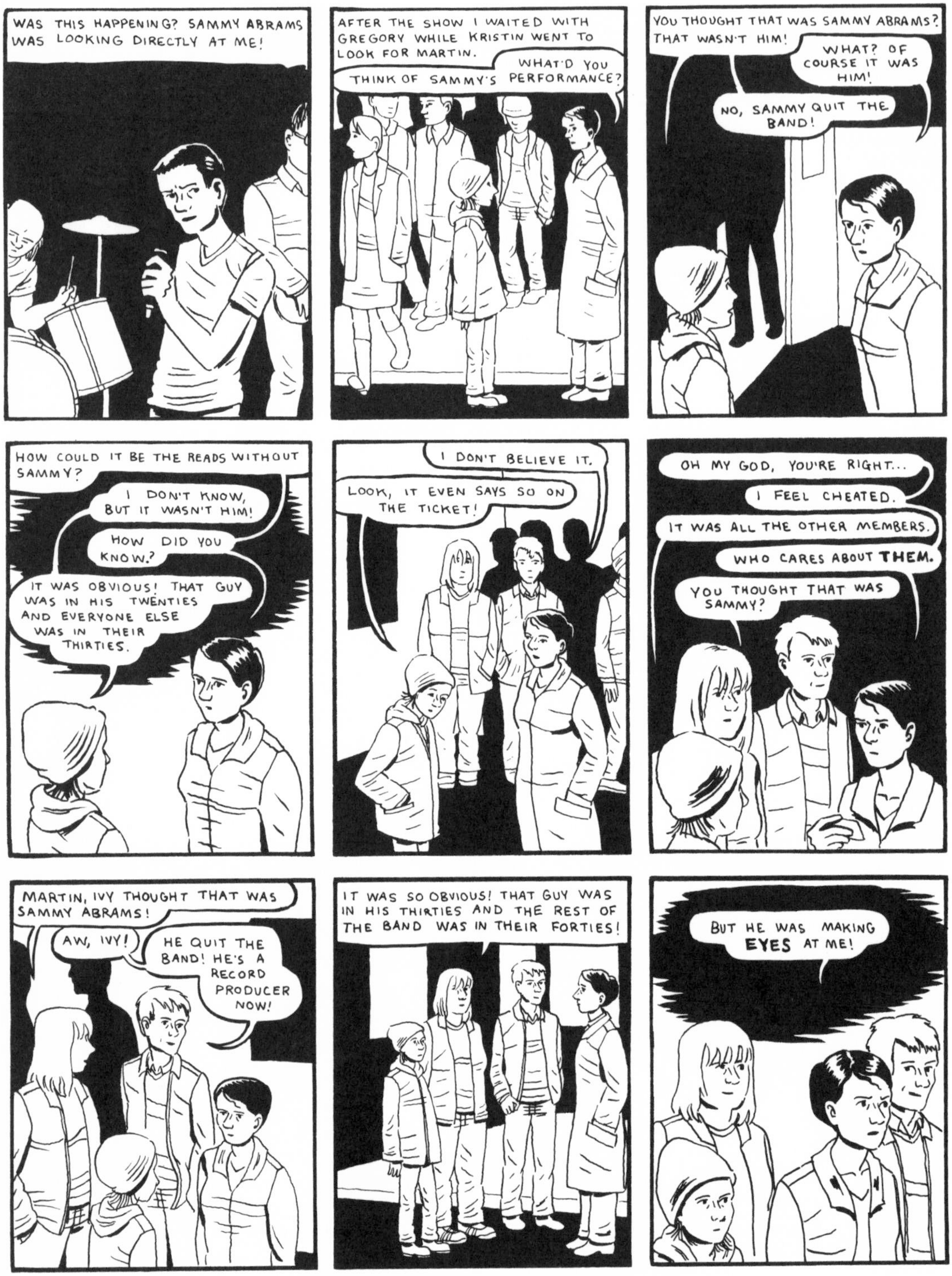
WAS THIS HAPPENING? SAMMY ABRAMS WAS LOOKING DIRECTLY AT ME!
AFTER THE SHOW I WAITED WITH GREGORY WHILE KRISTIN WENT TO LOOK FOR MARTIN.
WHAT'D YOU THINK OF SAMMY'S PERFORMANCE?
YOU THOUGHT THAT WAS SAMMY ABRAMS? THAT WASN'T HIM!
WHAT? OF COURSE IT WAS HIM!
NO, SAMMY QUIT THE BAND!
HOW COULD IT BE THE READS WITHOUT SAMMY?
I DON'T KNOW, BUT IT WASN'T HIM!
HOW DID YOU KNOW?
IT WAS OBVIOUS! THAT GUY WAS IN HIS TWENTIES AND EVERYONE ELSE WAS IN THEIR THIRTIES.
I DON'T BELIEVE IT.
LOOK, IT EVEN SAYS SO ON THE TICKET!
OH MY GOD, YOU'RE RIGHT...
I FEEL CHEATED.
IT WAS ALL THE OTHER MEMBERS.
WHO CARES ABOUT THEM.
YOU THOUGHT THAT WAS SAMMY?
MARTIN, IVY THOUGHT THAT WAS SAMMY ABRAMS!
AW, IVY!
HE QUIT THE BAND! HE'S A RECORD PRODUCER NOW!
IT WAS SO OBVIOUS! THAT GUY WAS IN HIS THIRTIES AND THE REST OF THE BAND WAS IN THEIR FORTIES!
BUT HE WAS MAKING EYES AT ME!

My Affliction

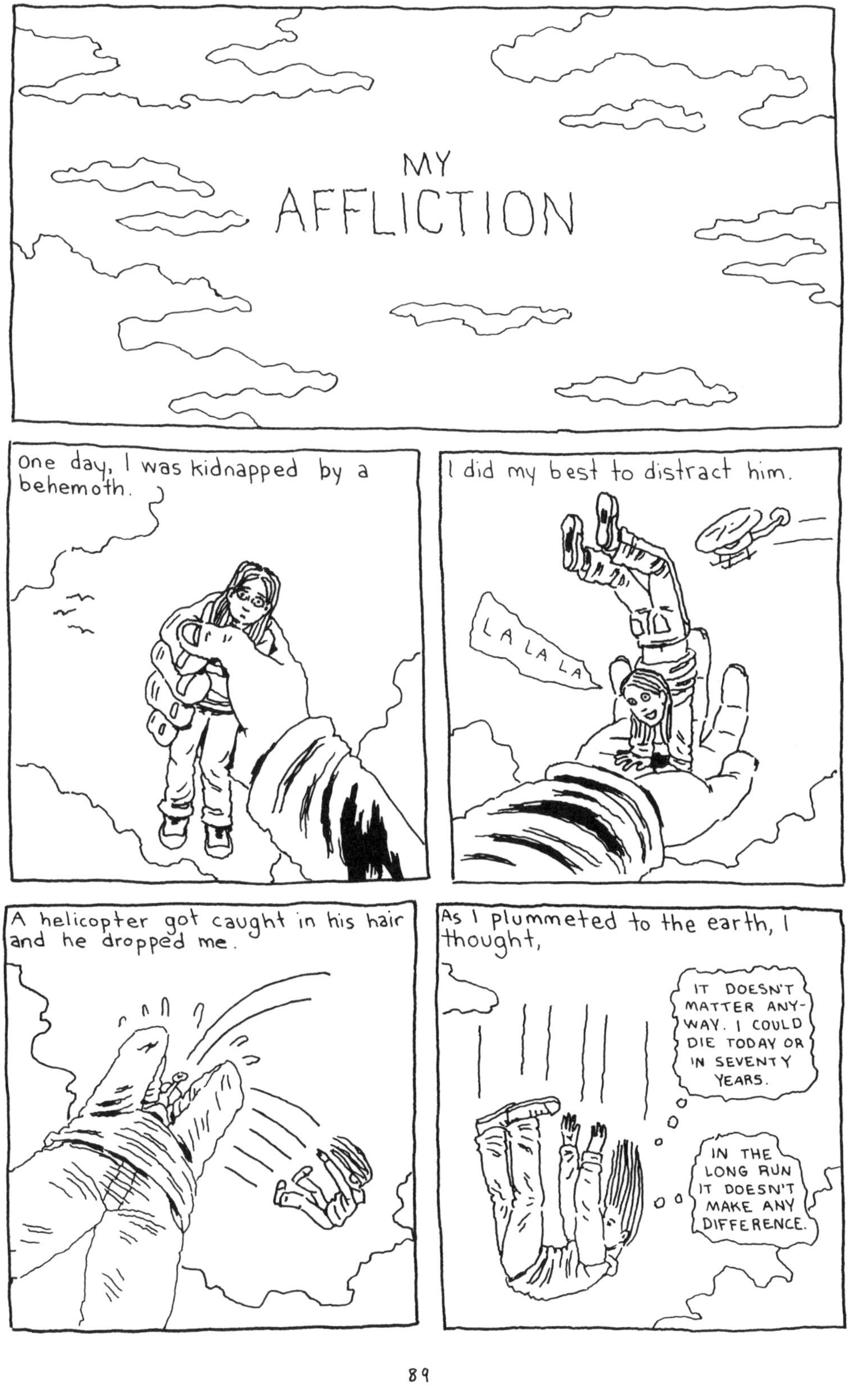
MY AFFLICTION
One day, I was kidnapped by a behemoth.
I did my best to distract him.
LA LA LA LA
A helicopter got caught in his hair and he dropped me.
As I plummeted to the earth, I thought,
IT DOESN'T MATTER ANYWAY. I COULD DIE TODAY OR IN SEVENTY YEARS.
IN THE LONG RUN IT DOESN'T MAKE ANY DIFFERENCE.

Something weird happened. I slowed down in midair.

Then I stopped entirely.

I stayed there for several days. The sun burned me. The night chilled me. Sometimes a strong wind lurched me this way and that.

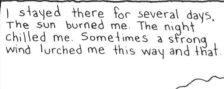

One morning a heavy rain pushed me downwards.

When the rain stopped I was almost down.

I climbed down a tree in Central Park.

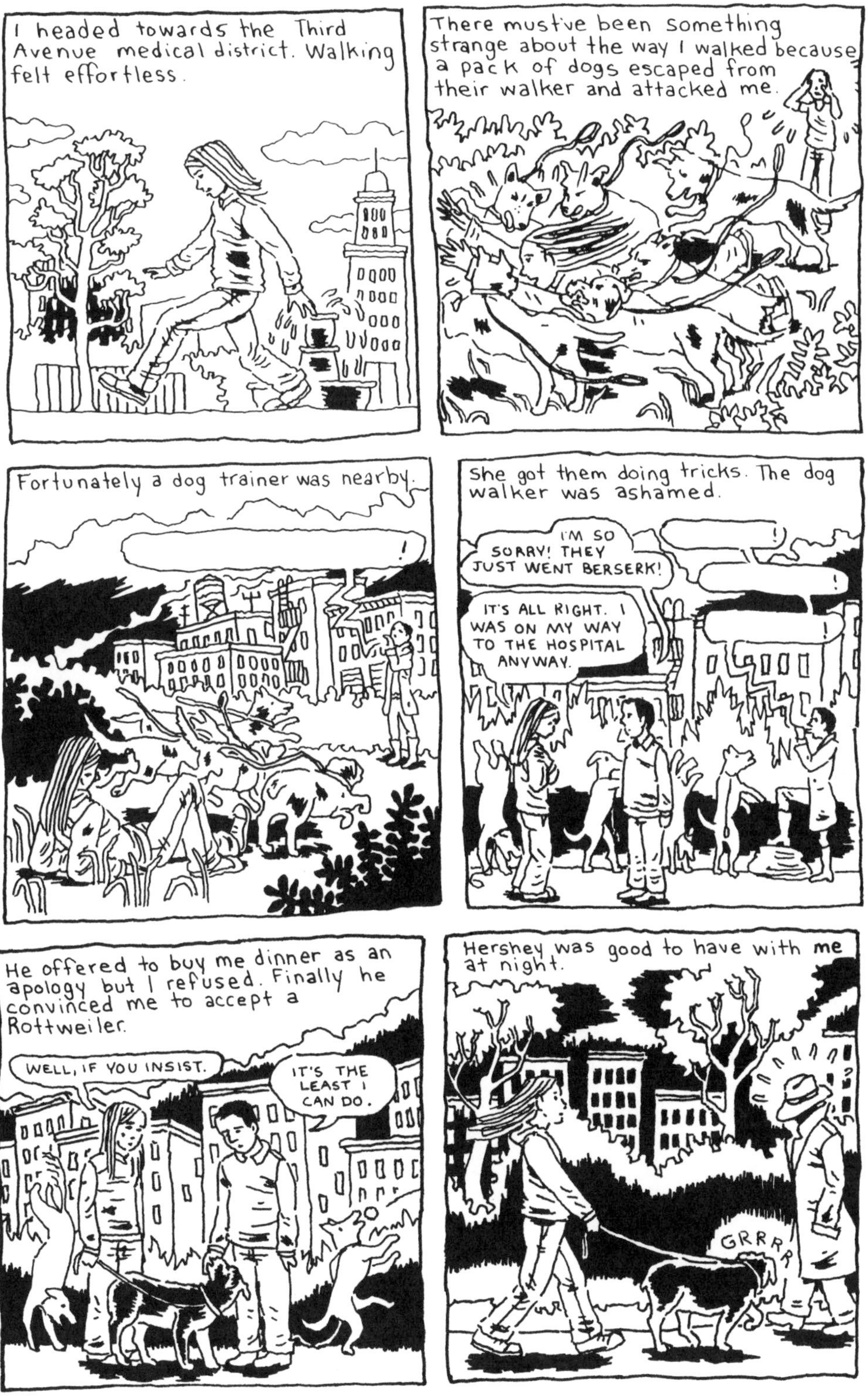
I headed towards the Third Avenue medical district. Walking felt effortless.
There mustve been something strange about the way I walked because a pack of dogs escaped from their walker and attacked me.
Fortunately a dog trainer was nearby.
She got them doing tricks. The dog walker was ashamed.
I'M SO SORRY! THEY JUST WENT BERSERK!
IT'S ALL RIGHT. I WAS ON MY WAY TO THE HOSPITAL ANYWAY.
He offered to buy me dinner as an apology but I refused. Finally he convinced me to accept a Rottweiler.
WELL, IF YOU INSIST.
IT'S THE LEAST I CAN DO.
Hershey was good to have with me at night.
GRRRR

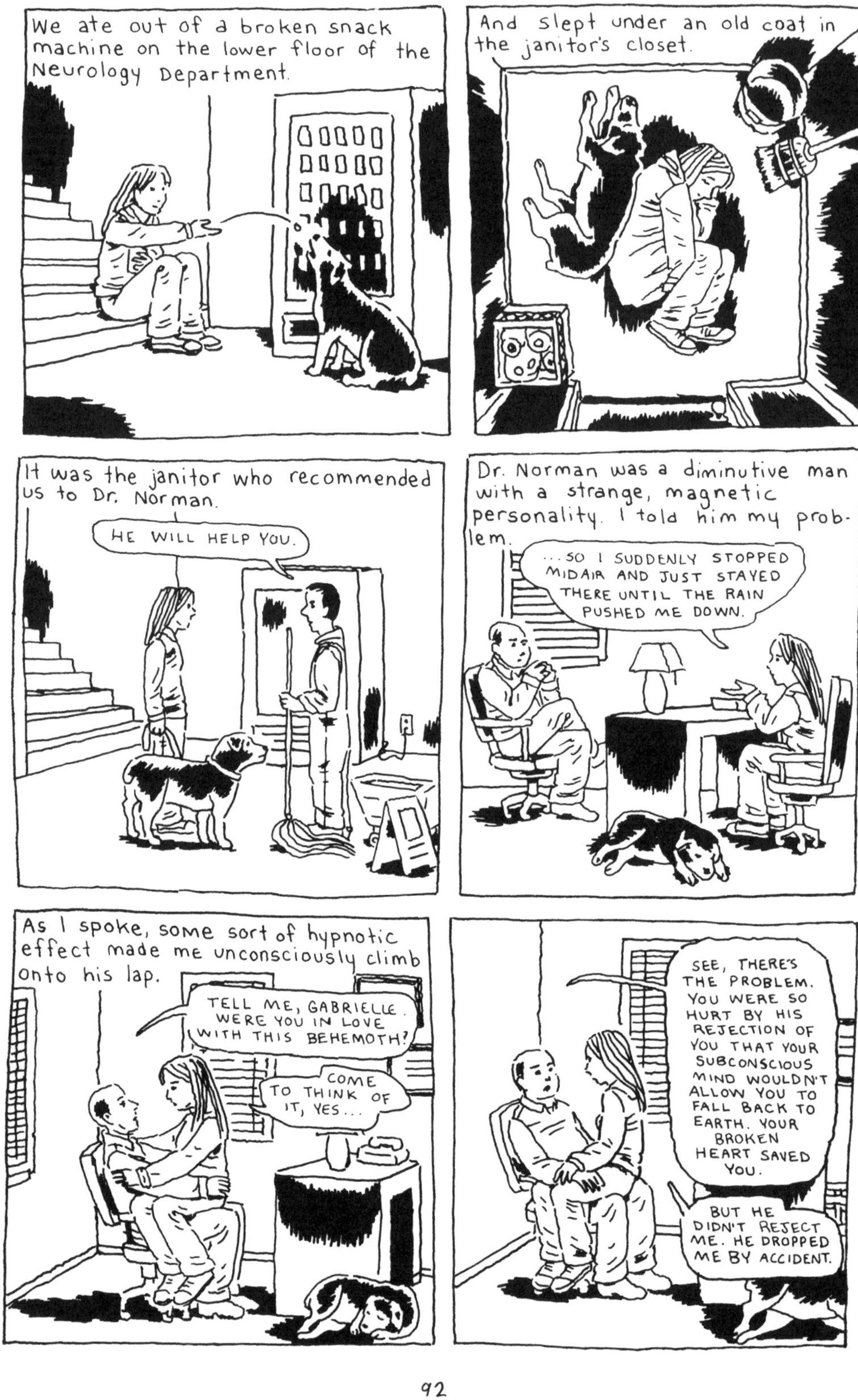

We ate out of a broken snack machine on the lower floor of the Neurology Department.
And slept under an old coat in the janitor's closet.
It was the janitor who recommended us to Dr. Norman.
HE WILL HELP YOU.
Dr. Norman was a diminutive man with a strange, magnetic personality. I told him my problem.
...SO I SUDDENLY STOPPED MIDAIR AND JUST STAYED THERE UNTIL THE RAIN PUSHED ME DOWN.
As I spoke, some sort of hypnotic effect made me unconsciously climb onto his lap.
TELL ME, GABRIELLE. WERE YOU IN LOVE WITH THIS BEHEMOTH?
COME TO THINK OF IT, YES...
SEE, THERE'S THE PROBLEM. YOU WERE SO HURT BY HIS REJECTION OF YOU THAT YOUR SUBCONSCIOUS MIND WOULDN'T ALLOW YOU TO FALL BACK TO EARTH. YOUR BROKEN HEART SAVED YOU.
BUT HE DIDN'T REJECT ME. HE DROPPED ME BY ACCIDENT.

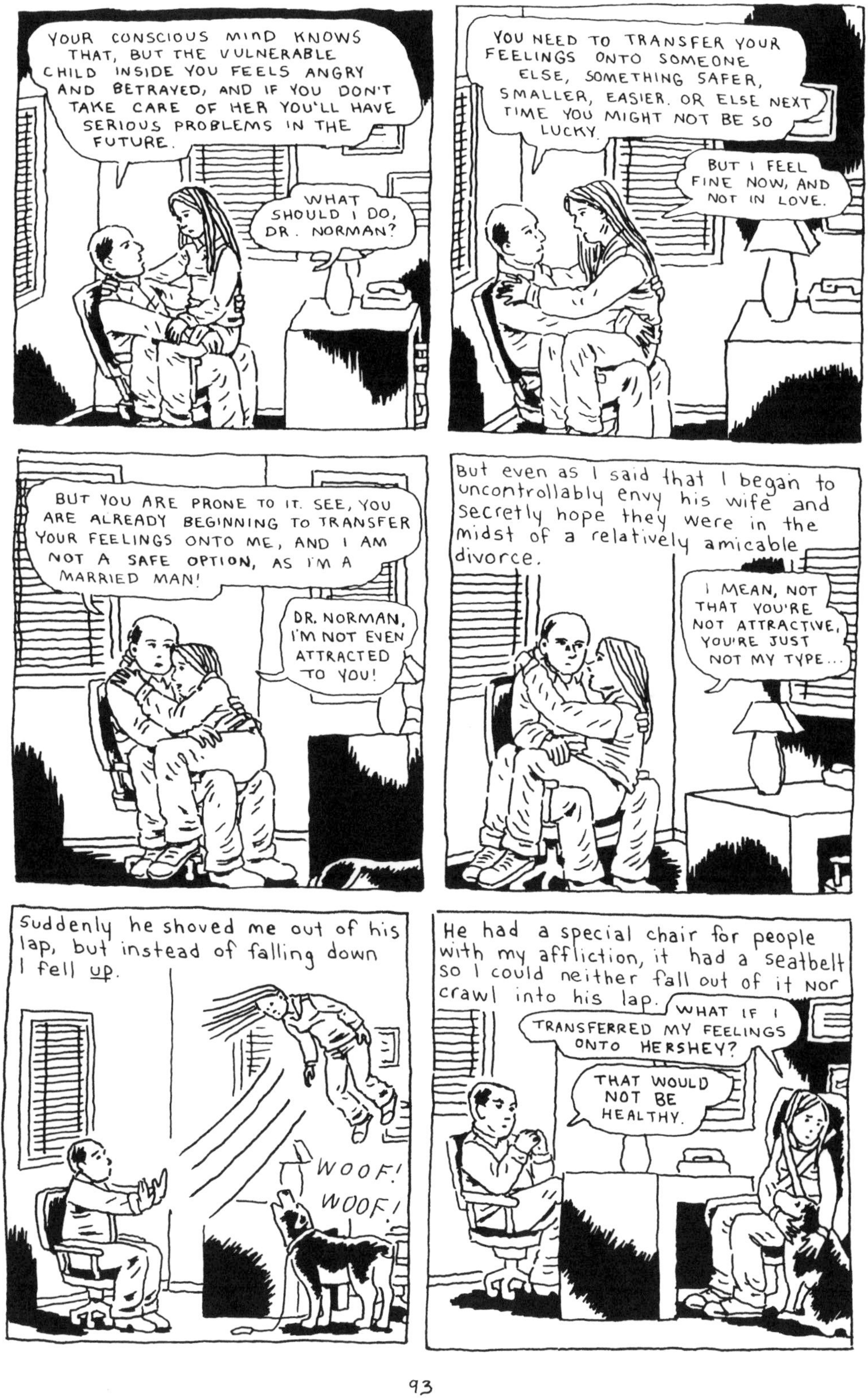
YOUR CONSCIOUS MIND KNOWS THAT, BUT THE VULNERABLE CHILD INSIDE YOU FEELS ANGRY AND BETRAYED, AND IF YOU DON'T TAKE CARE OF HER YOU'LL HAVE SERIOUS PROBLEMS IN THE FUTURE.
WHAT SHOULD I DO, DR. NORMAN?
YOU NEED TO TRANSFER YOUR FEELINGS ONTO SOMEONE ELSE, SOMETHING SAFER, SMALLER, EASIER. OR ELSE NEXT TIME YOU MIGHT NOT BE SO LUCKY.
BUT I FEEL FINE NOW, AND NOT IN LOVE.
BUT YOU ARE PRONE TO IT. SEE, YOU ARE ALREADY BEGINNING TO TRANSFER YOUR FEELINGS ONTO ME, AND I AM NOT A SAFE OPTION, AS I'M A MARRIED MAN!
DR. NORMAN, I'M NOT EVEN ATTRACTED TO YOU!
But even as I said that I began to uncontrollably envy his wife and secretly hope they were in the midst of a relatively amicable divorce.
I MEAN, NOT THAT YOU'RE NOT ATTRACTIVE, YOU'RE JUST NOT MY TYPE...
Suddenly he shoved me out of his lap, but instead of falling down I fell up.
WOOF!
WOOF!
He had a special chair for people with my affliction, it had a seatbelt so I could neither fall out of it nor crawl into his lap.
WHAT IF I TRANSFERRED MY FEELINGS ONTO HERSHEY?
THAT WOULD NOT BE HEALTHY.

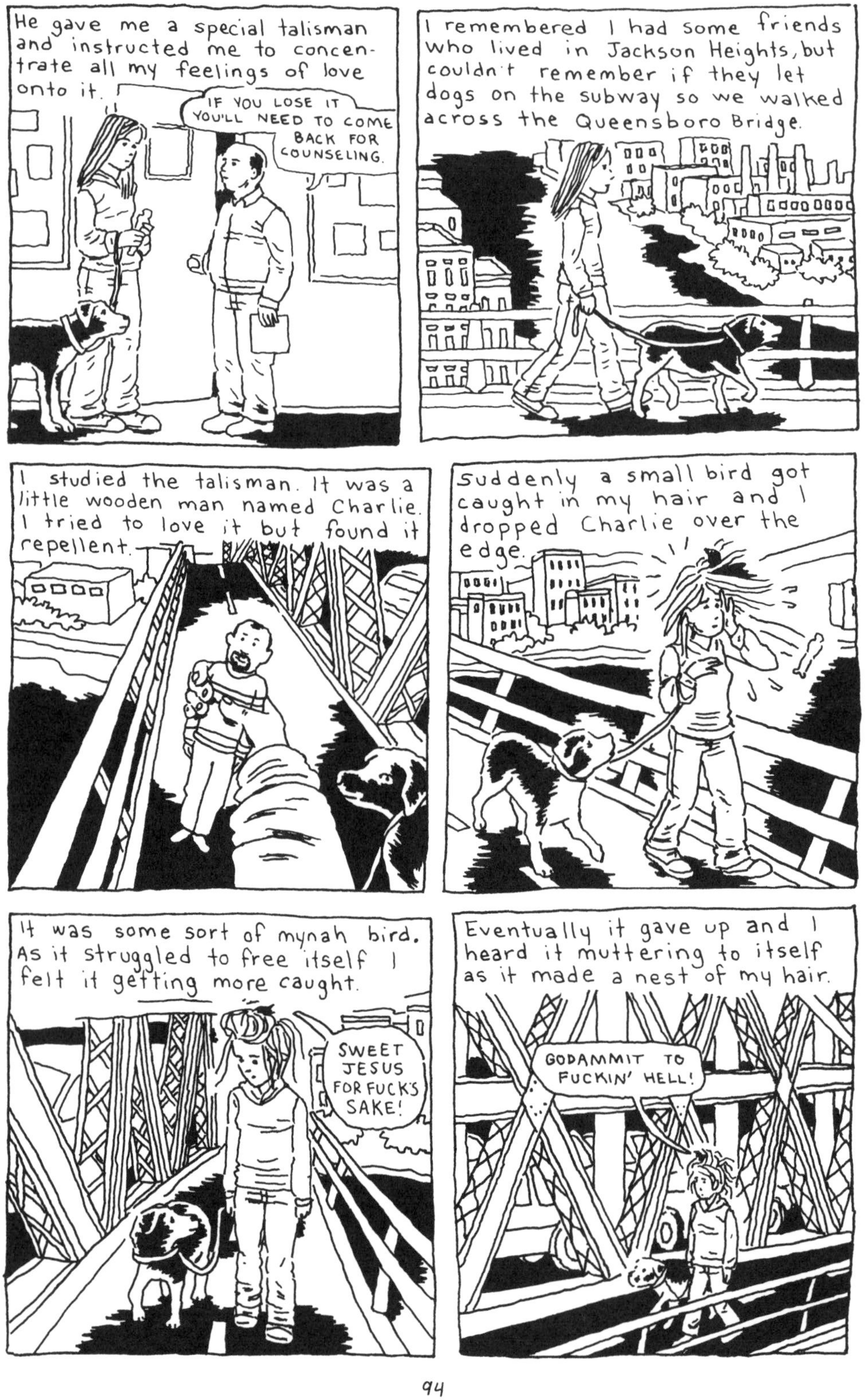
He gave me a special talisman and instructed me to concentrate all my feelings of love onto it.
IF YOU LOSE IT YOU'LL NEED TO COME BACK FOR COUNSELING.
I remembered I had some friends who lived in Jackson Heights, but couldn't remember if they let dogs on the subway so we walked across the Queensboro Bridge.
I studied the talisman. It was a little wooden man named Charlie. I tried to love it but found it repellent.
Suddenly a small bird got caught in my hair and I dropped Charlie over the edge.
It was some sort of mynah bird. As it struggled to free itself I felt it getting more caught.
SWEET JESUS FOR FUCK'S SAKE!
Eventually it gave up and I heard it muttering to itself as it made a nest of my hair.
GODAMMIT TO FUCKIN' HELL!

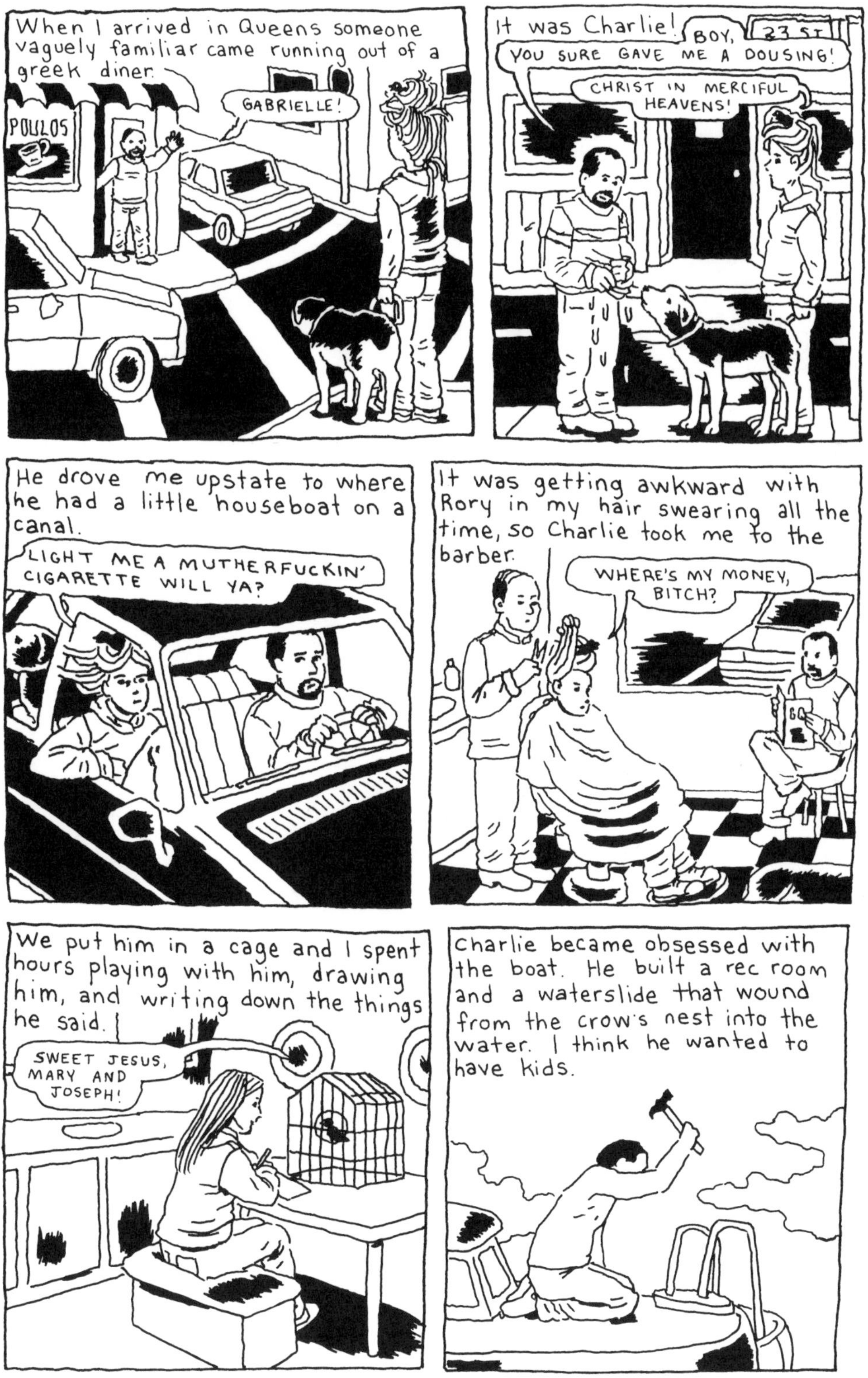
When I arrived in Queens someone vaguely familiar came running out of a greek diner.
POULOS
GABRIELLE!
It was Charlie!
BOY, YOU SURE GAVE ME A DOUSING!
23 ST
CHRIST IN MERCIFUL HEAVENS!
He drove me upstate to where he had a little houseboat on a canal.
LIGHT ME A MUTHERFUCKIN' CIGARETTE WILL YA?
It was getting awkward with Rory in my hair swearing all the time, so Charlie took me to the barber.
WHERE'S MY MONEY, BITCH?
GQ
We put him in a cage and I spent hours playing with him, drawing him, and writing down the things he said.
SWEET JESUS, MARY AND JOSEPH!
Charlie became obsessed with the boat. He built a rec room and a waterslide that wound from the crow's nest into the water. I think he wanted to have kids.

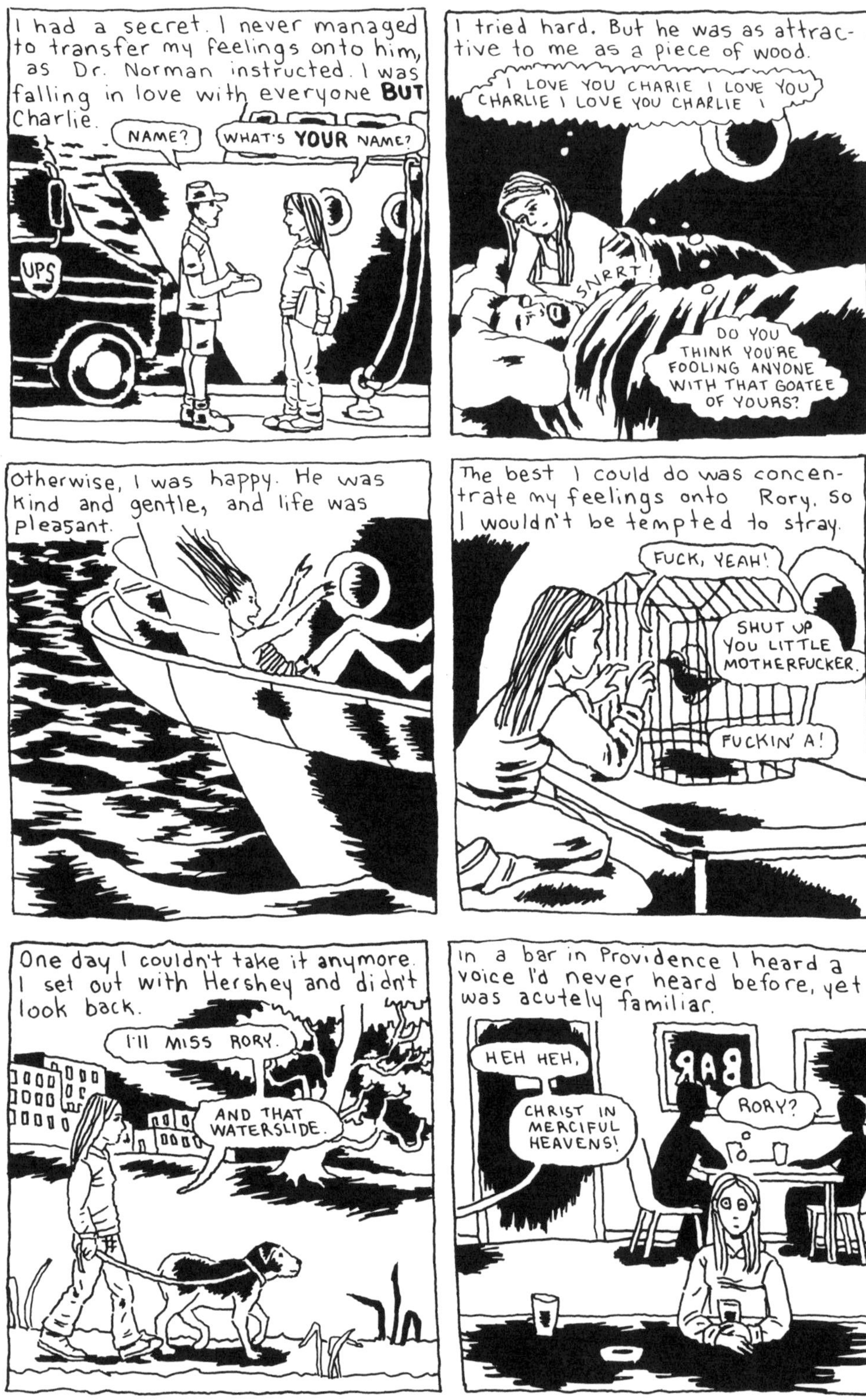
I had a secret. I never managed to transfer my feelings onto him, as Dr. Norman instructed. I was falling in love with everyone BUT Charlie.
NAME?
WHAT'S YOUR NAME?
I tried hard. But he was as attractive to me as a piece of wood.
I LOVE YOU CHARIE I LOVE YOU CHARLIE I LOVE YOU CHARLIE I
SNRRT!
DO YOU THINK YOU'RE FOOLING ANYONE WITH THAT GOATEE OF YOURS?
Otherwise, I was happy. He was kind and gentle, and life was pleasant.
The best I could do was concentrate my feelings onto Rory, so I wouldn't be tempted to stray.
FUCK, YEAH!
SHUT UP YOU LITTLE MOTHERFUCKER.
FUCKIN' A!
One day I couldn't take it anymore. I set out with Hershey and didn't look back.
I'LL MISS RORY.
AND THAT WATERSLIDE.
In a bar in Providence I heard a voice I'd never heard before, yet was acutely familiar.
HEH HEH.
CHRIST IN MERCIFUL HEAVENS!
RORY?
BAR

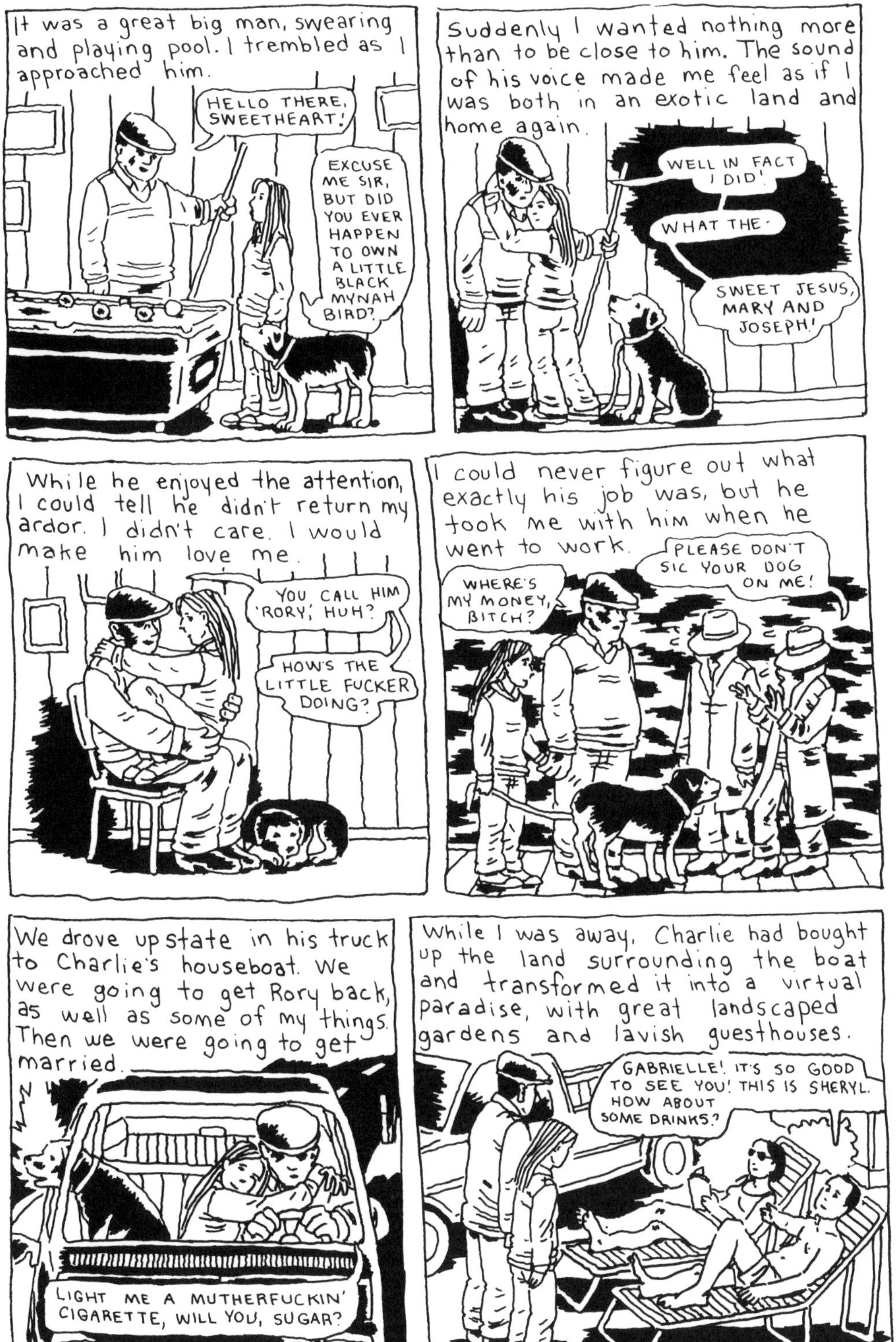
It was a great big man, swearing and playing pool. I trembled as I approached him.
HELLO THERE, SWEETHEART!
EXCUSE ME SIR, BUT DID YOU EVER HAPPEN TO OWN A LITTLE BLACK MYNAH BIRD?
Suddenly I wanted nothing more than to be close to him. The sound of his voice made me feel as if I was both in an exotic land and home again.
WELL IN FACT I DID!
WHAT THE-
SWEET JESUS, MARY AND JOSEPH!
While he enjoyed the attention, I could tell he didn't return my ardor. I didn't care. I would make him love me.
YOU CALL HIM 'RORY,' HUH?
HOW'S THE LITTLE FUCKER DOING?
I could never figure out what exactly his job was, but he took me with him when he went to work.
WHERE'S MY MONEY, BITCH?
PLEASE DON'T SIC YOUR DOG ON ME!
We drove upstate in his truck to Charlie's houseboat. We were going to get Rory back, as well as some of my things. Then we were going to get married.
LIGHT ME A MUTHERFUCKIN' CIGARETTE, WILL YOU, SUGAR?
While I was away, Charlie had bought up the land surrounding the boat and transformed it into a virtual paradise, with great landscaped gardens and lavish guesthouses.
GABRIELLE! IT'S SO GOOD TO SEE YOU! THIS IS SHERYL. HOW ABOUT SOME DRINKS?

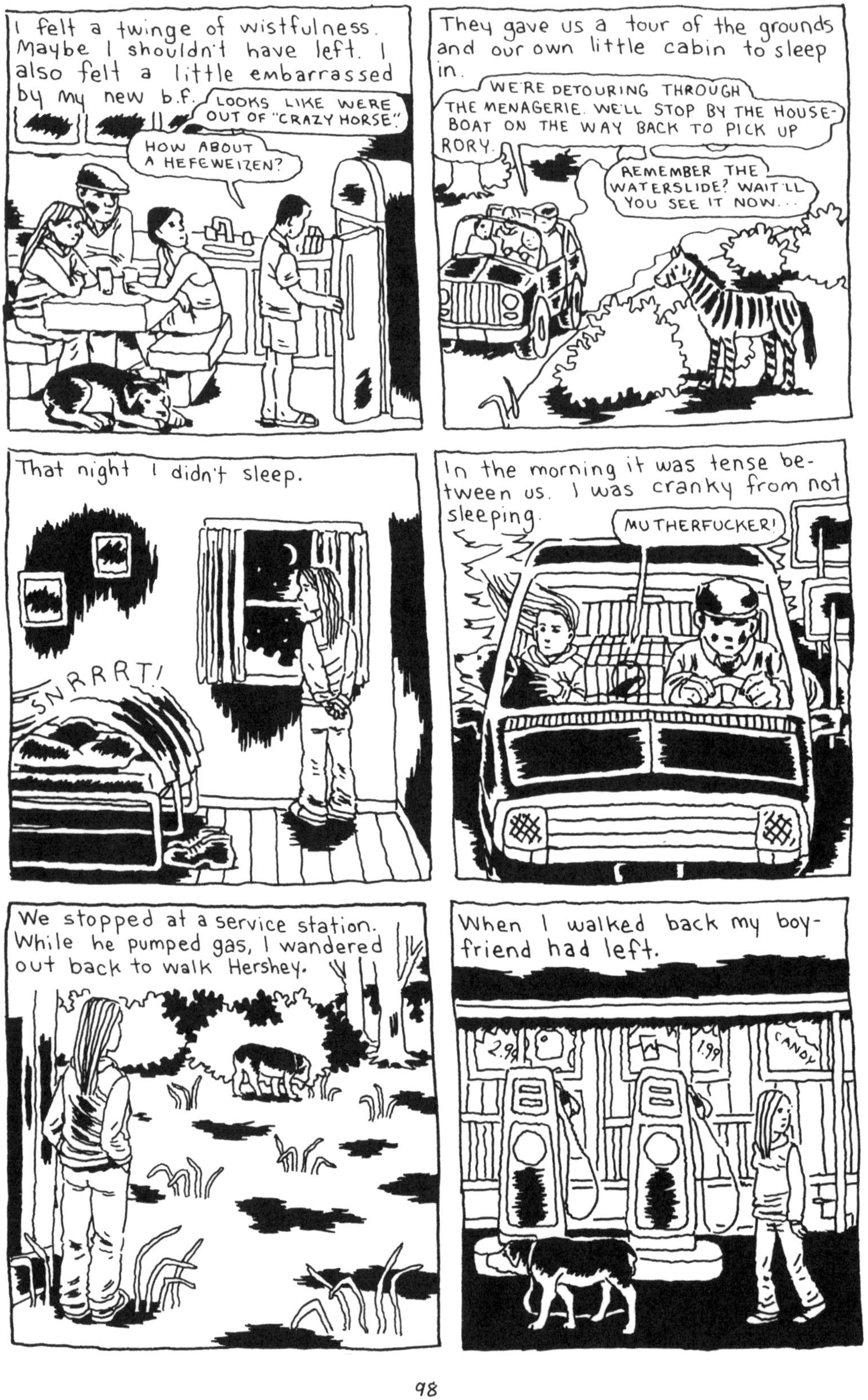
I felt a twinge of wistfulness. Maybe I shouldn't have left. I also felt a little embarrassed by my new b.f.
LOOKS LIKE WERE OUT OF "CRAZY HORSE"
HOW ABOUT A HEFEWEIZEN?
They gave us a tour of the grounds and our own little cabin to sleep in.
WE'RE DETOURING THROUGH THE MENAGERIE. WE'LL STOP BY THE HOUSE-BOAT ON THE WAY BACK TO PICK UP RORY.
REMEMBER THE WATERSLIDE? WAIT'LL YOU SEE IT NOW...
That night I didn't sleep.
SNRRRT!
In the morning it was tense between us. I was cranky from not sleeping.
MUTHERFUCKER!
We stopped at a service station. While he pumped gas, I wandered out back to walk Hershey.
When I walked back my boyfriend had left.
2.99
1.99
CANDY

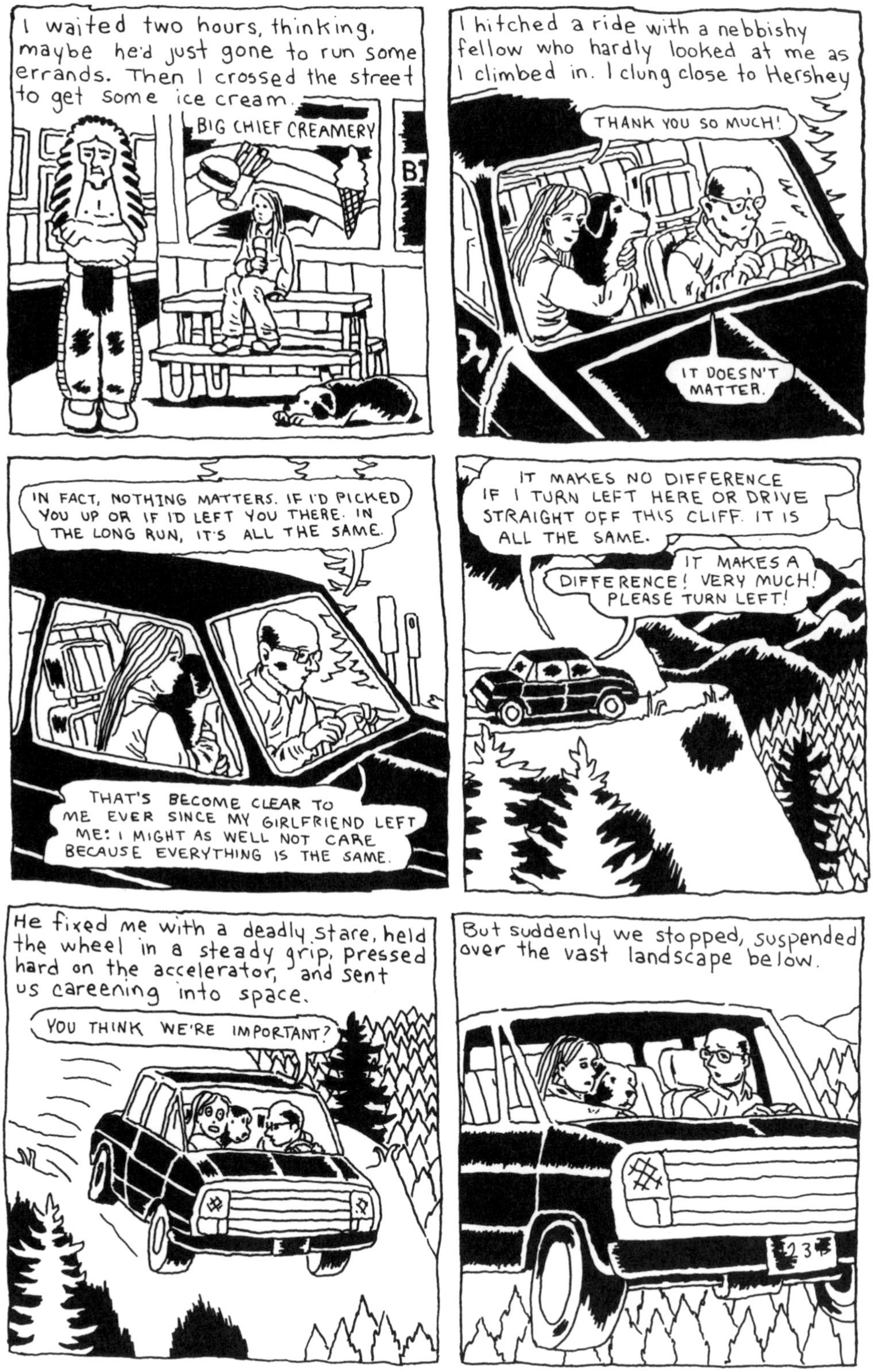
I waited two hours, thinking, maybe he'd just gone to run some errands. Then I crossed the street to get some ice cream.
BIG CHIEF CREAMERY
I hitched a ride with a nebbishy fellow who hardly looked at me as I climbed in. I clung close to Hershey
THANK YOU SO MUCH!
IT DOESN'T MATTER.
IN FACT, NOTHING MATTERS. IF I'D PICKED YOU UP OR IF I'D LEFT YOU THERE. IN THE LONG RUN, IT'S ALL THE SAME.
THAT'S BECOME CLEAR TO ME EVER SINCE MY GIRLFRIEND LEFT ME: I MIGHT AS WELL NOT CARE BECAUSE EVERYTHING IS THE SAME.
IT MAKES NO DIFFERENCE IF I TURN LEFT HERE OR DRIVE STRAIGHT OFF THIS CLIFF. IT IS ALL THE SAME.
IT MAKES A DIFFERENCE! VERY MUCH! PLEASE TURN LEFT!
He fixed me with a deadly stare, held the wheel in a steady grip, pressed hard on the accelerator, and sent us careening into space.
YOU THINK WE'RE IMPORTANT?
But suddenly we stopped, suspended over the vast landscape below.

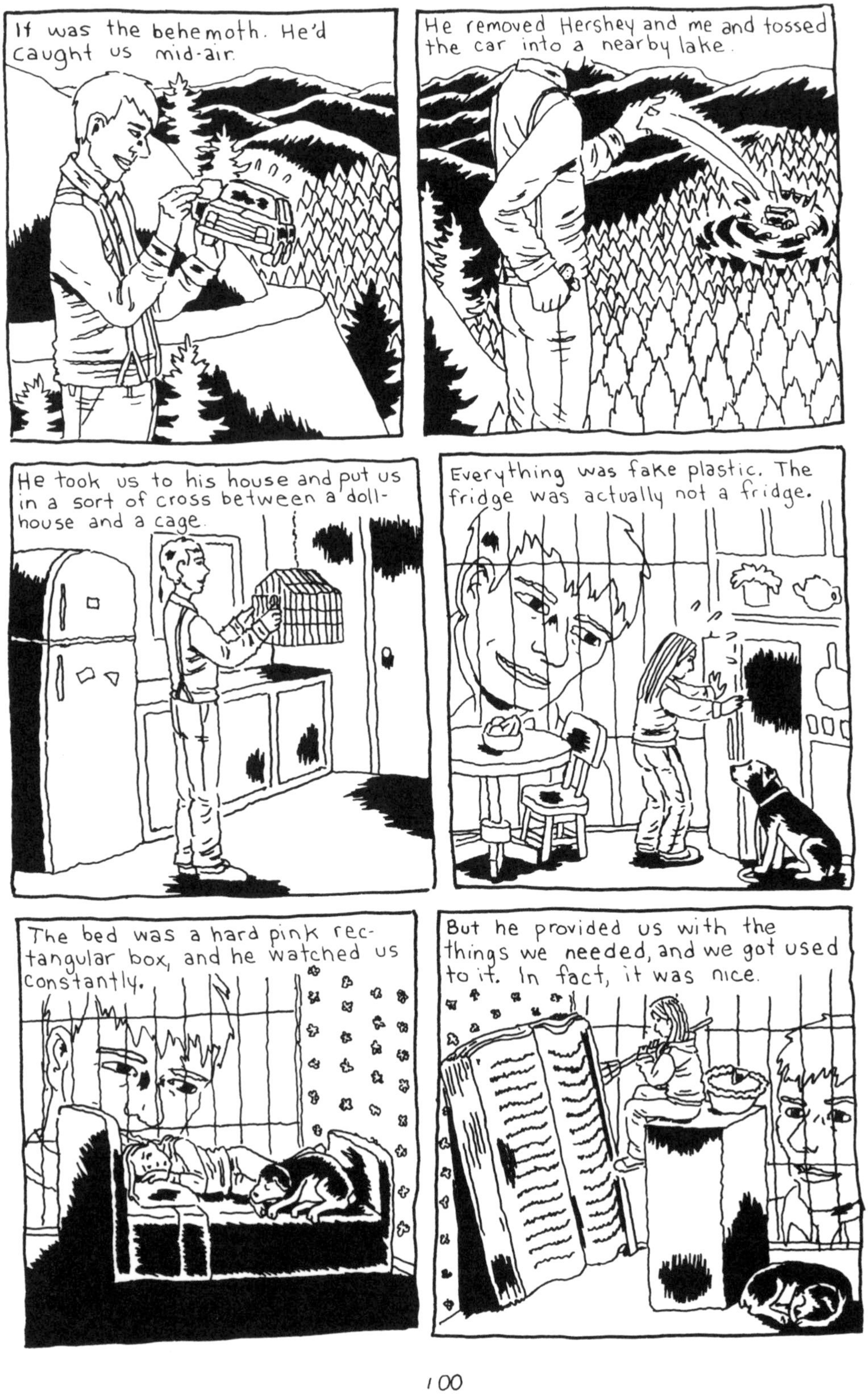
It was the behemoth. He'd caught us mid-air.
He removed Hershey and me and tossed the car into a nearby lake.
He took us to his house and put us in a sort of cross between a doll-house and a cage.
Everything was fake plastic. The fridge was actually not a fridge.
The bed was a hard pink rec-tangular box, and he watched us constantly.
But he provided us with the things we needed, and we got used to it. In fact, it was nice.

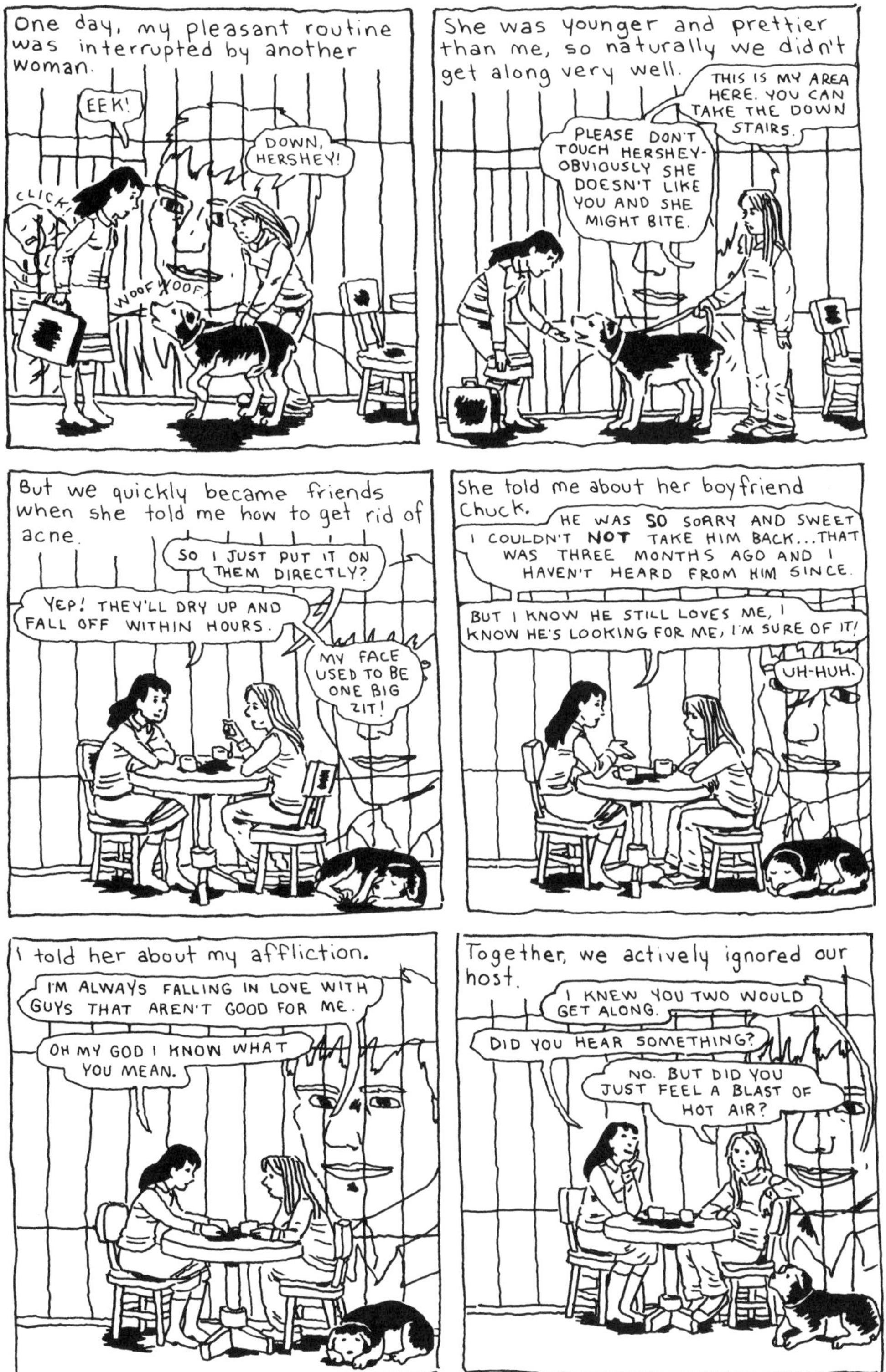
One day, my pleasant routine was interrupted by another woman.
EEK!
DOWN, HERSHEY!
CLICK!
WOOF WOOF!
She was younger and prettier than me, so naturally we didn't get along very well.
THIS IS MY AREA HERE. YOU CAN TAKE THE DOWN STAIRS.
PLEASE DON'T TOUCH HERSHEY- OBVIOUSLY SHE DOESN'T LIKE YOU AND SHE MIGHT BITE.
But we quickly became friends when she told me how to get rid of acne.
SO I JUST PUT IT ON THEM DIRECTLY?
YEP! THEY'LL DRY UP AND FALL OFF WITHIN HOURS.
MY FACE USED TO BE ONE BIG ZIT!
She told me about her boyfriend Chuck.
HE WAS SO SORRY AND SWEET I COULDN'T NOT TAKE HIM BACK...THAT WAS THREE MONTHS AGO AND I HAVEN'T HEARD FROM HIM SINCE.
BUT I KNOW HE STILL LOVES ME, I KNOW HE'S LOOKING FOR ME, I'M SURE OF IT!
UH-HUH.
I told her about my affliction.
I'M ALWAYS FALLING IN LOVE WITH GUYS THAT AREN'T GOOD FOR ME.
OH MY GOD I KNOW WHAT YOU MEAN.
Together, we actively ignored our host.
I KNEW YOU TWO WOULD GET ALONG.
DID YOU HEAR SOMETHING?
NO. BUT DID YOU JUST FEEL A BLAST OF HOT AIR?

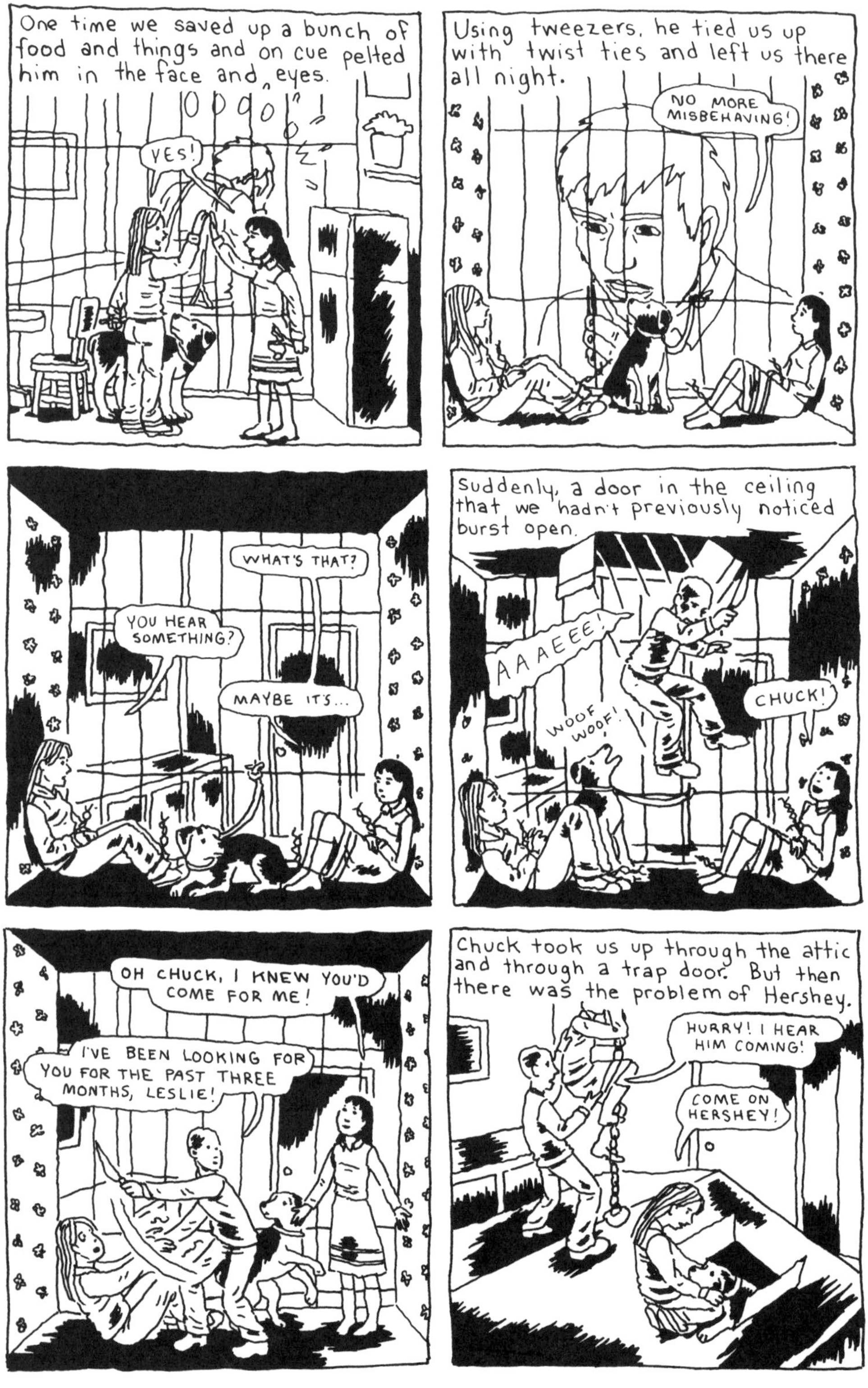
One time we saved up a bunch of food and things and on cue pelted him in the face and eyes.
YES!
Using tweezers, he tied us up with twist ties and left us there all night.
NO MORE MISBEHAVING!
YOU HEAR SOMETHING?
WHAT'S THAT?
MAYBE IT'S...
Suddenly, a door in the ceiling that we hadn't previously noticed burst open.
AAAEEE!
WOOF WOOF!
CHUCK!
OH CHUCK, I KNEW YOU'D COME FOR ME!
I'VE BEEN LOOKING FOR YOU FOR THE PAST THREE MONTHS, LESLIE!
Chuck took us up through the attic and through a trap door. But then there was the problem of Hershey.
HURRY! I HEAR HIM COMING!
COME ON HERSHEY!

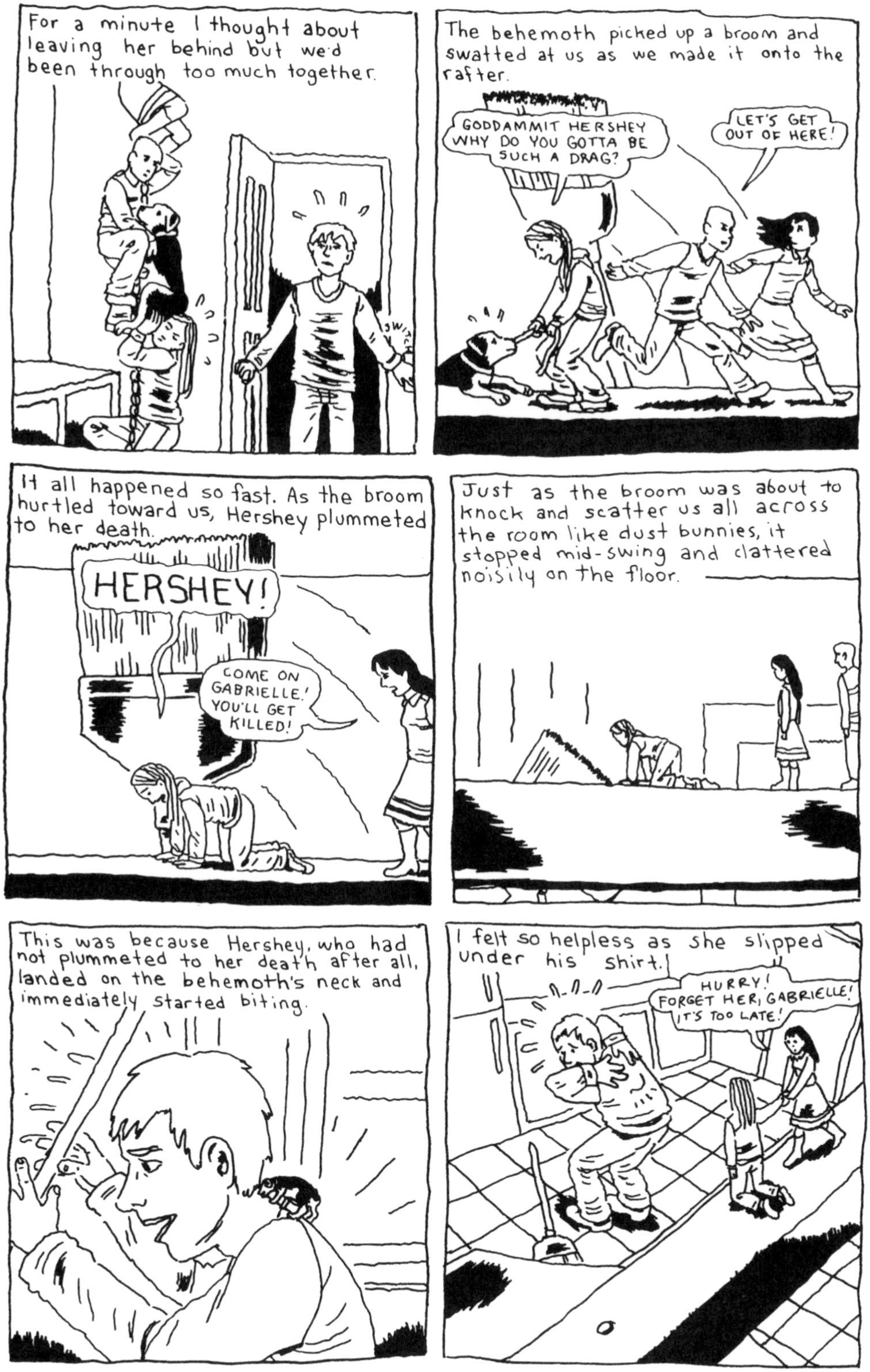
For a minute I thought about leaving her behind but we'd been through too much together.
SWITCH
The behemoth picked up a broom and swatted at us as we made it onto the rafter.
GODDAMMIT HERSHEY WHY DO YOU GOTTA BE SUCH A DRAG?
LET'S GET OUT OF HERE!
It all happened so fast. As the broom hurtled toward us, Hershey plummeted to her death.
HERSHEY!
COME ON GABRIELLE! YOU'LL GET KILLED!
Just as the broom was about to knock and scatter us all across the room like dust bunnies, it stopped mid-swing and clattered noisily on the floor.
This was because Hershey, who had not plummeted to her death after all, landed on the behemoth's neck and immediately started biting.
I felt so helpless as she slipped under his shirt.
HURRY! FORGET HER, GABRIELLE! IT'S TOO LATE!

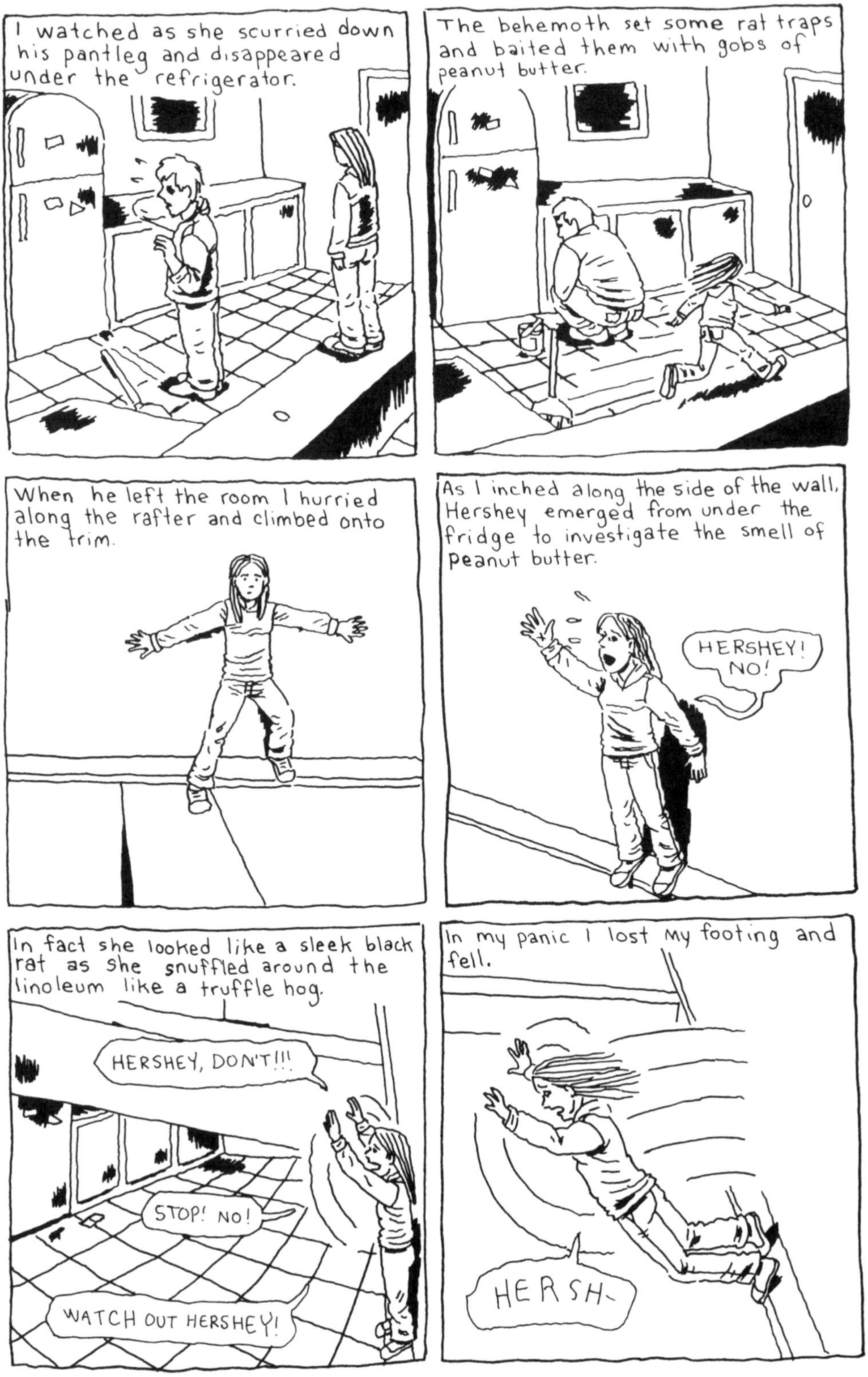
I watched as she scurried down his pantleg and disappeared under the refrigerator.
The behemoth set some rat traps and baited them with gobs of peanut butter.
When he left the room I hurried along the rafter and climbed onto the trim.
As I inched along the side of the wall, Hershey emerged from under the fridge to investigate the smell of peanut butter.
HERSHEY! NO!
In fact she looked like a sleek black rat as she snuffled around the linoleum like a truffle hog.
HERSHEY, DON'T!!!
STOP! NO!
WATCH OUT HERSHEY!
In my panic I lost my footing and fell.
HERSH-

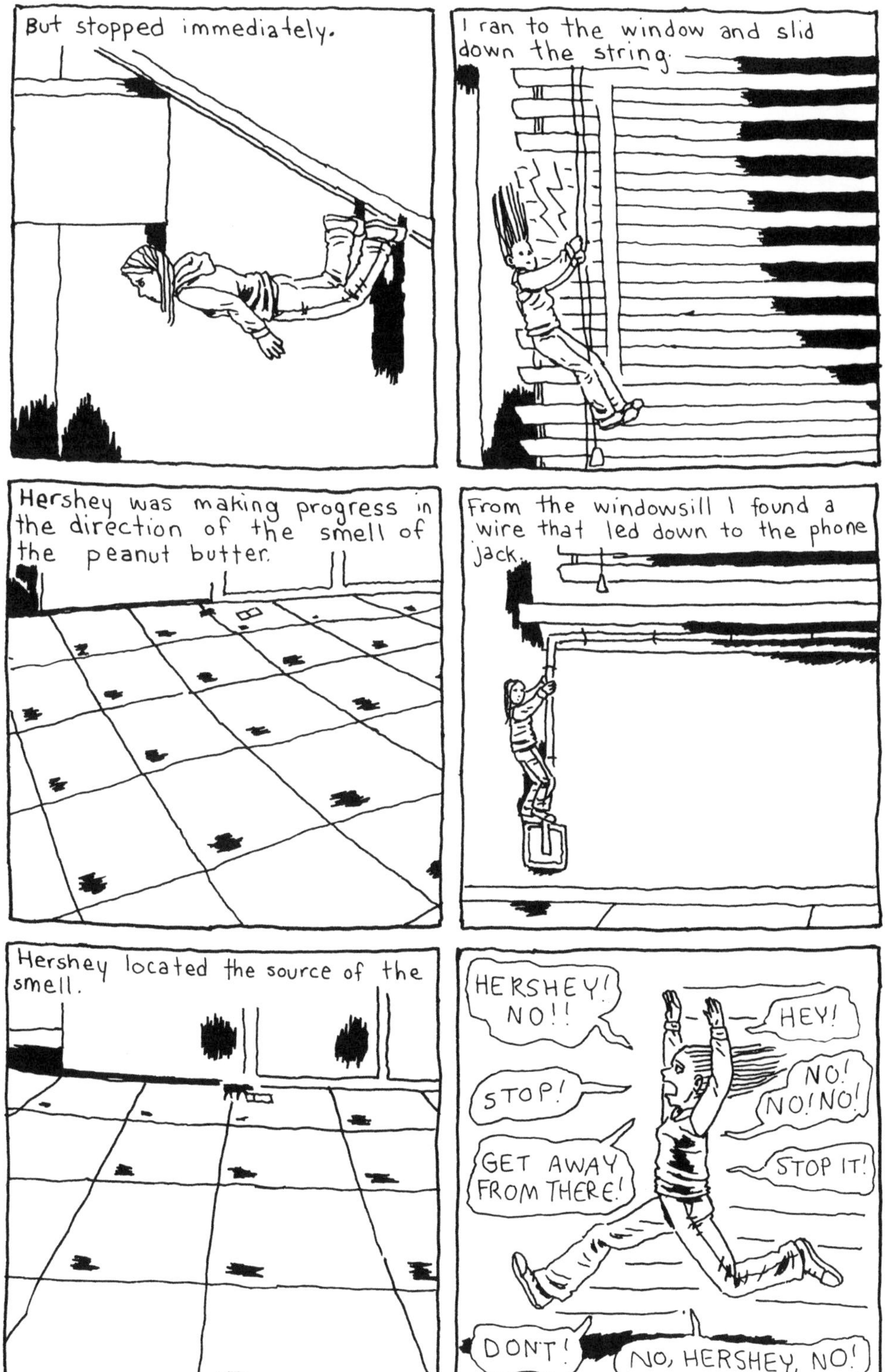

But stopped immediately.
I ran to the window and slid down the string.
Hershey was making progress in the direction of the smell of the peanut butter.
From the windowsill I found a wire that led down to the phone jack.
Hershey located the source of the smell.
HERSHEY! NO!!
STOP!
GET AWAY FROM THERE!
HEY!
NO! NO! NO!
STOP IT!
DONT!
NO, HERSHEY, NO!

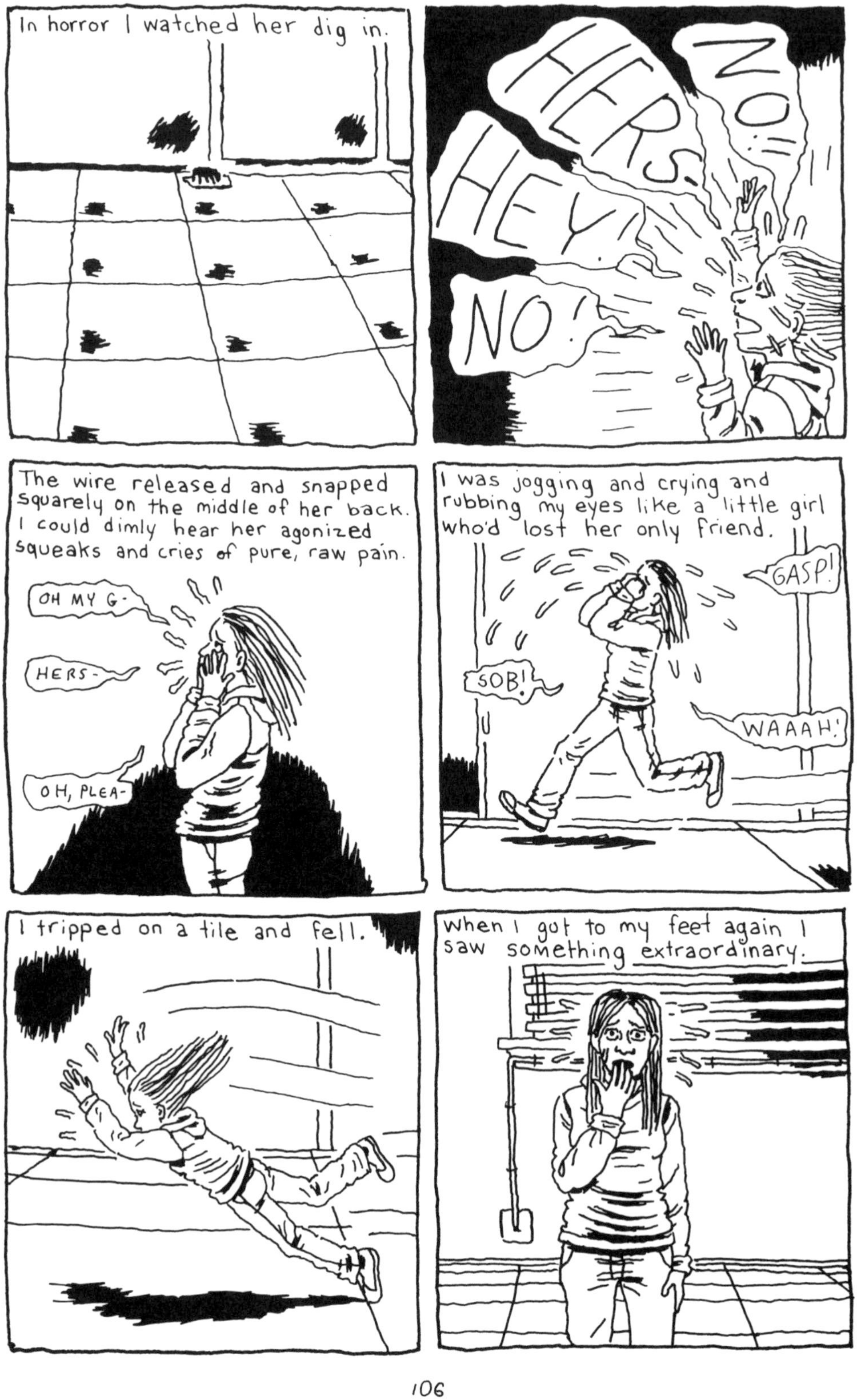

In horror I watched her dig in.
NO!
HERS-
HEY!
NO!
The wire released and snapped squarely on the middle of her back. I could dimly hear her agonized squeaks and cries of pure, raw pain.
OH MY G-
HERS-
OH, PLEA-
I was jogging and crying and rubbing my eyes like a little girl who'd lost her only friend.
GASP!
SOB!
WAAAH!
I tripped on a tile and fell.
When I got to my feet again I saw something extraordinary.

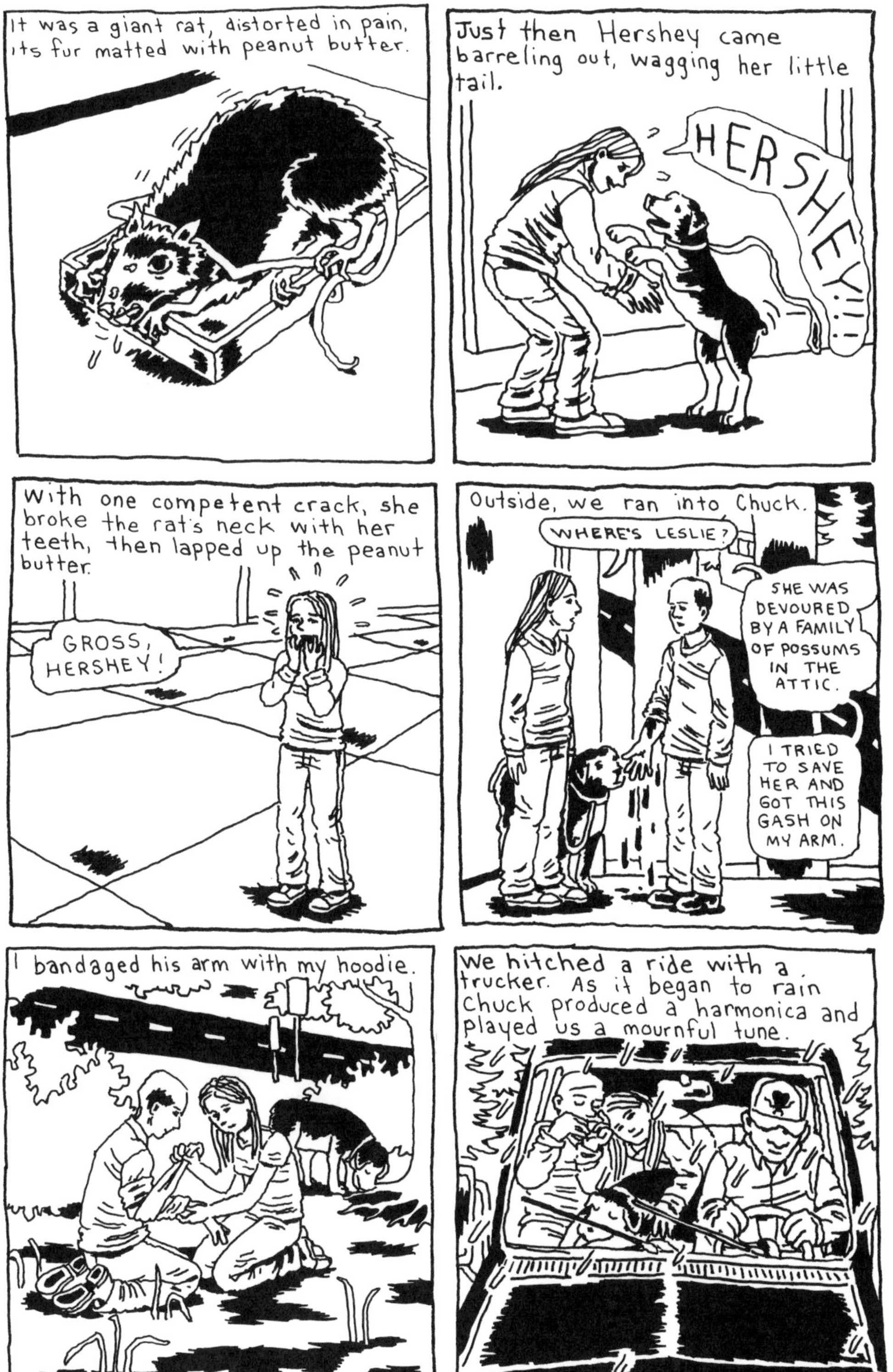

It was a giant rat, distorted in pain, its fur matted with peanut butter.
Just then Hershey came barreling out, wagging her little tail.
HERSHEY!!!
With one competent crack, she broke the rat's neck with her teeth, then lapped up the peanut butter.
GROSS, HERSHEY!
Outside, we ran into Chuck.
WHERE'S LESLIE?
SHE WAS DEVOURED BY A FAMILY OF POSSUMS IN THE ATTIC.
I TRIED TO SAVE HER AND GOT THIS GASH ON MY ARM.
I bandaged his arm with my hoodie.
We hitched a ride with a trucker. As it began to rain Chuck produced a harmonica and played us a mournful tune.
Gabrielle Bell

Summer Camp

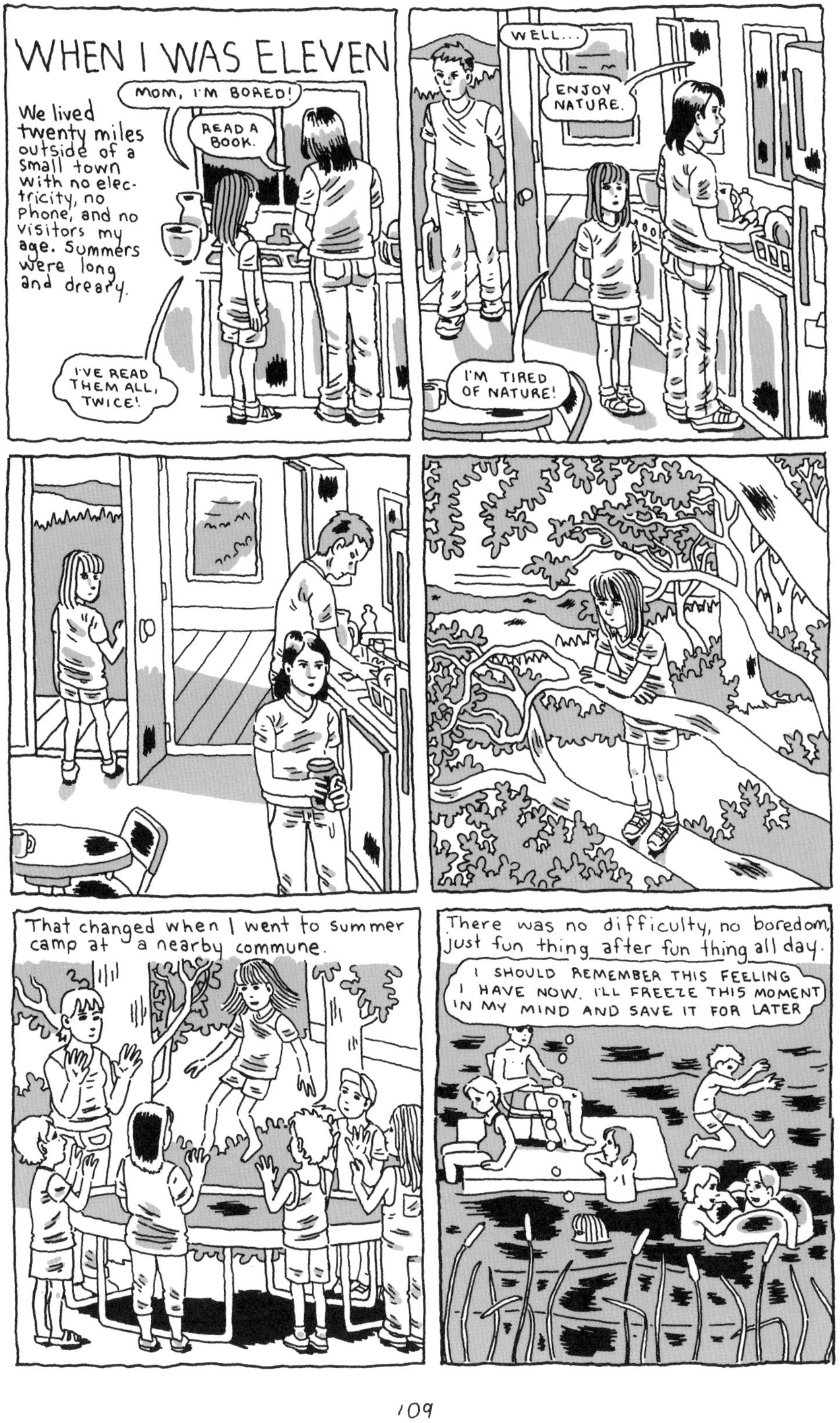
WHEN I WAS ELEVEN
We lived twenty miles outside of a small town with no electricity, no phone, and no visitors my age. Summers were long and dreary.
MOM, I'M BORED!
READ A BOOK.
I'VE READ THEM ALL, TWICE!
WELL...
ENJOY NATURE.
I'M TIRED OF NATURE!
That changed when I went to summer camp at a nearby commune.
There was no difficulty, no boredom, just fun thing after fun thing all day.
I SHOULD REMEMBER THIS FEELING I HAVE NOW. I'LL FREEZE THIS MOMENT IN MY MIND AND SAVE IT FOR LATER

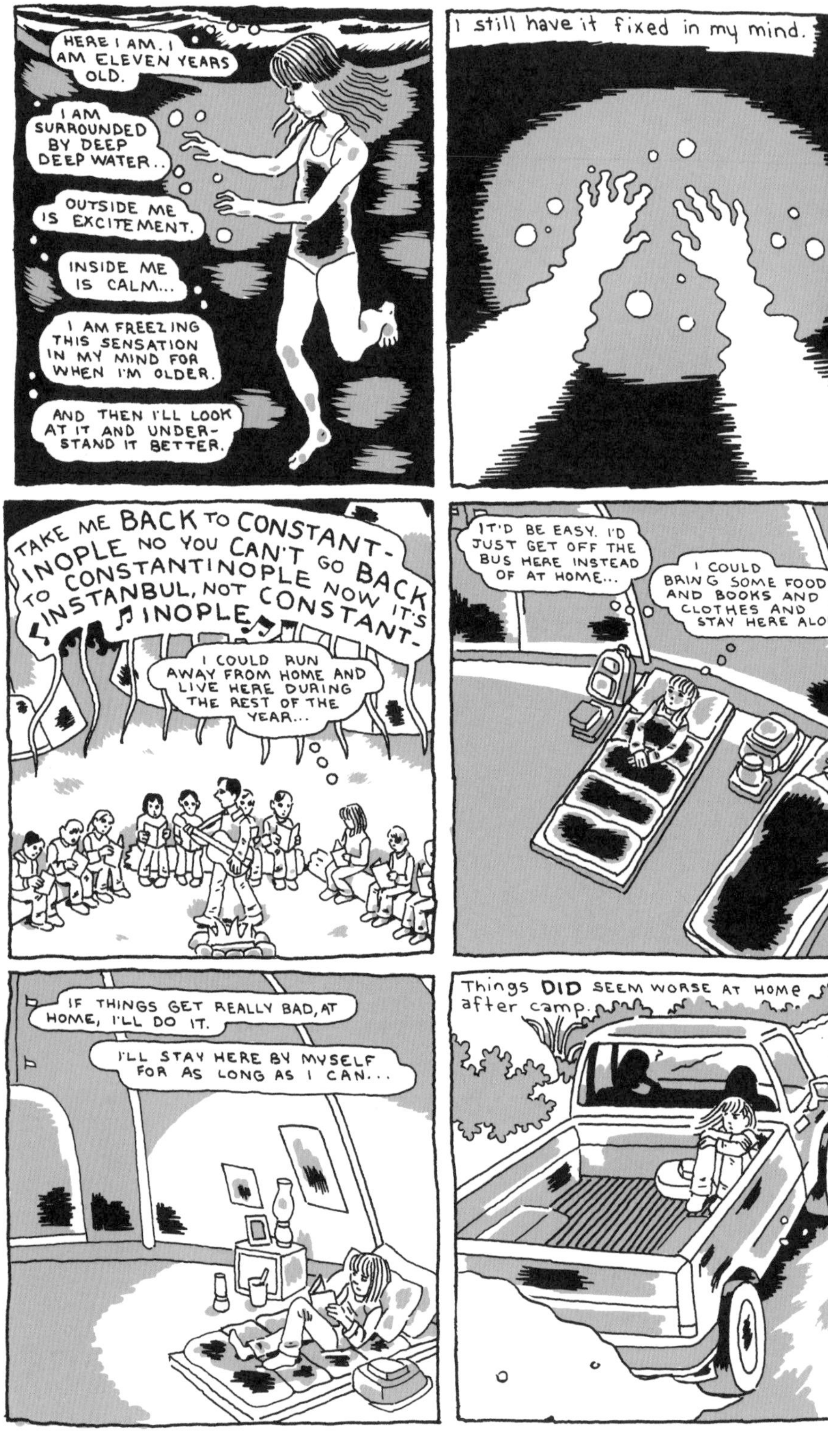
HERE I AM. I AM ELEVEN YEARS OLD.
I AM SURROUNDED BY DEEP DEEP WATER..
OUTSIDE ME IS EXCITEMENT.
INSIDE ME IS CALM...
I AM FREEZING THIS SENSATION IN MY MIND FOR WHEN I'M OLDER.
AND THEN I'LL LOOK AT IT AND UNDERSTAND IT BETTER.
I still have it fixed in my mind.
TAKE ME BACK TO CONSTANTINOPLE NO YOU CAN'T GO BACK TO CONSTANTINOPLE NOW IT'S ISTANBUL, NOT CONSTANTINOPLE
I COULD RUN AWAY FROM HOME AND LIVE HERE DURING THE REST OF THE YEAR...
IT'D BE EASY. I'D JUST GET OFF THE BUS HERE INSTEAD OF AT HOME...
I COULD BRING SOME FOOD AND BOOKS AND CLOTHES AND STAY HERE ALONE.
IF THINGS GET REALLY BAD, AT HOME, I'LL DO IT.
I'LL STAY HERE BY MYSELF FOR AS LONG AS I CAN...
Things DID seem worse at home after camp.

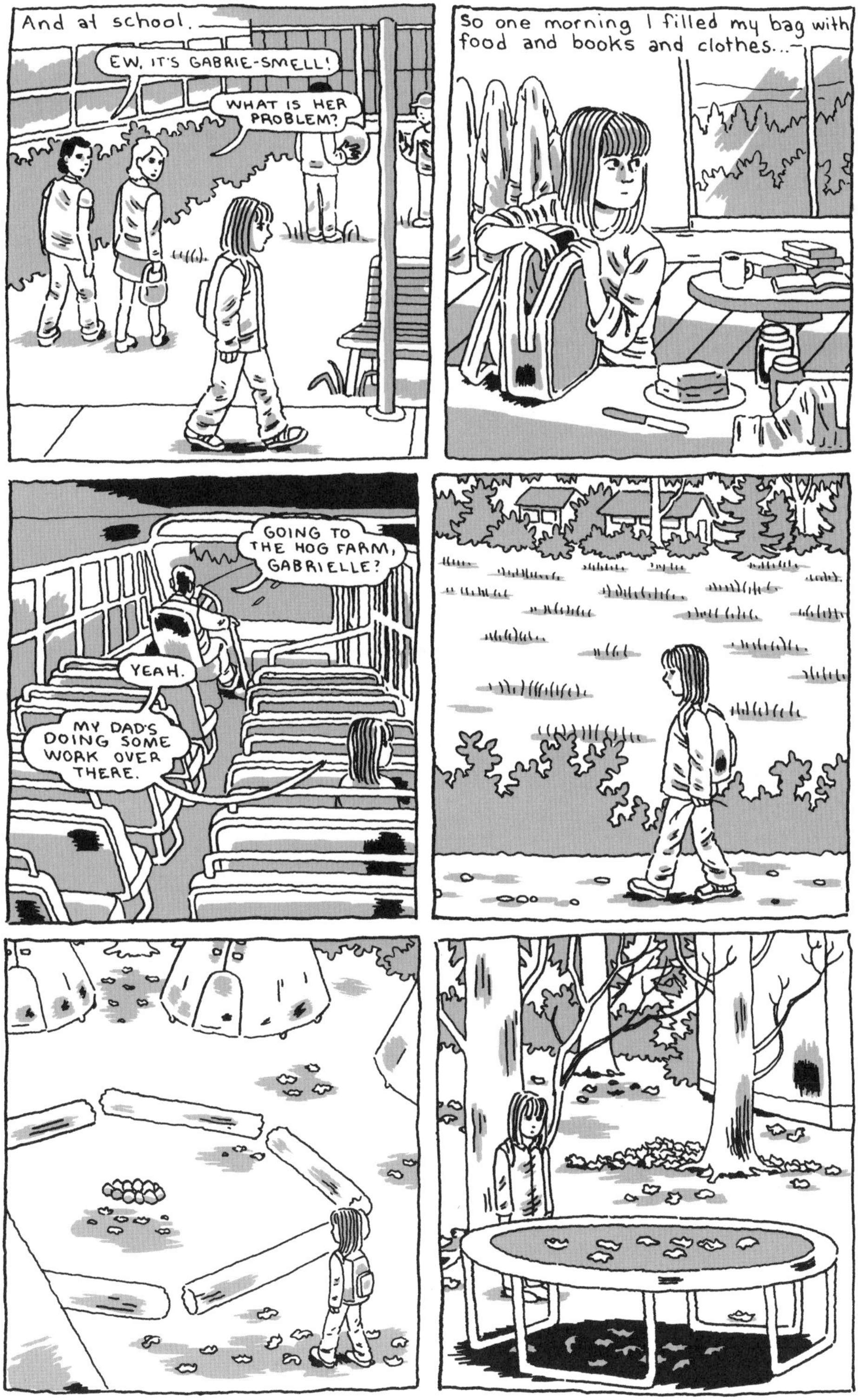
And at school.
EW, IT'S GABRIE-SMELL!
WHAT IS HER PROBLEM?
So one morning I filled my bag with food and books and clothes...
GOING TO THE HOG FARM, GABRIELLE?
YEAH.
MY DAD'S DOING SOME WORK OVER THERE.

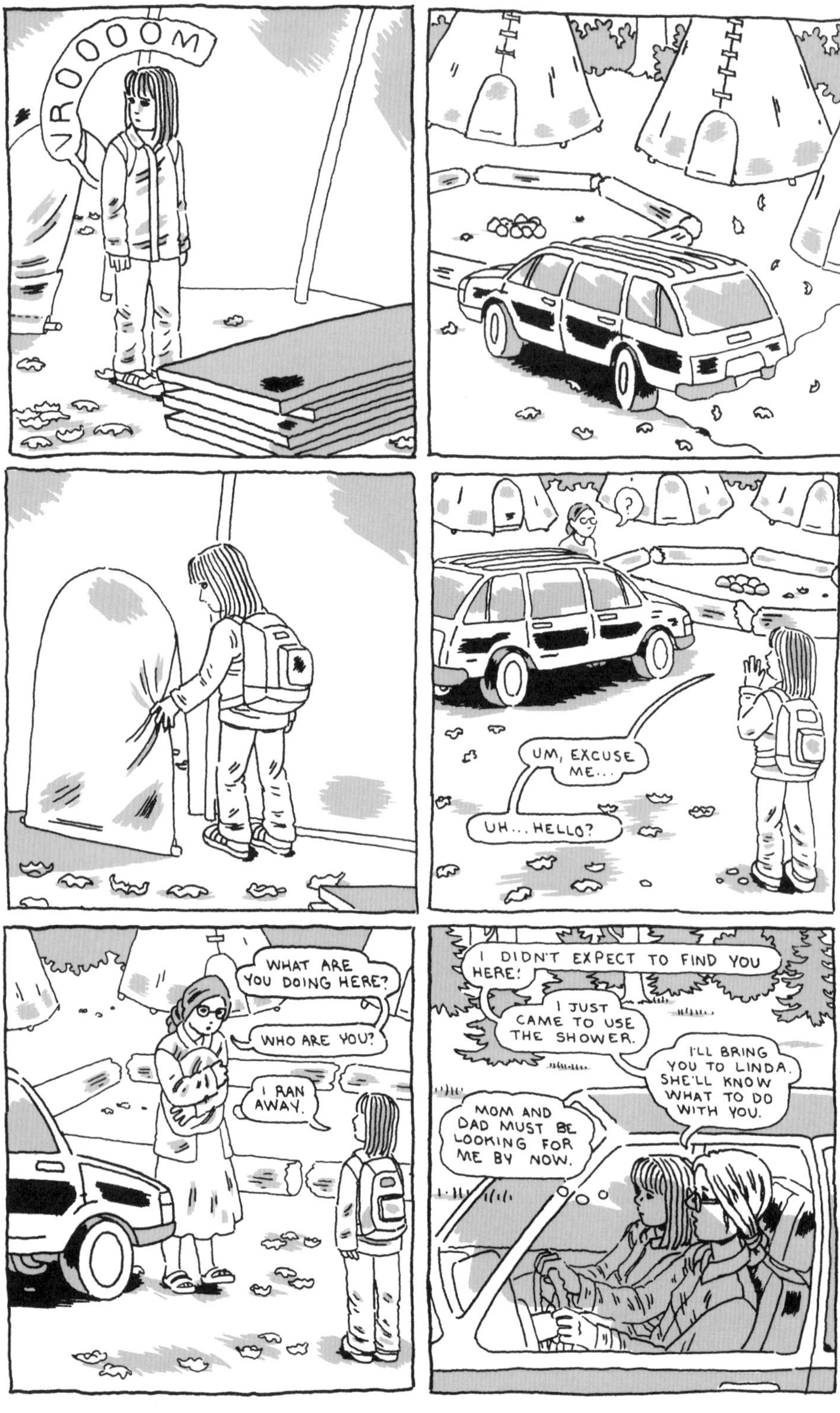
VROOOOM
?
UM, EXCUSE ME...
UH... HELLO?
WHAT ARE YOU DOING HERE?
WHO ARE YOU?
I RAN AWAY.
I DIDN'T EXPECT TO FIND YOU HERE!
I JUST CAME TO USE THE SHOWER.
I'LL BRING YOU TO LINDA. SHE'LL KNOW WHAT TO DO WITH YOU.
MOM AND DAD MUST BE LOOKING FOR ME BY NOW.

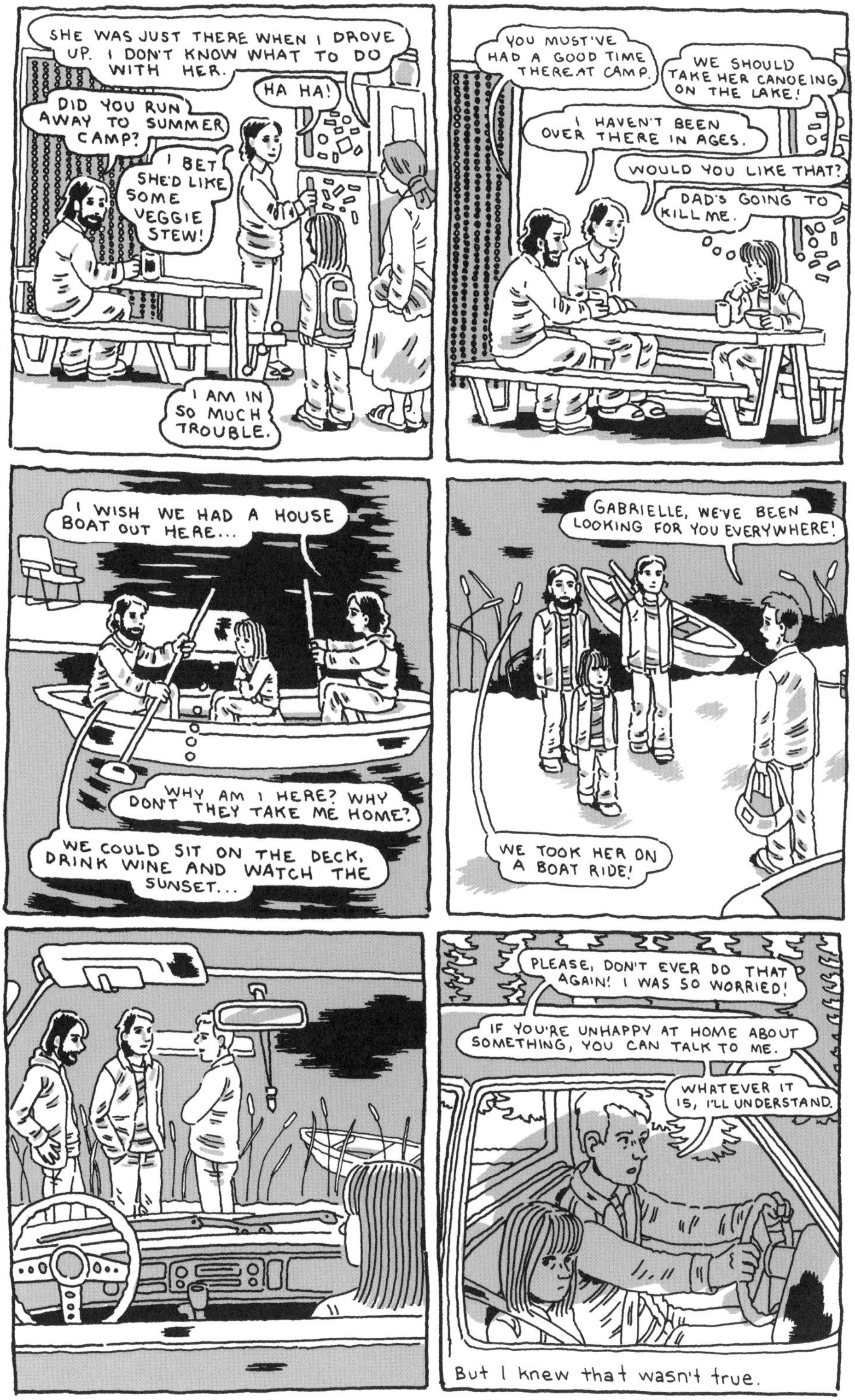
SHE WAS JUST THERE WHEN I DROVE UP. I DON'T KNOW WHAT TO DO WITH HER.
DID YOU RUN AWAY TO SUMMER CAMP?
HA HA!
I BET SHE'D LIKE SOME VEGGIE STEW!
I AM IN SO MUCH TROUBLE.
YOU MUST'VE HAD A GOOD TIME THERE AT CAMP.
WE SHOULD TAKE HER CANOEING ON THE LAKE!
I HAVEN'T BEEN OVER THERE IN AGES.
WOULD YOU LIKE THAT?
DAD'S GOING TO KILL ME.
I WISH WE HAD A HOUSE BOAT OUT HERE...
WHY AM I HERE? WHY DON'T THEY TAKE ME HOME?
WE COULD SIT ON THE DECK, DRINK WINE AND WATCH THE SUNSET...
GABRIELLE, WE'VE BEEN LOOKING FOR YOU EVERYWHERE!
WE TOOK HER ON A BOAT RIDE!
PLEASE, DON'T EVER DO THAT AGAIN! I WAS SO WORRIED!
IF YOU'RE UNHAPPY AT HOME ABOUT SOMETHING, YOU CAN TALK TO ME.
WHATEVER IT IS, I'LL UNDERSTAND.
But I knew that wasn't true.

Hit Me

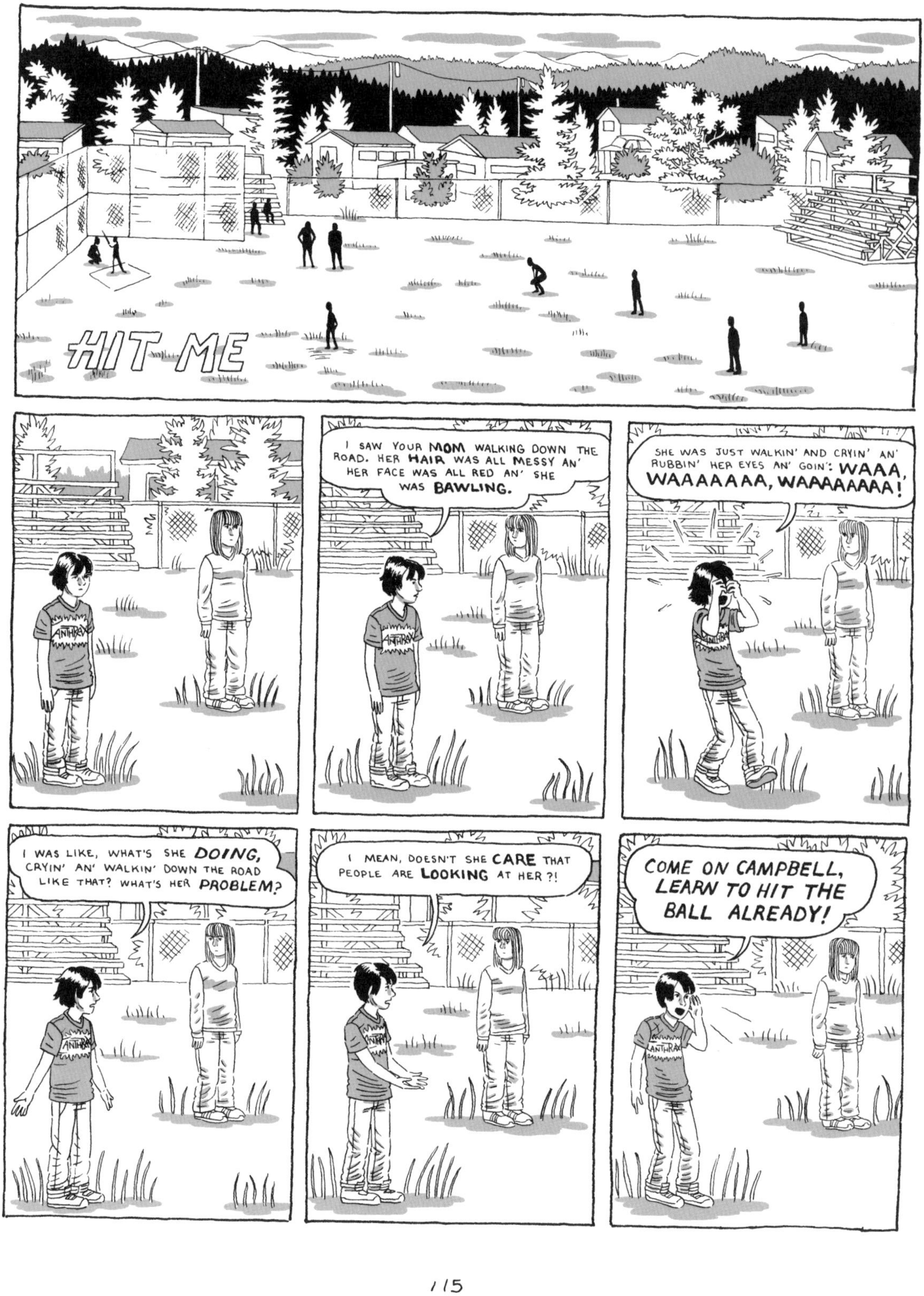
HIT ME
I SAW YOUR MOM WALKING DOWN THE ROAD. HER HAIR WAS ALL MESSY AN' HER FACE WAS ALL RED AN' SHE WAS BAWLING.
SHE WAS JUST WALKIN' AND CRYIN' AN' RUBBIN' HER EYES AN' GOIN': WAAA, WAAAAAAA, WAAAAAAAA!
I WAS LIKE, WHAT'S SHE DOING, CRYIN' AN' WALKIN' DOWN THE ROAD LIKE THAT? WHAT'S HER PROBLEM?
I MEAN, DOESN'T SHE CARE THAT PEOPLE ARE LOOKING AT HER?!
COME ON CAMPBELL, LEARN TO HIT THE BALL ALREADY!

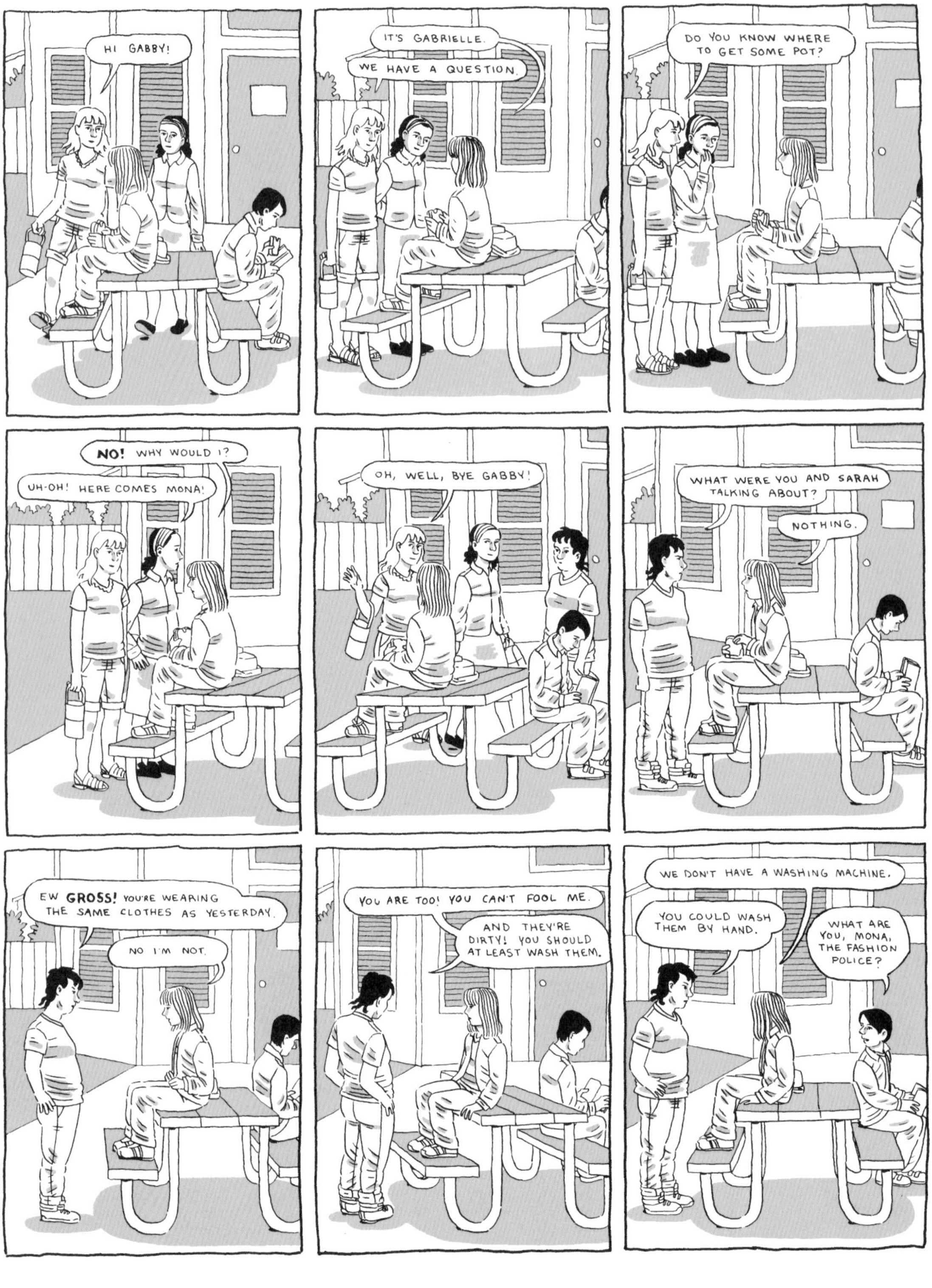
HI GABBY!
IT'S GABRIELLE.
WE HAVE A QUESTION.
DO YOU KNOW WHERE TO GET SOME POT?
NO! WHY WOULD I?
UH-OH! HERE COMES MONA!
OH, WELL, BYE GABBY!
WHAT WERE YOU AND SARAH TALKING ABOUT?
NOTHING.
EW GROSS! YOU'RE WEARING THE SAME CLOTHES AS YESTERDAY.
NO I'M NOT.
YOU ARE TOO! YOU CAN'T FOOL ME.
AND THEY'RE DIRTY! YOU SHOULD AT LEAST WASH THEM.
WE DON'T HAVE A WASHING MACHINE.
YOU COULD WASH THEM BY HAND.
WHAT ARE YOU, MONA, THE FASHION POLICE?

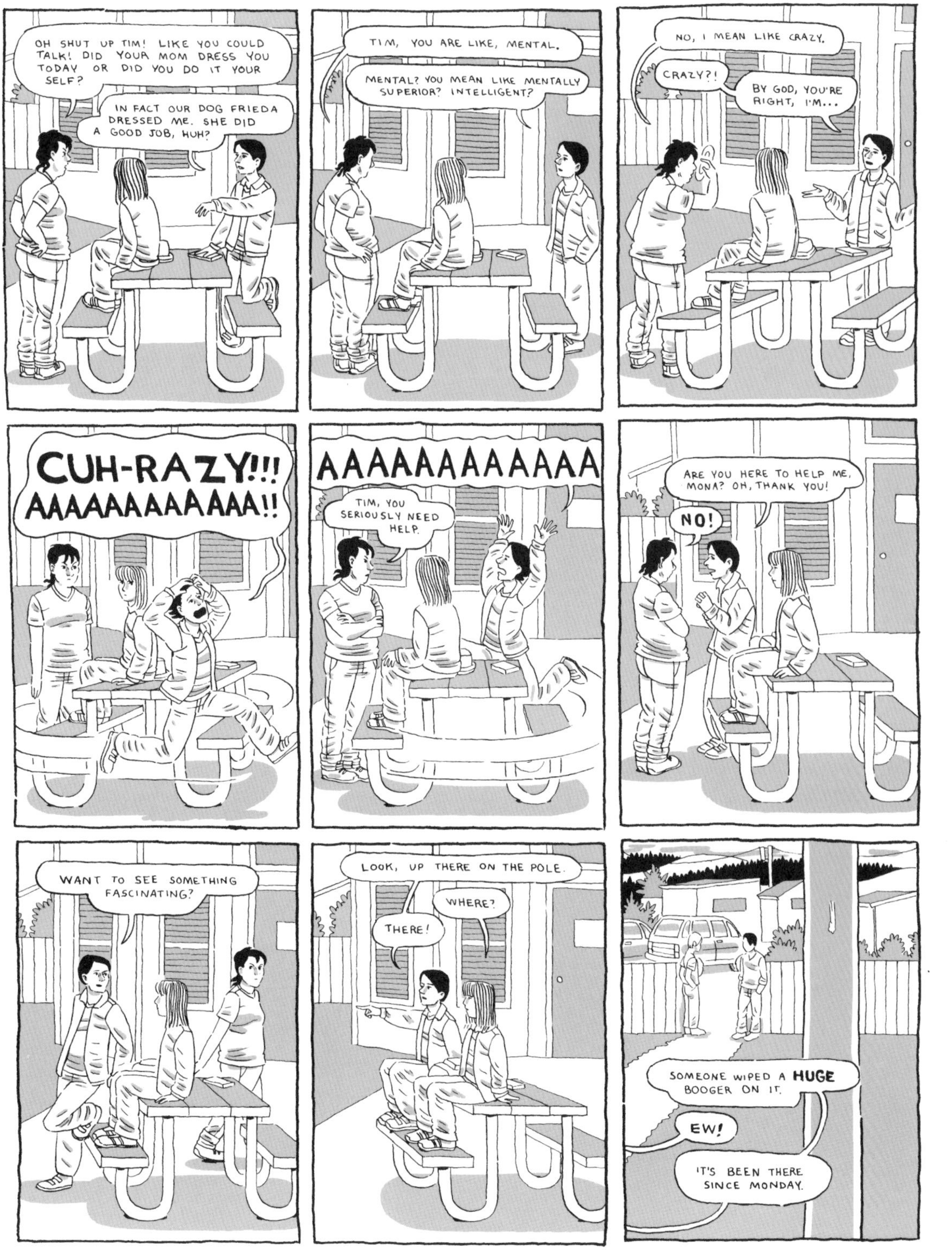
OH SHUT UP TIM! LIKE YOU COULD TALK! DID YOUR MOM DRESS YOU TODAY OR DID YOU DO IT YOUR SELF?
IN FACT OUR DOG FRIEDA DRESSED ME. SHE DID A GOOD JOB, HUH?
TIM, YOU ARE LIKE, MENTAL.
MENTAL? YOU MEAN LIKE MENTALLY SUPERIOR? INTELLIGENT?
NO, I MEAN LIKE CRAZY.
CRAZY?!
BY GOD, YOU'RE RIGHT, I'M...
CUH-RAZY!!! AAAAAAAAAAAA!!
AAAAAAAAAAAA
TIM, YOU SERIOUSLY NEED HELP.
ARE YOU HERE TO HELP ME, MONA? OH, THANK YOU!
NO!
WANT TO SEE SOMETHING FASCINATING?
LOOK, UP THERE ON THE POLE.
WHERE?
THERE!
SOMEONE WIPED A HUGE BOOGER ON IT.
EW!
IT'S BEEN THERE SINCE MONDAY.

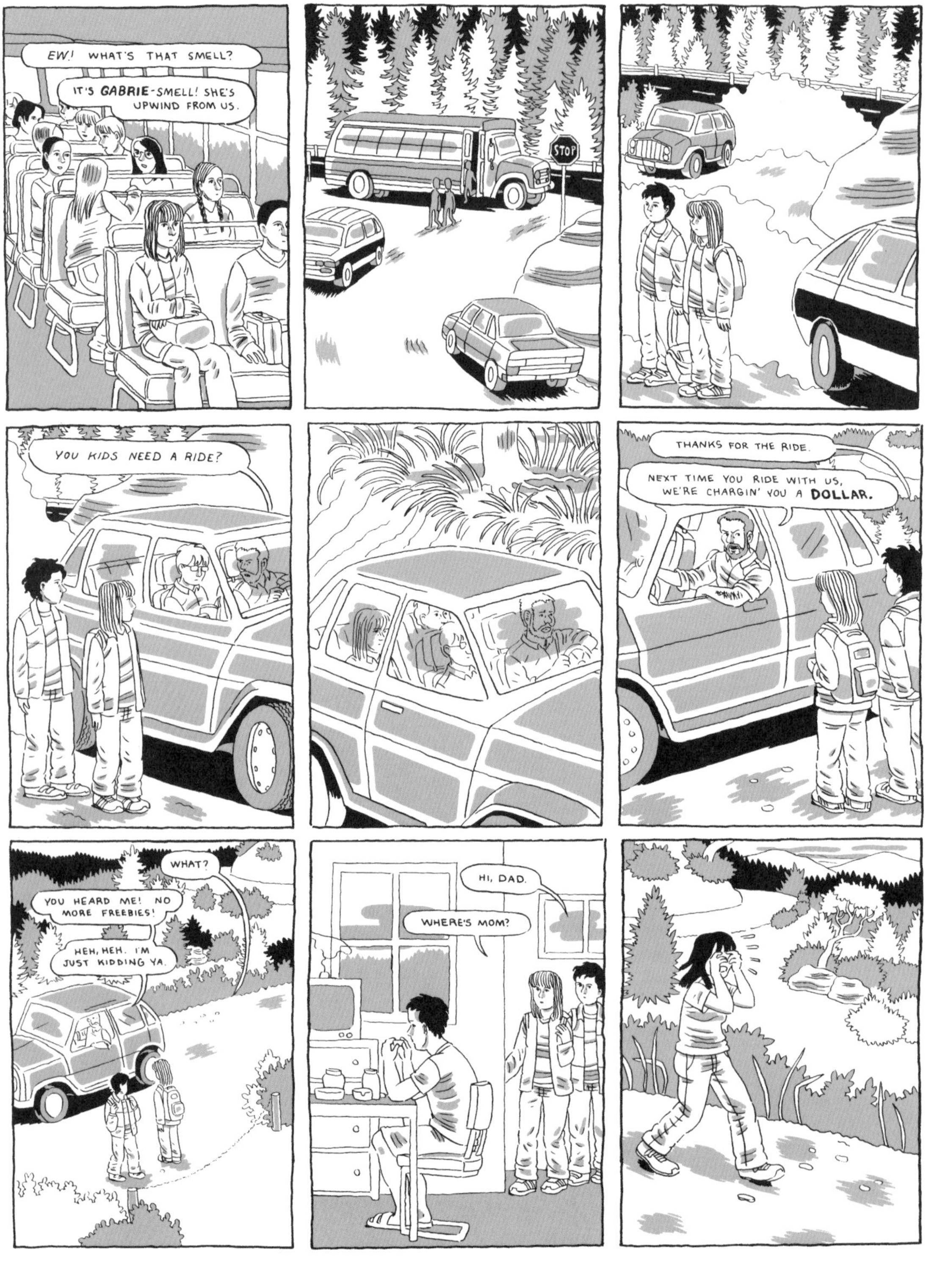
EW! WHAT'S THAT SMELL?
IT'S GABRIE-SMELL! SHE'S UPWIND FROM US.
STOP
YOU KIDS NEED A RIDE?
THANKS FOR THE RIDE.
NEXT TIME YOU RIDE WITH US, WE'RE CHARGIN' YOU A DOLLAR.
WHAT?
YOU HEARD ME! NO MORE FREEBIES!
HEH, HEH. I'M JUST KIDDING YA.
HI, DAD.
WHERE'S MOM?

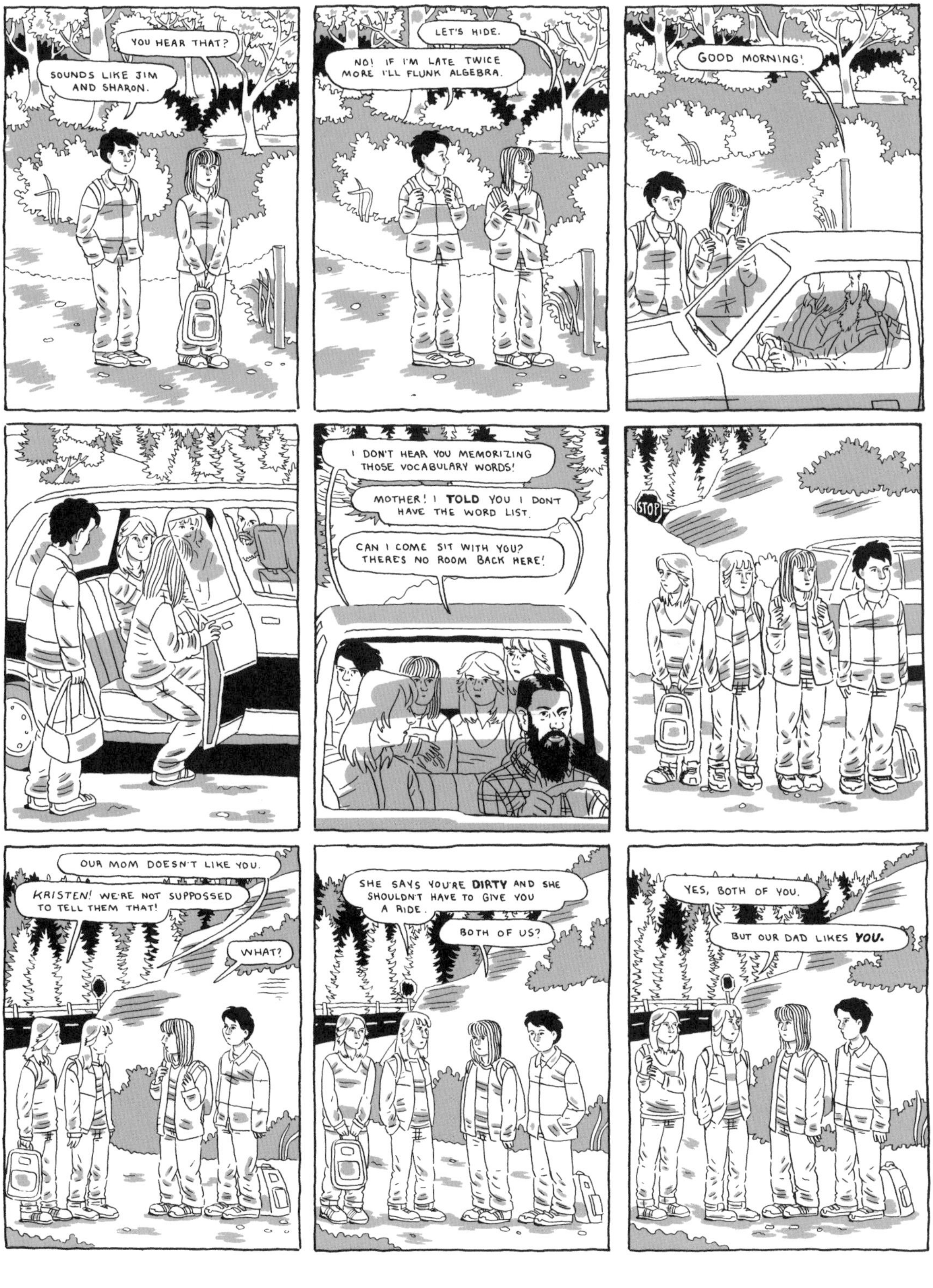
YOU HEAR THAT?
SOUNDS LIKE JIM AND SHARON.
LET'S HIDE.
NO! IF I'M LATE TWICE MORE I'LL FLUNK ALGEBRA.
GOOD MORNING!
I DON'T HEAR YOU MEMORIZING THOSE VOCABULARY WORDS!
MOTHER! I **TOLD** YOU I DON'T HAVE THE WORD LIST.
CAN I COME SIT WITH YOU? THERE'S NO ROOM BACK HERE!
STOP
OUR MOM DOESN'T LIKE YOU.
KRISTEN! WE'RE NOT SUPPOSSED TO TELL THEM THAT!
WHAT?
SHE SAYS YOU'RE **DIRTY** AND SHE SHOULDN'T HAVE TO GIVE YOU A RIDE.
BOTH OF US?
YES, BOTH OF YOU.
BUT OUR DAD LIKES **YOU.**

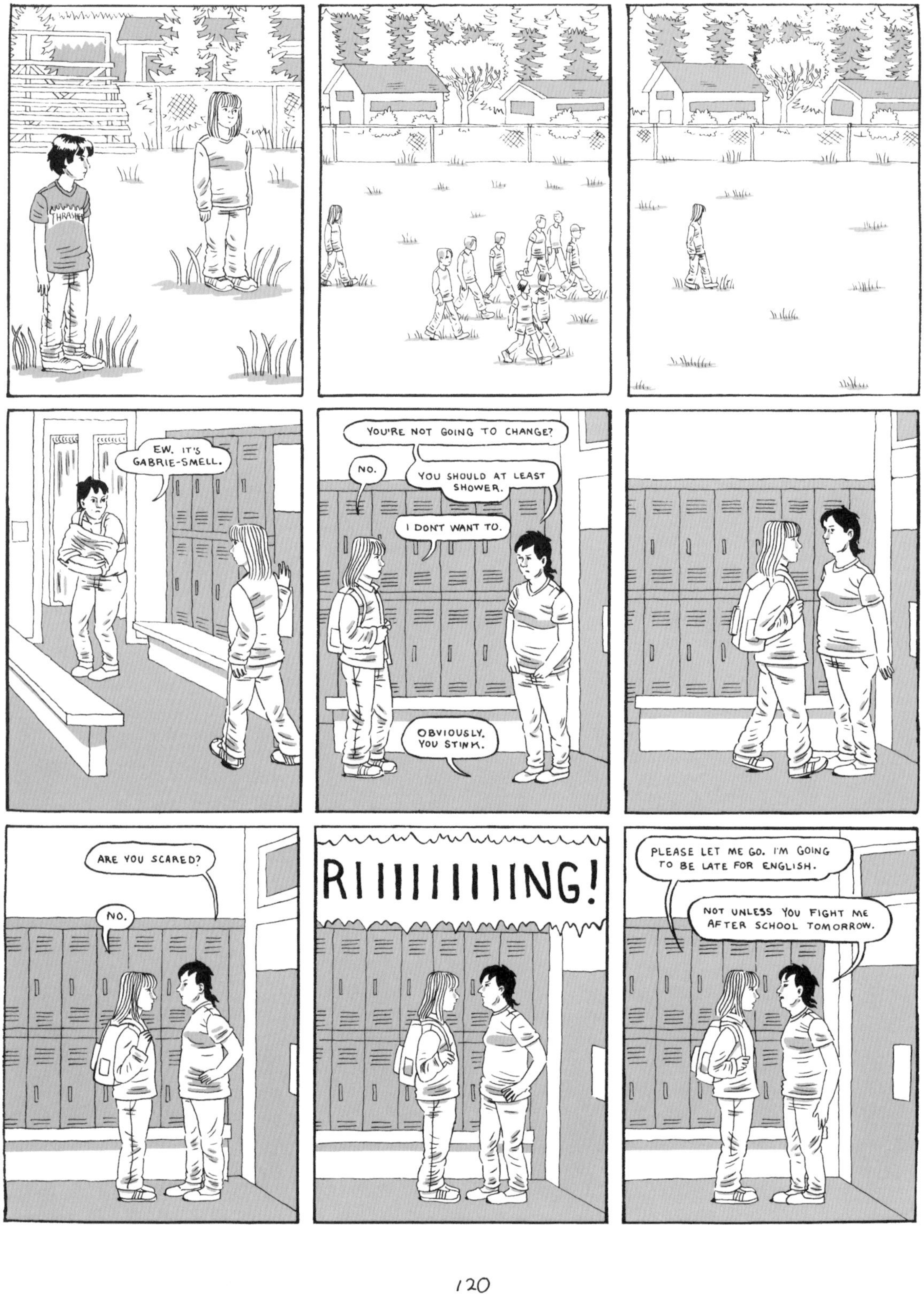
THRASHER
EW. IT'S GABRIE-SMELL.
YOU'RE NOT GOING TO CHANGE?
NO.
YOU SHOULD AT LEAST SHOWER.
I DON'T WANT TO.
OBVIOUSLY. YOU STINK.
ARE YOU SCARED?
NO.
RIIIIIIIIING!
PLEASE LET ME GO. I'M GOING TO BE LATE FOR ENGLISH.
NOT UNLESS YOU FIGHT ME AFTER SCHOOL TOMORROW.

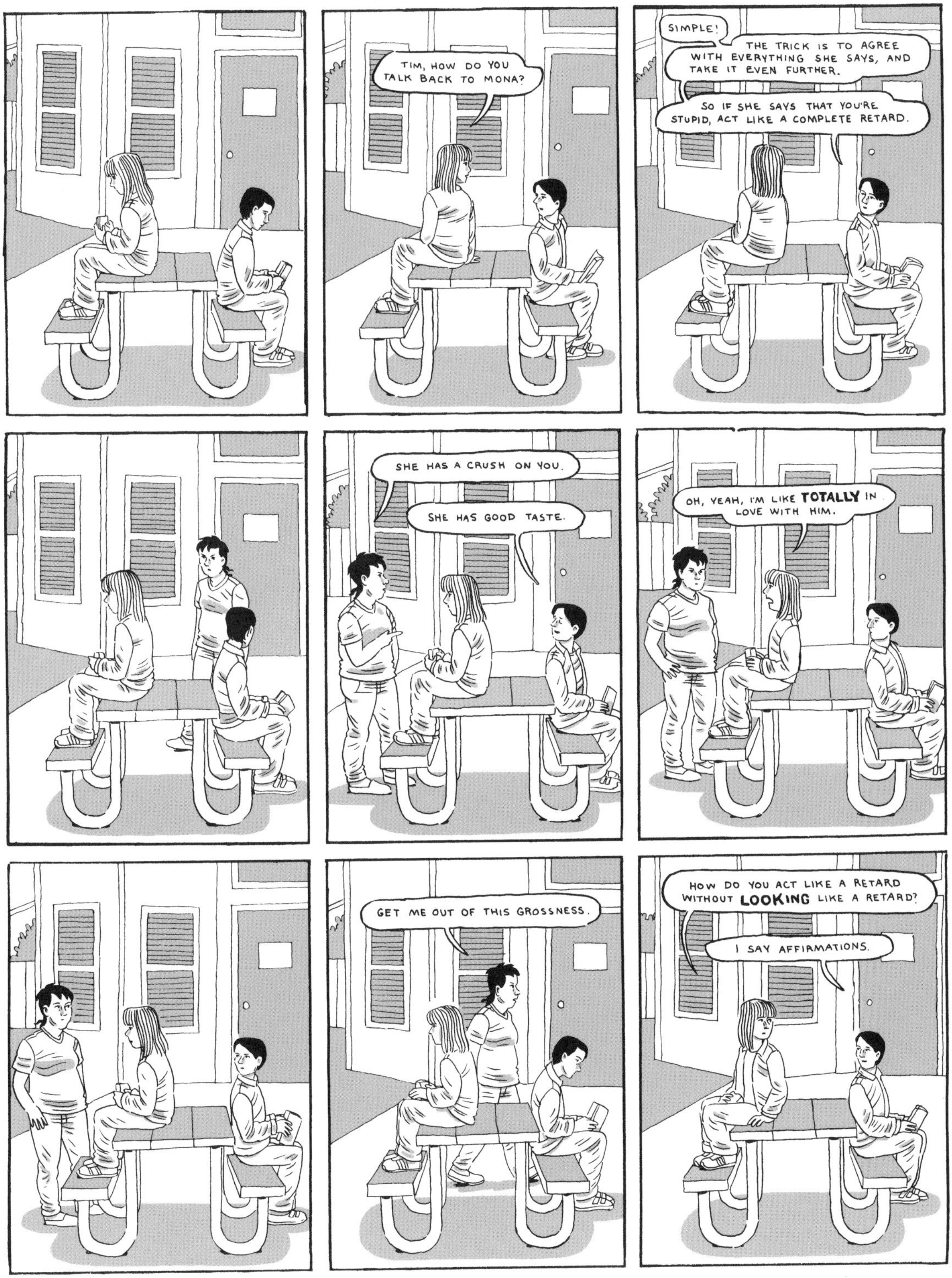
TIM, HOW DO YOU TALK BACK TO MONA?
SIMPLE!
THE TRICK IS TO AGREE WITH EVERYTHING SHE SAYS, AND TAKE IT EVEN FURTHER.
SO IF SHE SAYS THAT YOU'RE STUPID, ACT LIKE A COMPLETE RETARD.
SHE HAS A CRUSH ON YOU.
SHE HAS GOOD TASTE.
OH, YEAH, I'M LIKE TOTALLY IN LOVE WITH HIM.
GET ME OUT OF THIS GROSSNESS.
HOW DO YOU ACT LIKE A RETARD WITHOUT LOOKING LIKE A RETARD?
I SAY AFFIRMATIONS.

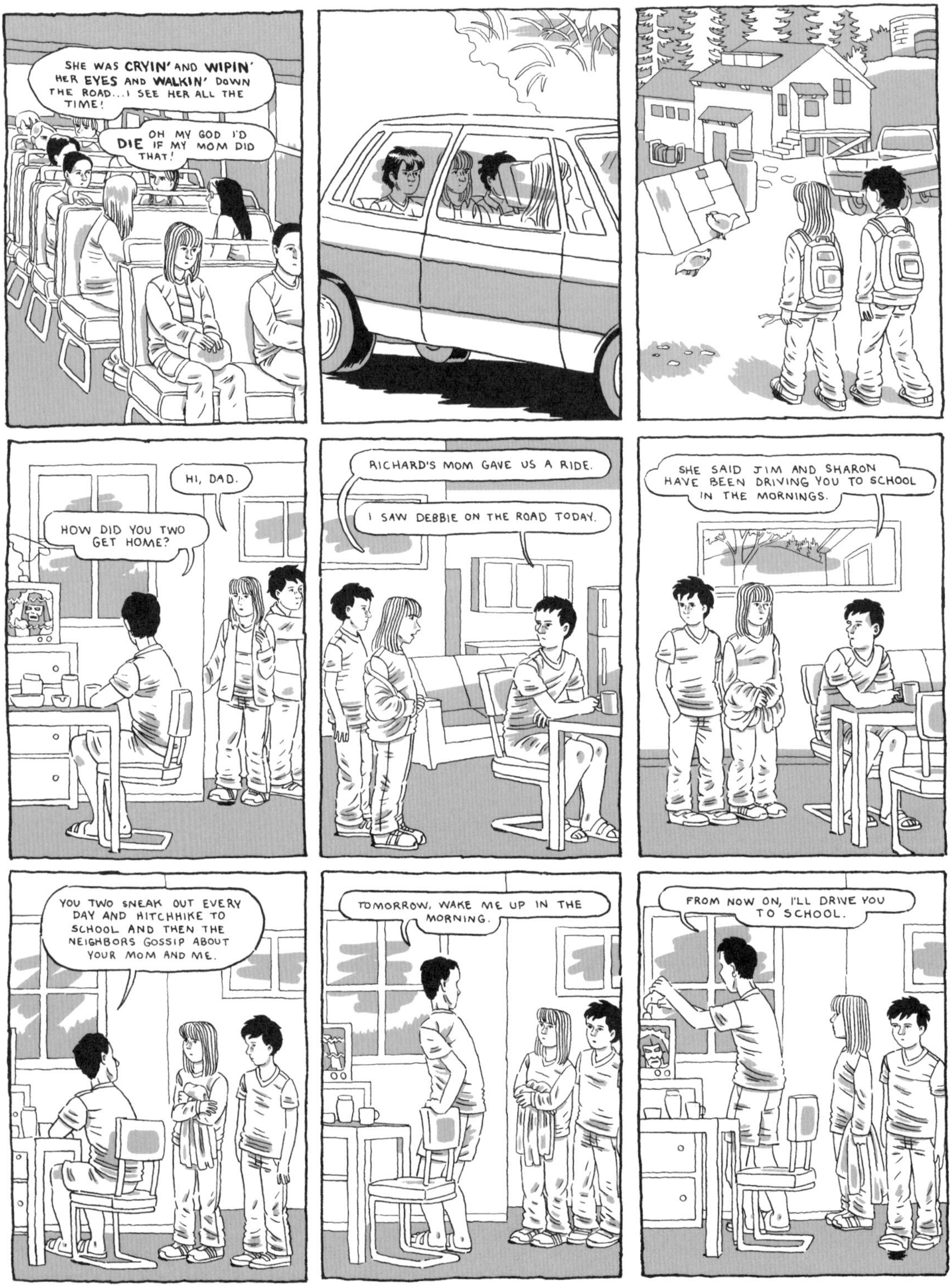
SHE WAS CRYIN' AND WIPIN' HER EYES AND WALKIN' DOWN THE ROAD... I SEE HER ALL THE TIME!
OH MY GOD I'D DIE IF MY MOM DID THAT!
HI, DAD.
HOW DID YOU TWO GET HOME?
RICHARD'S MOM GAVE US A RIDE.
I SAW DEBBIE ON THE ROAD TODAY.
SHE SAID JIM AND SHARON HAVE BEEN DRIVING YOU TO SCHOOL IN THE MORNINGS.
YOU TWO SNEAK OUT EVERY DAY AND HITCHHIKE TO SCHOOL AND THEN THE NEIGHBORS GOSSIP ABOUT YOUR MOM AND ME.
TOMORROW, WAKE ME UP IN THE MORNING.
FROM NOW ON, I'LL DRIVE YOU TO SCHOOL.

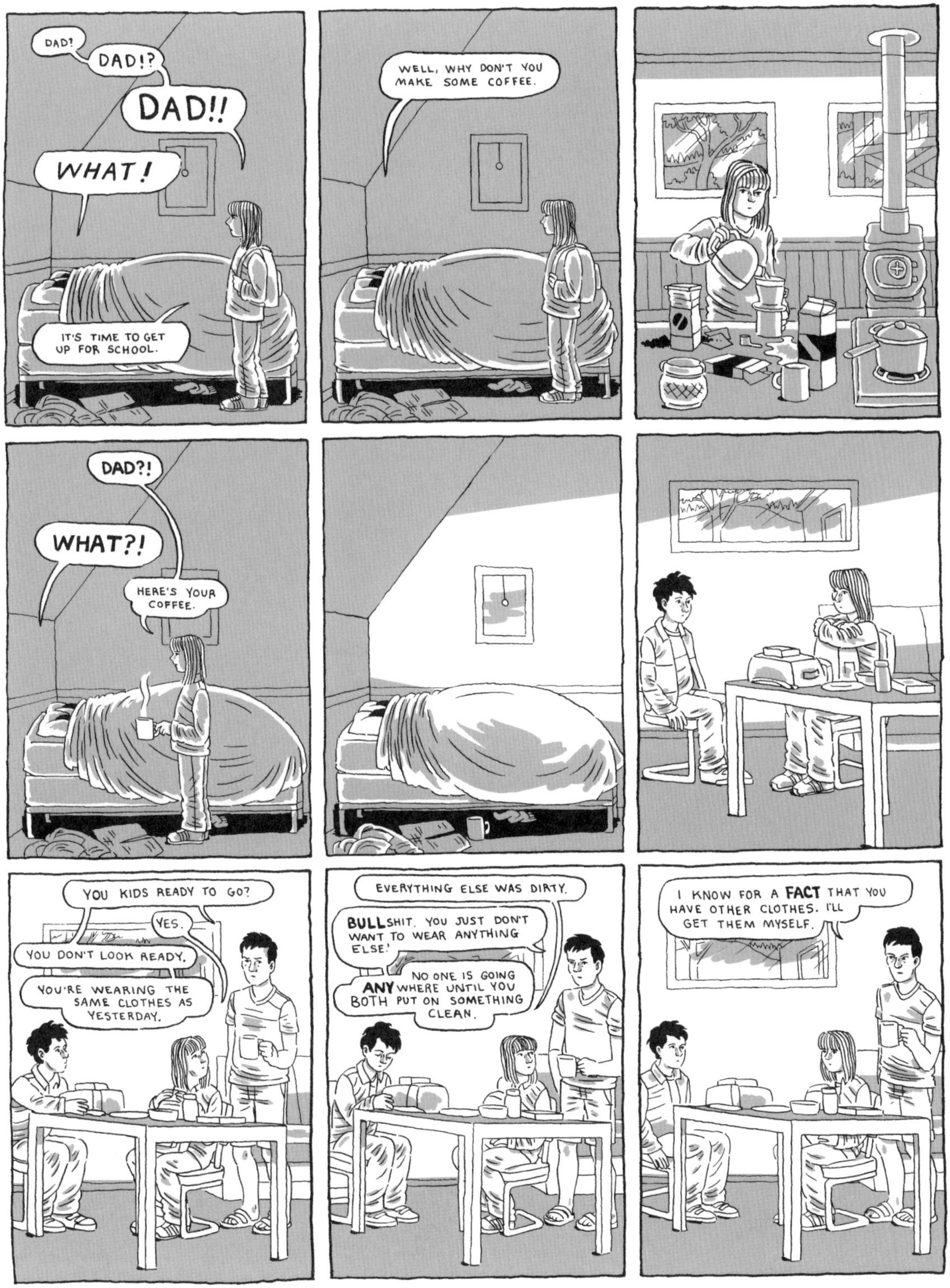
DAD?
DAD!?
DAD!!
WHAT!
IT'S TIME TO GET UP FOR SCHOOL.
WELL, WHY DON'T YOU MAKE SOME COFFEE.
DAD?!
WHAT?!
HERE'S YOUR COFFEE.
YOU KIDS READY TO GO?
YES.
YOU DON'T LOOK READY.
YOU'RE WEARING THE SAME CLOTHES AS YESTERDAY.
EVERYTHING ELSE WAS DIRTY.
BULLSHIT. YOU JUST DON'T WANT TO WEAR ANYTHING ELSE!
NO ONE IS GOING ANYWHERE UNTIL YOU BOTH PUT ON SOMETHING CLEAN.
I KNOW FOR A FACT THAT YOU HAVE OTHER CLOTHES. I'LL GET THEM MYSELF.

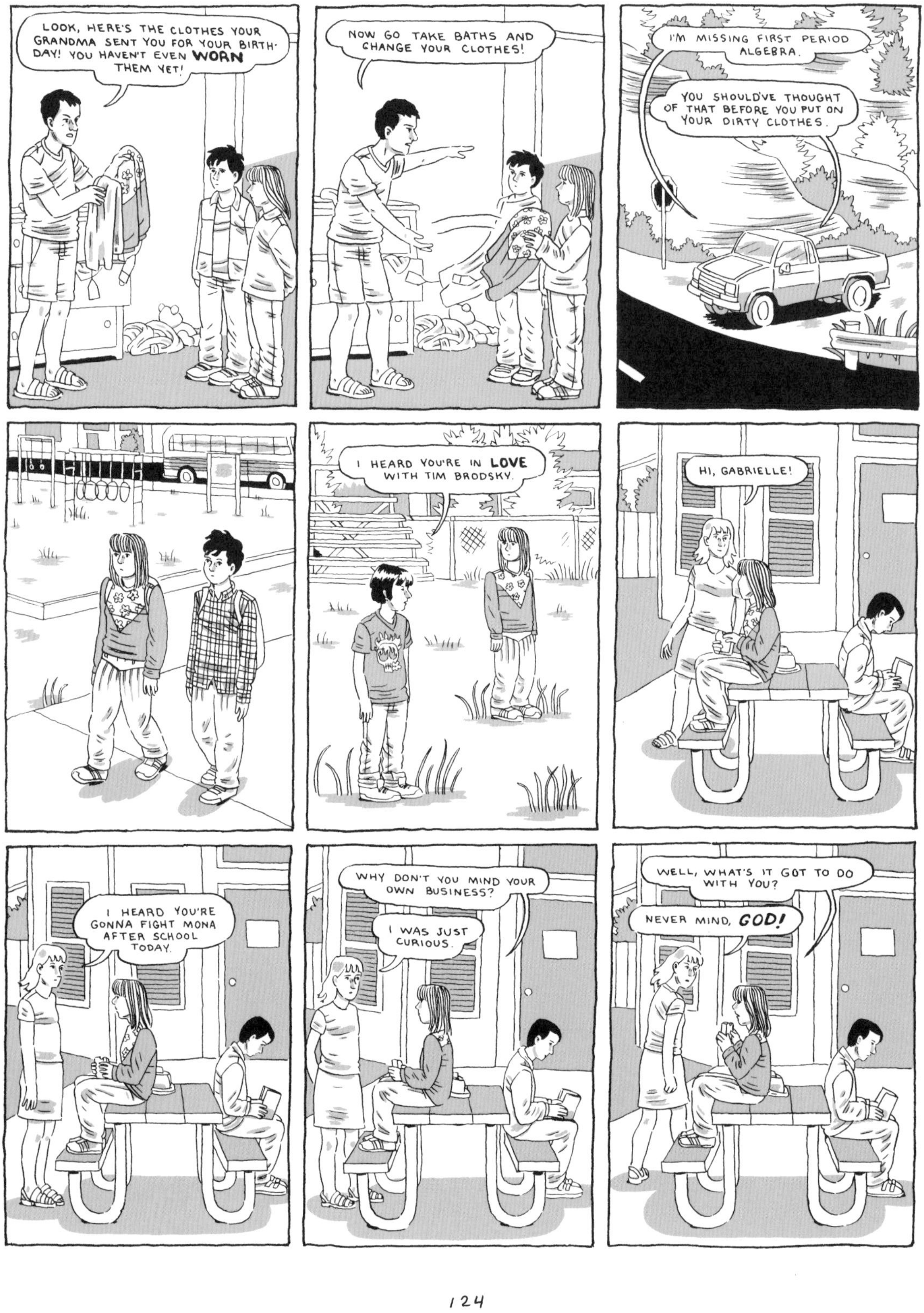
LOOK, HERE'S THE CLOTHES YOUR GRANDMA SENT YOU FOR YOUR BIRTHDAY! YOU HAVEN'T EVEN WORN THEM YET!
NOW GO TAKE BATHS AND CHANGE YOUR CLOTHES!
I'M MISSING FIRST PERIOD ALGEBRA.
YOU SHOULD'VE THOUGHT OF THAT BEFORE YOU PUT ON YOUR DIRTY CLOTHES.
I HEARD YOU'RE IN LOVE WITH TIM BRODSKY.
HI, GABRIELLE!
I HEARD YOU'RE GONNA FIGHT MONA AFTER SCHOOL TODAY.
WHY DON'T YOU MIND YOUR OWN BUSINESS?
I WAS JUST CURIOUS.
WELL, WHAT'S IT GOT TO DO WITH YOU?
NEVER MIND, GOD!

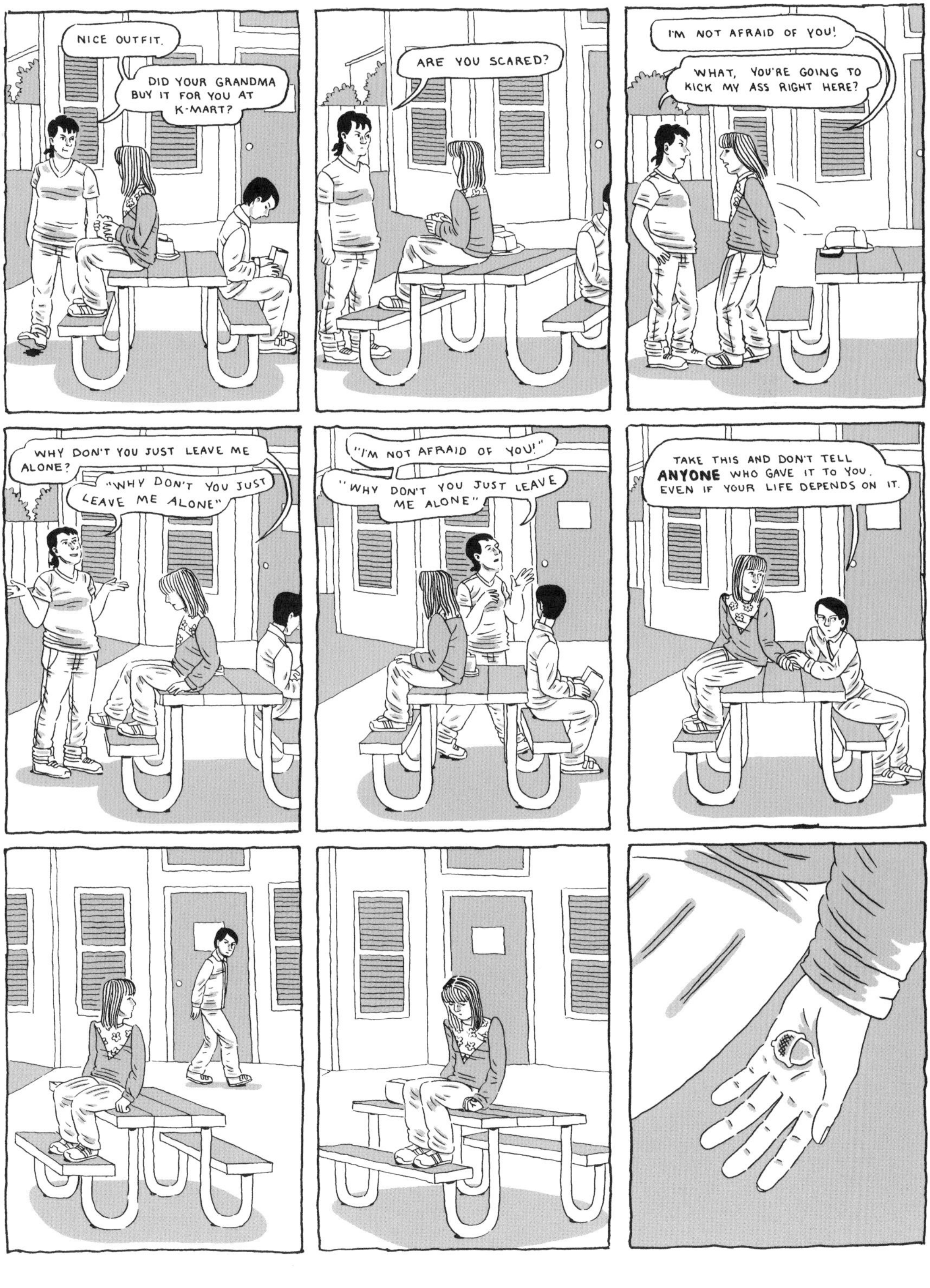
NICE OUTFIT.
DID YOUR GRANDMA BUY IT FOR YOU AT K-MART?
ARE YOU SCARED?
I'M NOT AFRAID OF YOU!
WHAT, YOU'RE GOING TO KICK MY ASS RIGHT HERE?
WHY DON'T YOU JUST LEAVE ME ALONE?
"WHY DON'T YOU JUST LEAVE ME ALONE"
"I'M NOT AFRAID OF YOU!"
"WHY DON'T YOU JUST LEAVE ME ALONE"
TAKE THIS AND DON'T TELL ANYONE WHO GAVE IT TO YOU. EVEN IF YOUR LIFE DEPENDS ON IT.

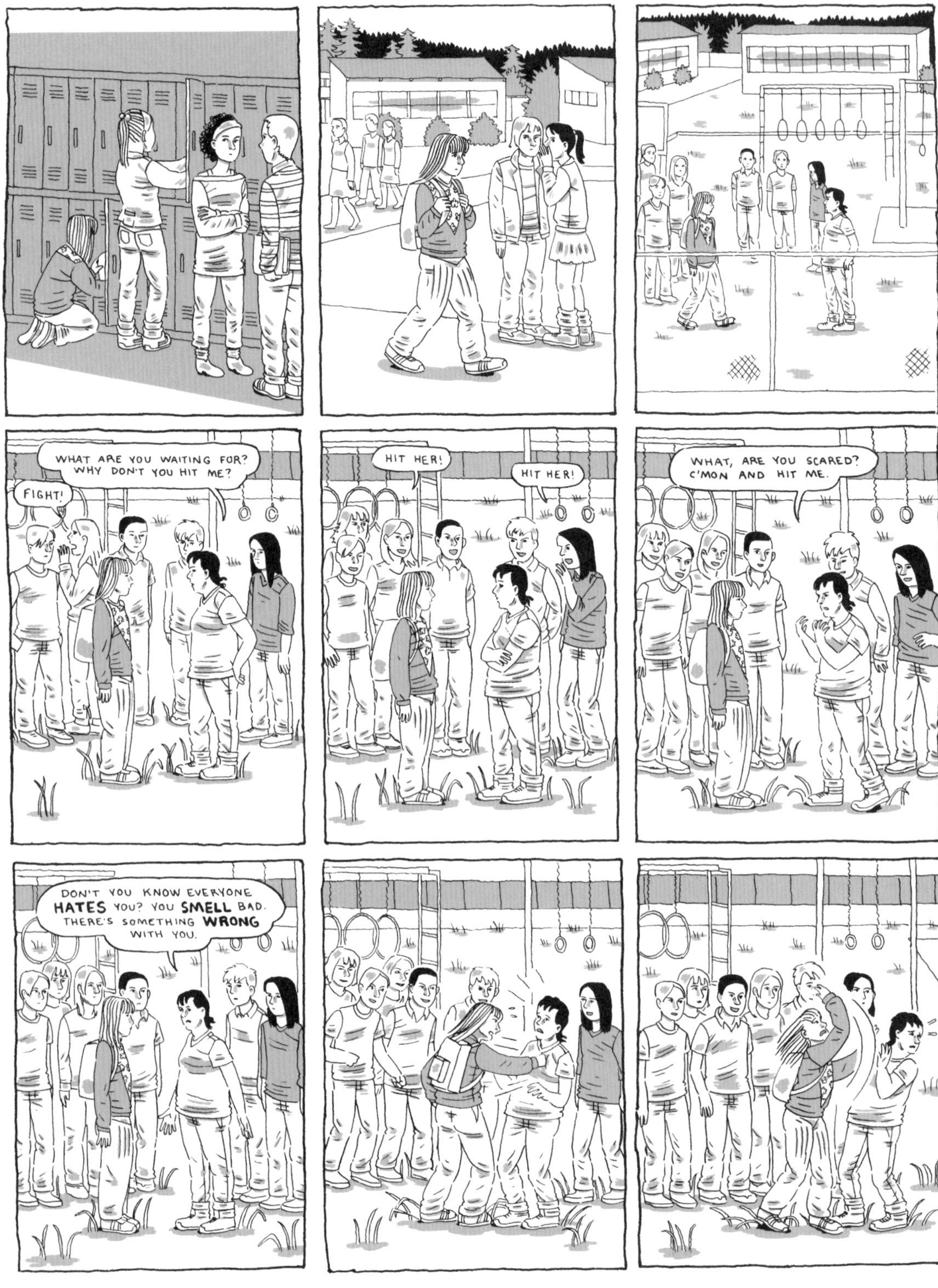
FIGHT!
WHAT ARE YOU WAITING FOR? WHY DON'T YOU HIT ME?
HIT HER!
HIT HER!
WHAT, ARE YOU SCARED? C'MON AND HIT ME.
DON'T YOU KNOW EVERYONE HATES YOU? YOU SMELL BAD. THERE'S SOMETHING WRONG WITH YOU.

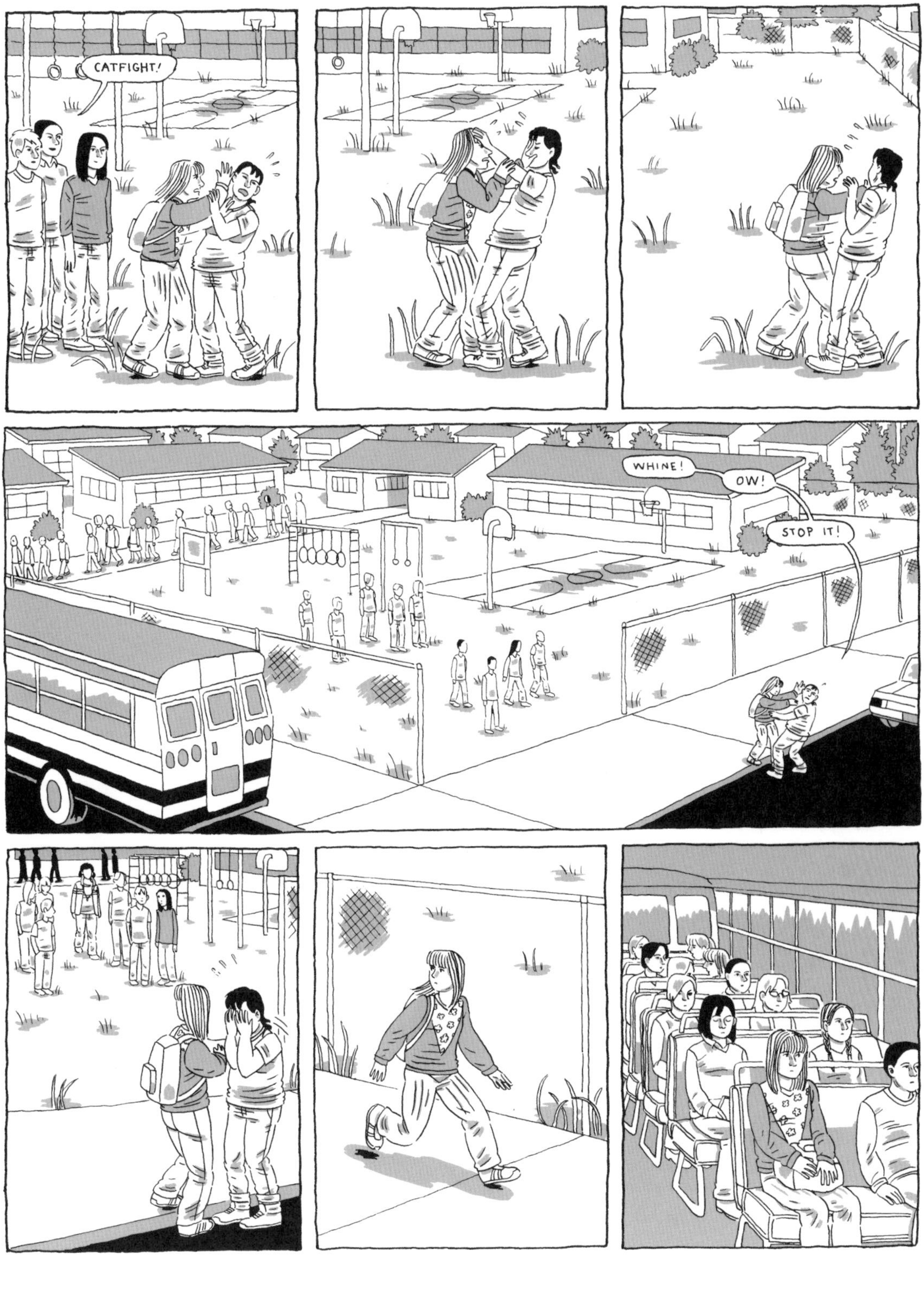
CATFIGHT!
WHINE!
OW!
STOP IT!

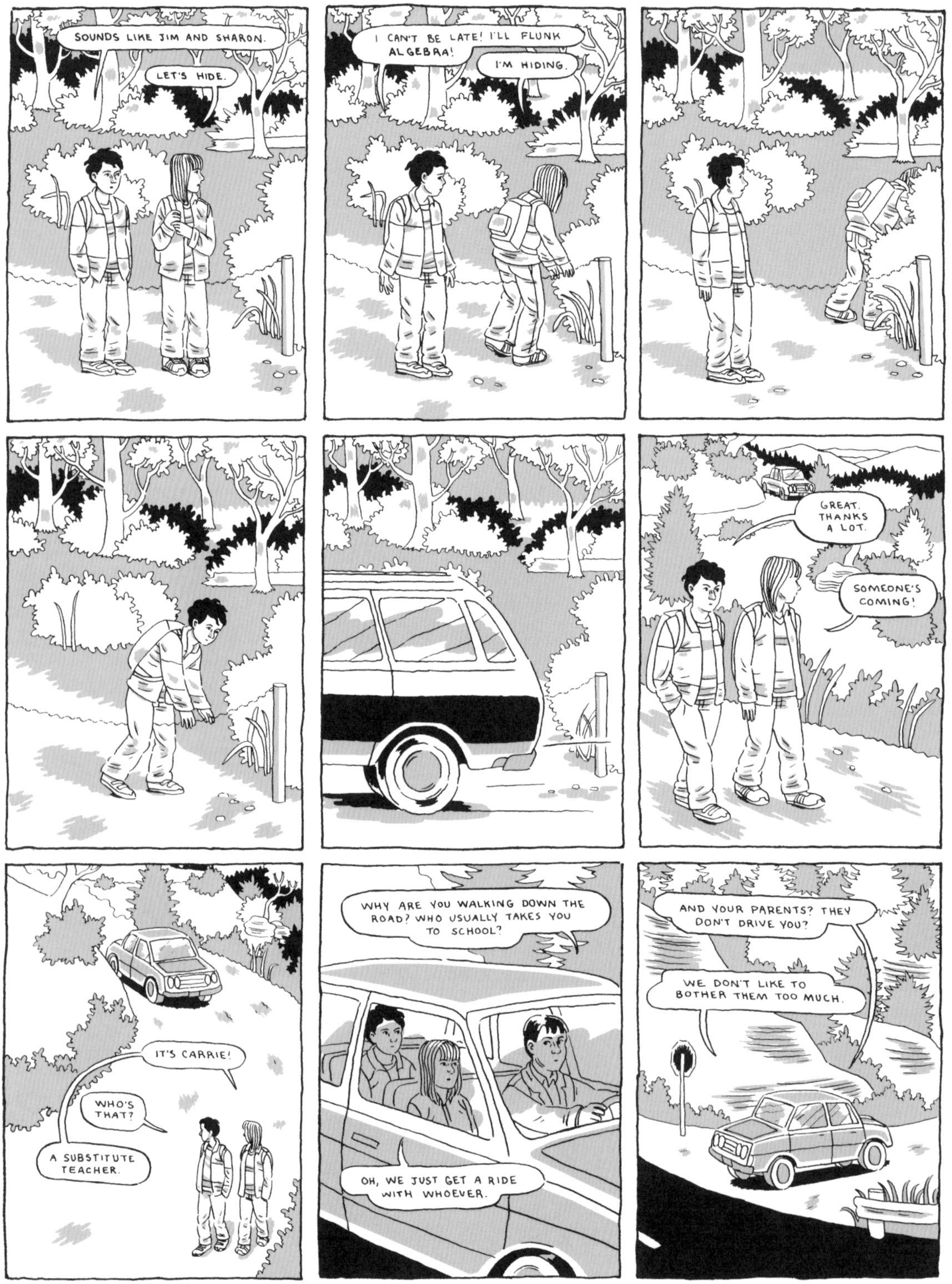
SOUNDS LIKE JIM AND SHARON.
LET'S HIDE.
I CAN'T BE LATE! I'LL FLUNK ALGEBRA!
I'M HIDING.
GREAT. THANKS A LOT.
SOMEONE'S COMING!
IT'S CARRIE!
WHO'S THAT?
A SUBSTITUTE TEACHER.
WHY ARE YOU WALKING DOWN THE ROAD? WHO USUALLY TAKES YOU TO SCHOOL?
OH, WE JUST GET A RIDE WITH WHOEVER.
AND YOUR PARENTS? THEY DON'T DRIVE YOU?
WE DON'T LIKE TO BOTHER THEM TOO MUCH.

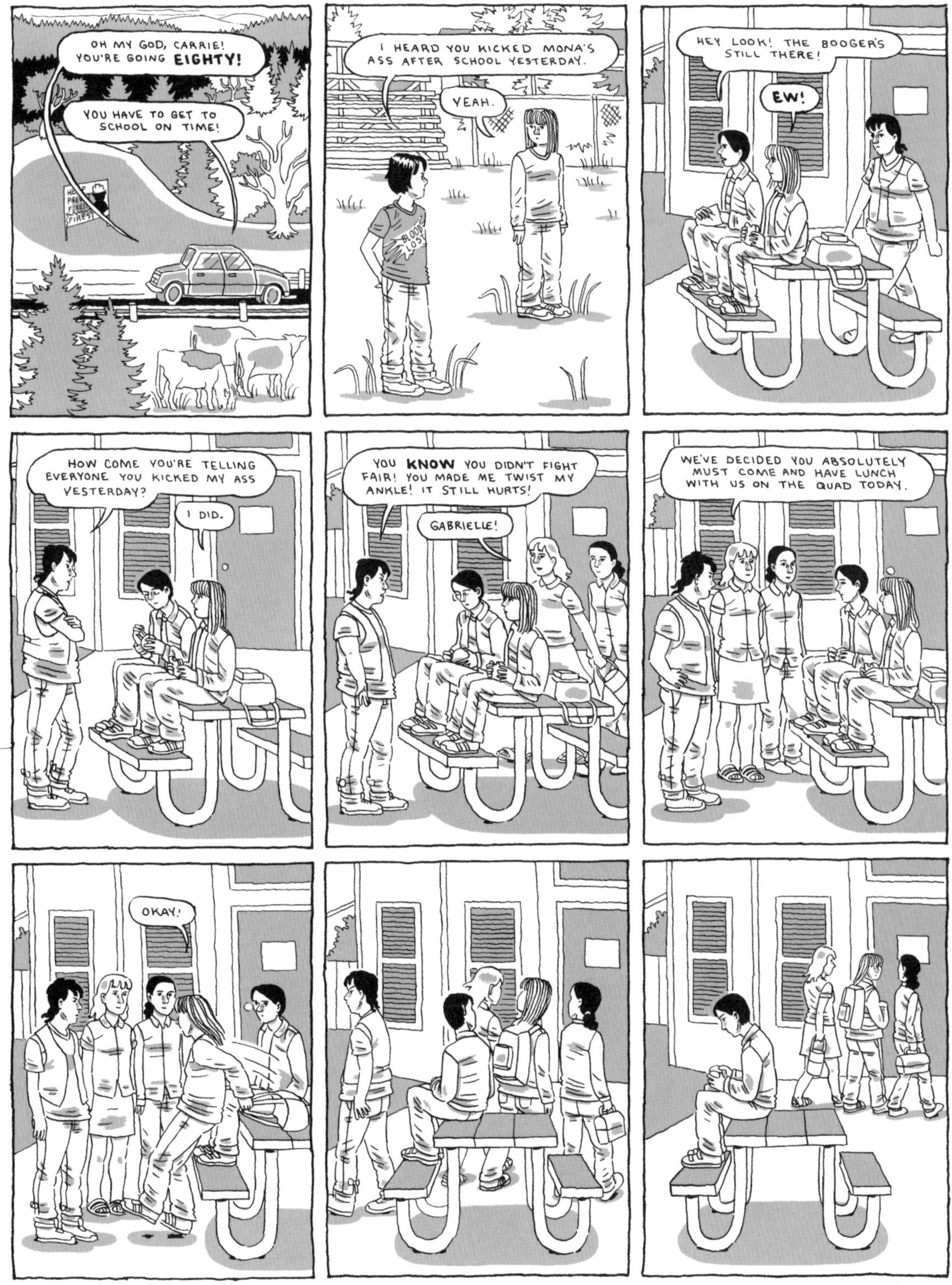
OH MY GOD, CARRIE! YOU'RE GOING EIGHTY!
YOU HAVE TO GET TO SCHOOL ON TIME!
I HEARD YOU KICKED MONA'S ASS AFTER SCHOOL YESTERDAY.
YEAH.
HEY LOOK! THE BOOGER'S STILL THERE!
EW!
HOW COME YOU'RE TELLING EVERYONE YOU KICKED MY ASS YESTERDAY?
I DID.
YOU KNOW YOU DIDN'T FIGHT FAIR! YOU MADE ME TWIST MY ANKLE! IT STILL HURTS!
GABRIELLE!
WE'VE DECIDED YOU ABSOLUTELY MUST COME AND HAVE LUNCH WITH US ON THE QUAD TODAY.
OKAY!

Gabrielle Bell 2006

Gabrielle the Third

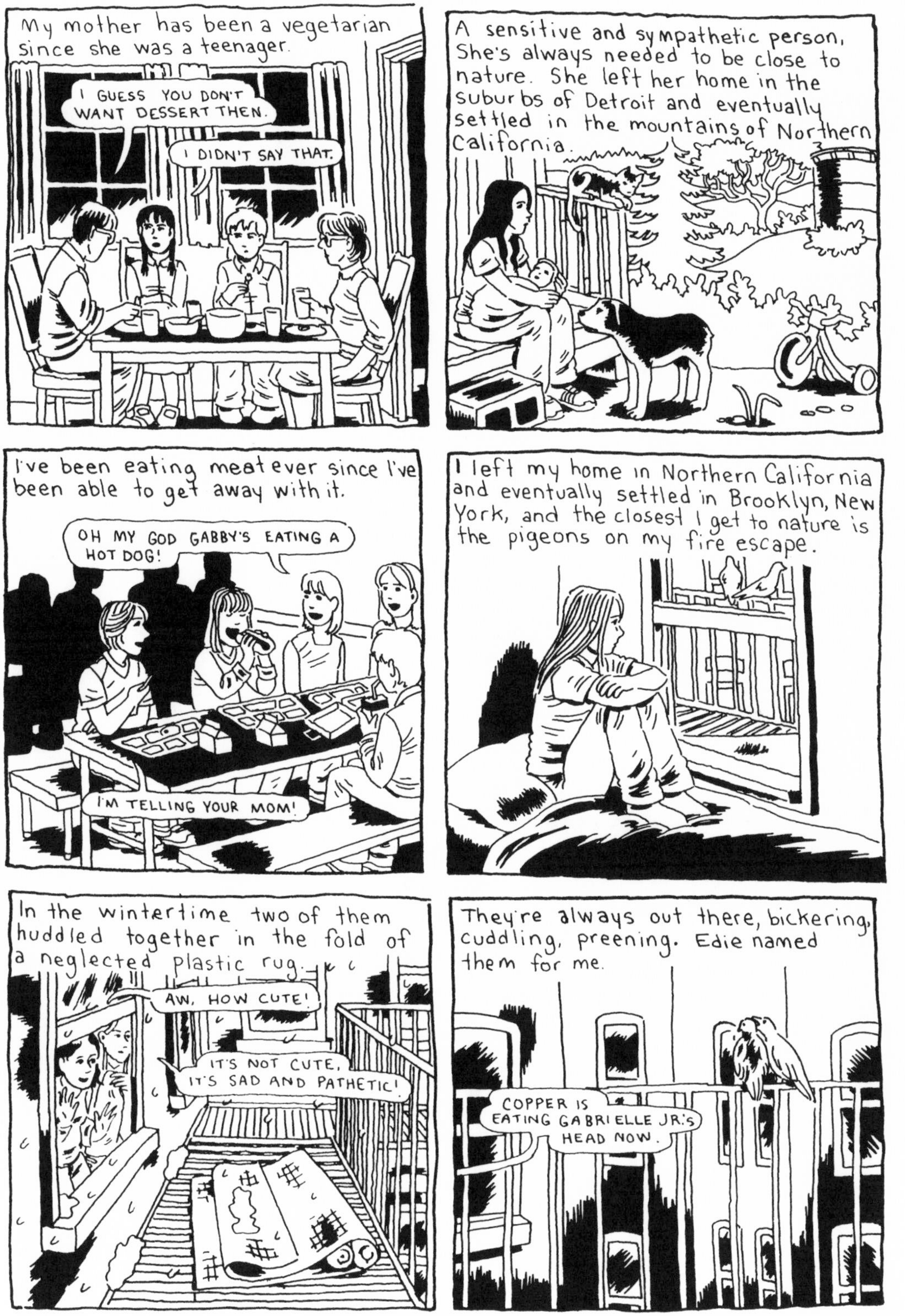
My mother has been a vegetarian since she was a teenager.
I GUESS YOU DON'T WANT DESSERT THEN.
I DIDN'T SAY THAT.
A sensitive and sympathetic person, She's always needed to be close to nature. She left her home in the suburbs of Detroit and eventually settled in the mountains of Northern California.
I've been eating meat ever since I've been able to get away with it.
OH MY GOD GABBY'S EATING A HOT DOG!
I'M TELLING YOUR MOM!
I left my home in Northern California and eventually settled in Brooklyn, New York, and the closest I get to nature is the pigeons on my fire escape.
In the wintertime two of them huddled together in the fold of a neglected plastic rug.
AW, HOW CUTE!
IT'S NOT CUTE, IT'S SAD AND PATHETIC!
They're always out there, bickering, cuddling, preening. Edie named them for me.
COPPER IS EATING GABRIELLE JR.'S HEAD NOW.

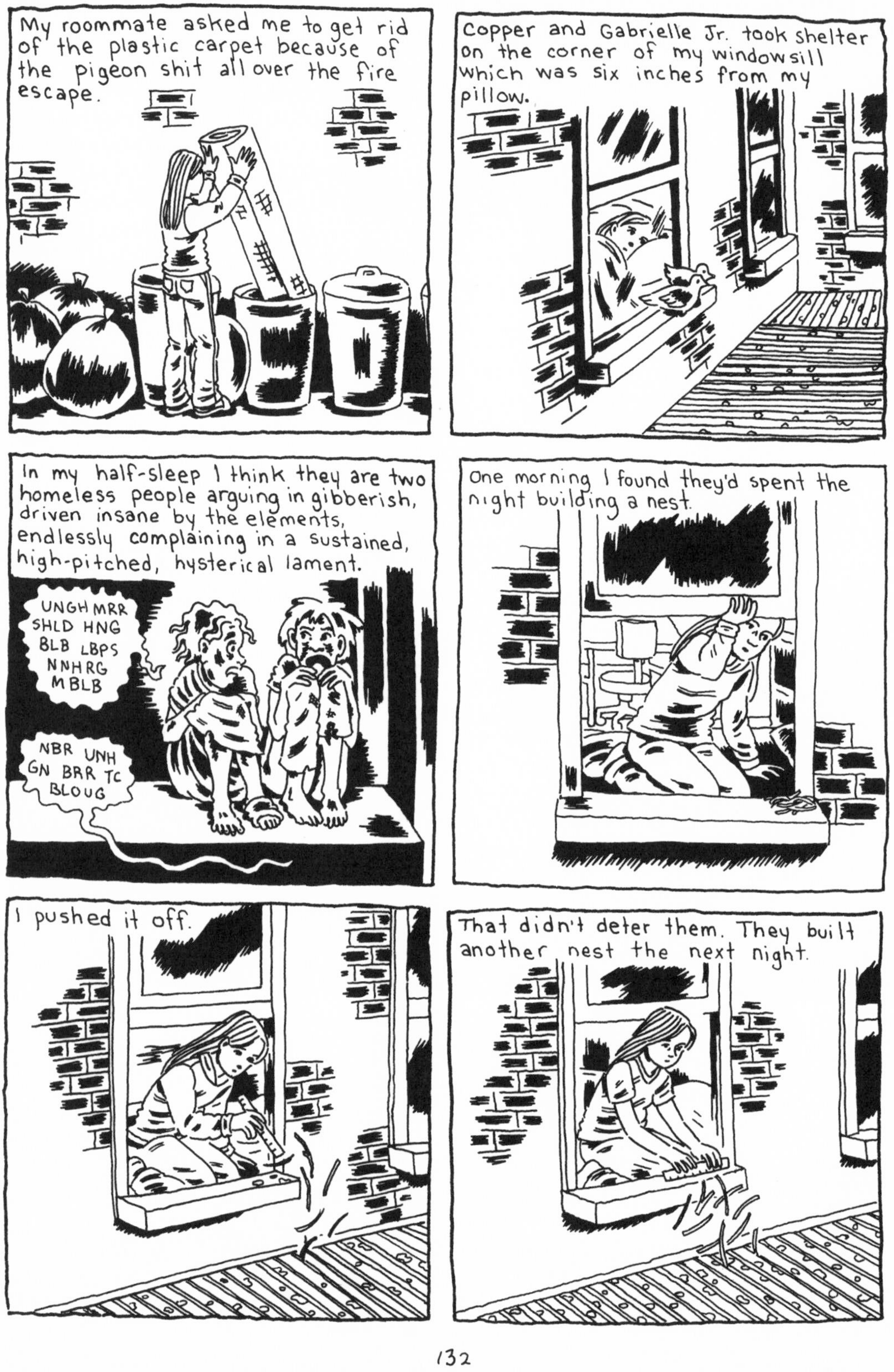

My roommate asked me to get rid of the plastic carpet because of the pigeon shit all over the fire escape.
Copper and Gabrielle Jr. took shelter on the corner of my windowsill which was six inches from my pillow.
In my half-sleep I think they are two homeless people arguing in gibberish, driven insane by the elements, endlessly complaining in a sustained, high-pitched, hysterical lament.
UNGH MRR SHLD HNG BLB LBPS NNHRG MBLB
NBR UNH GN BRR TC BLOUG
One morning I found they'd spent the night building a nest.
I pushed it off.
That didn't deter them. They built another nest the next night.

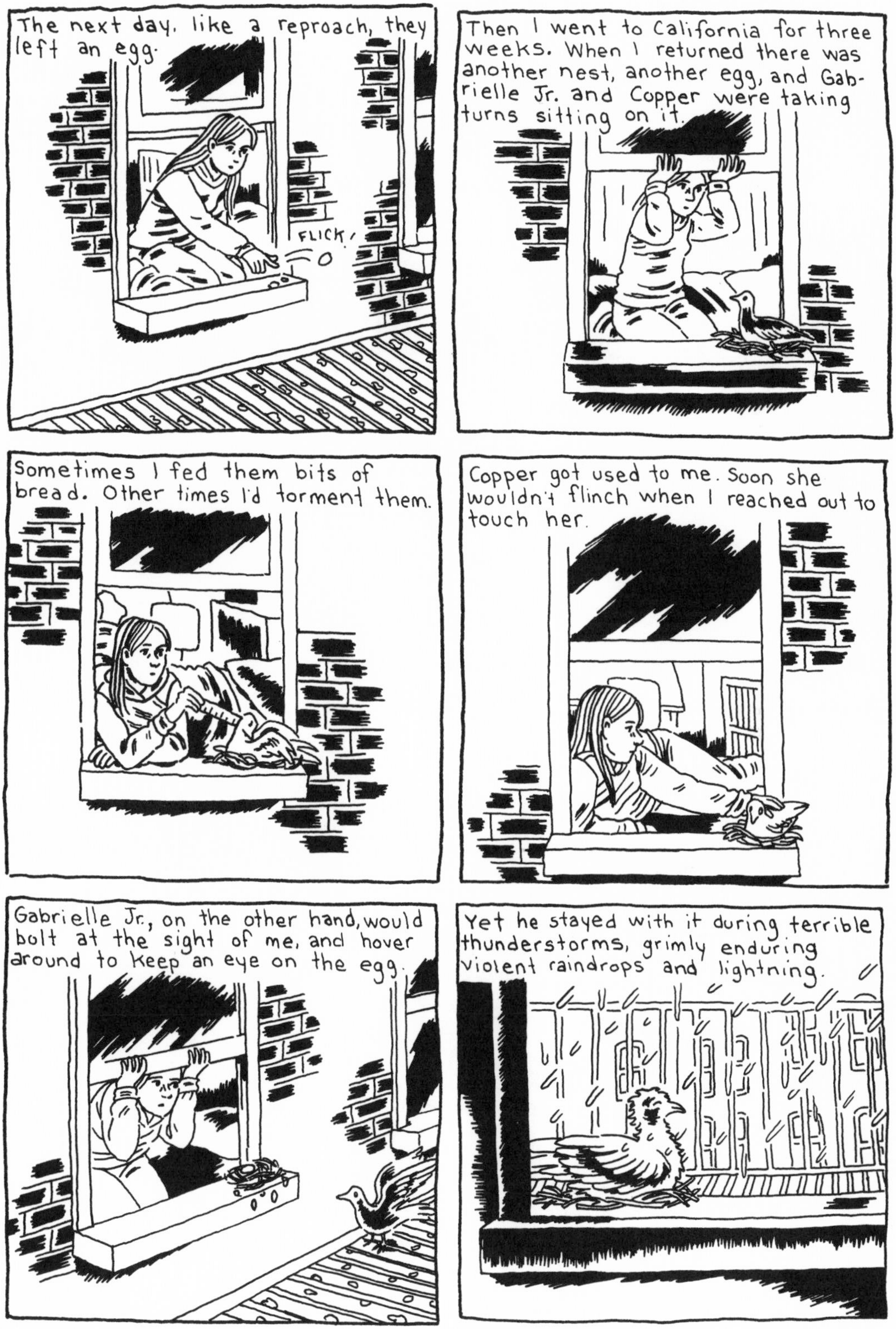
The next day, like a reproach, they left an egg.
FLICK!
Then I went to California for three weeks. When I returned there was another nest, another egg, and Gabrielle Jr. and Copper were taking turns sitting on it.
Sometimes I fed them bits of bread. Other times I'd torment them.
Copper got used to me. Soon she wouldn't flinch when I reached out to touch her.
Gabrielle Jr., on the other hand, would bolt at the sight of me, and hover around to keep an eye on the egg.
Yet he stayed with it during terrible thunderstorms, grimly enduring violent raindrops and lightning.

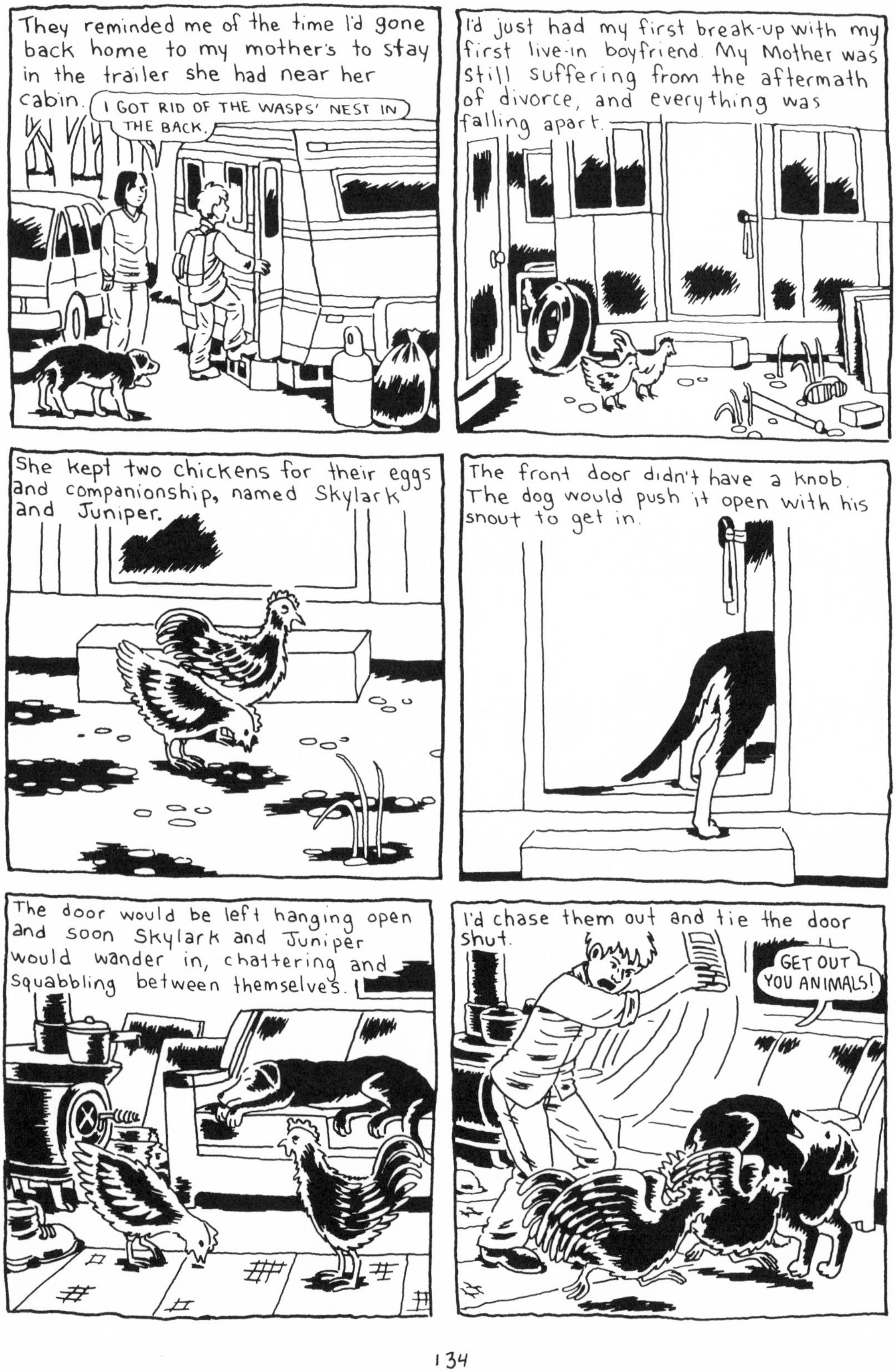
They reminded me of the time I'd gone back home to my mother's to stay in the trailer she had near her cabin.
I GOT RID OF THE WASPS' NEST IN THE BACK.
I'd just had my first break-up with my first live-in boyfriend. My Mother was still suffering from the aftermath of divorce, and everything was falling apart.
She kept two chickens for their eggs and companionship, named Skylark and Juniper.
The front door didn't have a knob. The dog would push it open with his snout to get in.
The door would be left hanging open and soon Skylark and Juniper would wander in, chattering and squabbling between themselves.
I'd chase them out and tie the door shut.
GET OUT YOU ANIMALS!

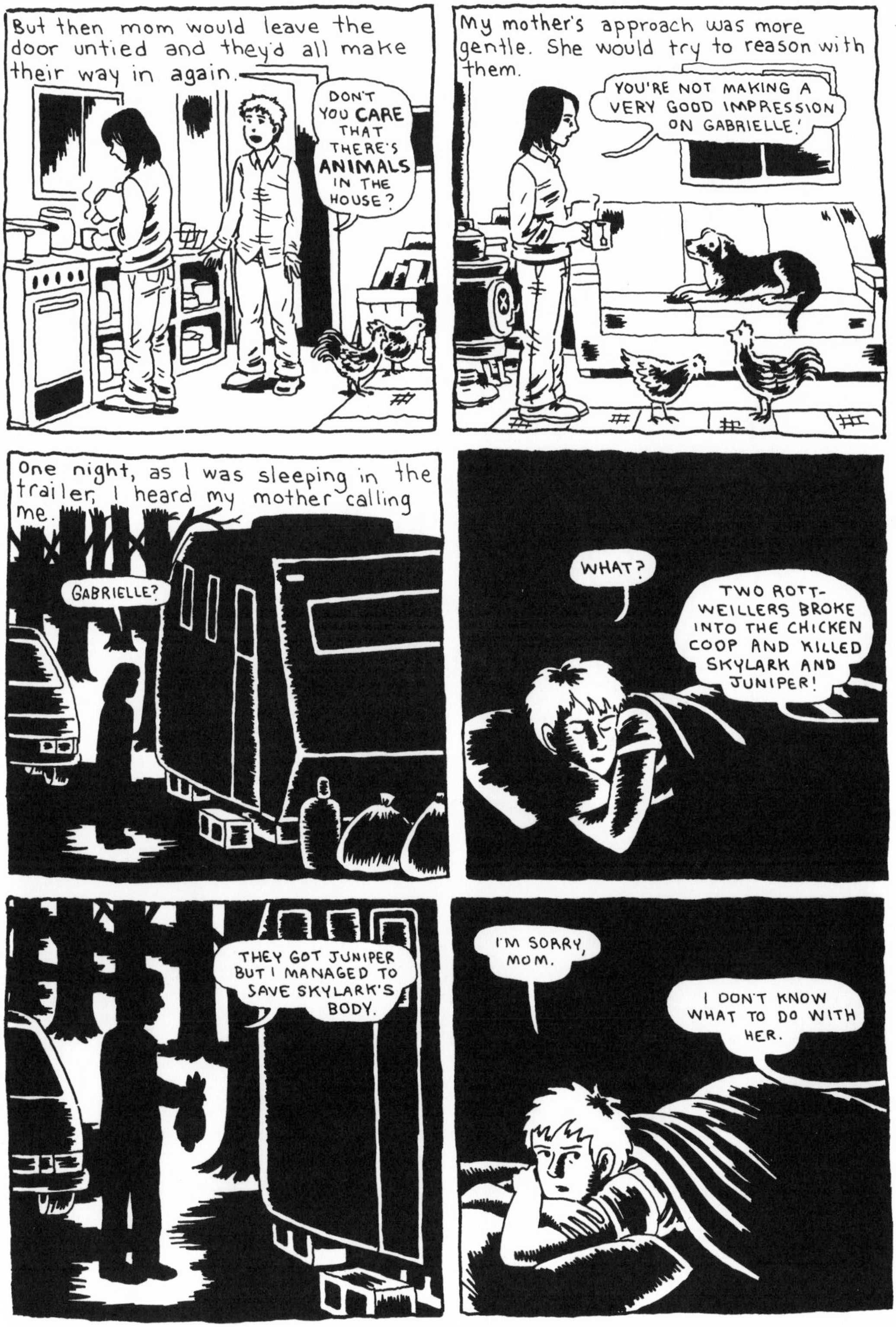
But then mom would leave the door untied and they'd all make their way in again.
DON'T YOU CARE THAT THERE'S ANIMALS IN THE HOUSE?
My mother's approach was more gentle. She would try to reason with them.
YOU'RE NOT MAKING A VERY GOOD IMPRESSION ON GABRIELLE!
One night, as I was sleeping in the trailer, I heard my mother calling me.
GABRIELLE?
WHAT?
TWO ROTT-WEILLERS BROKE INTO THE CHICKEN COOP AND KILLED SKYLARK AND JUNIPER!
THEY GOT JUNIPER BUT I MANAGED TO SAVE SKYLARK'S BODY.
I'M SORRY, MOM.
I DON'T KNOW WHAT TO DO WITH HER.

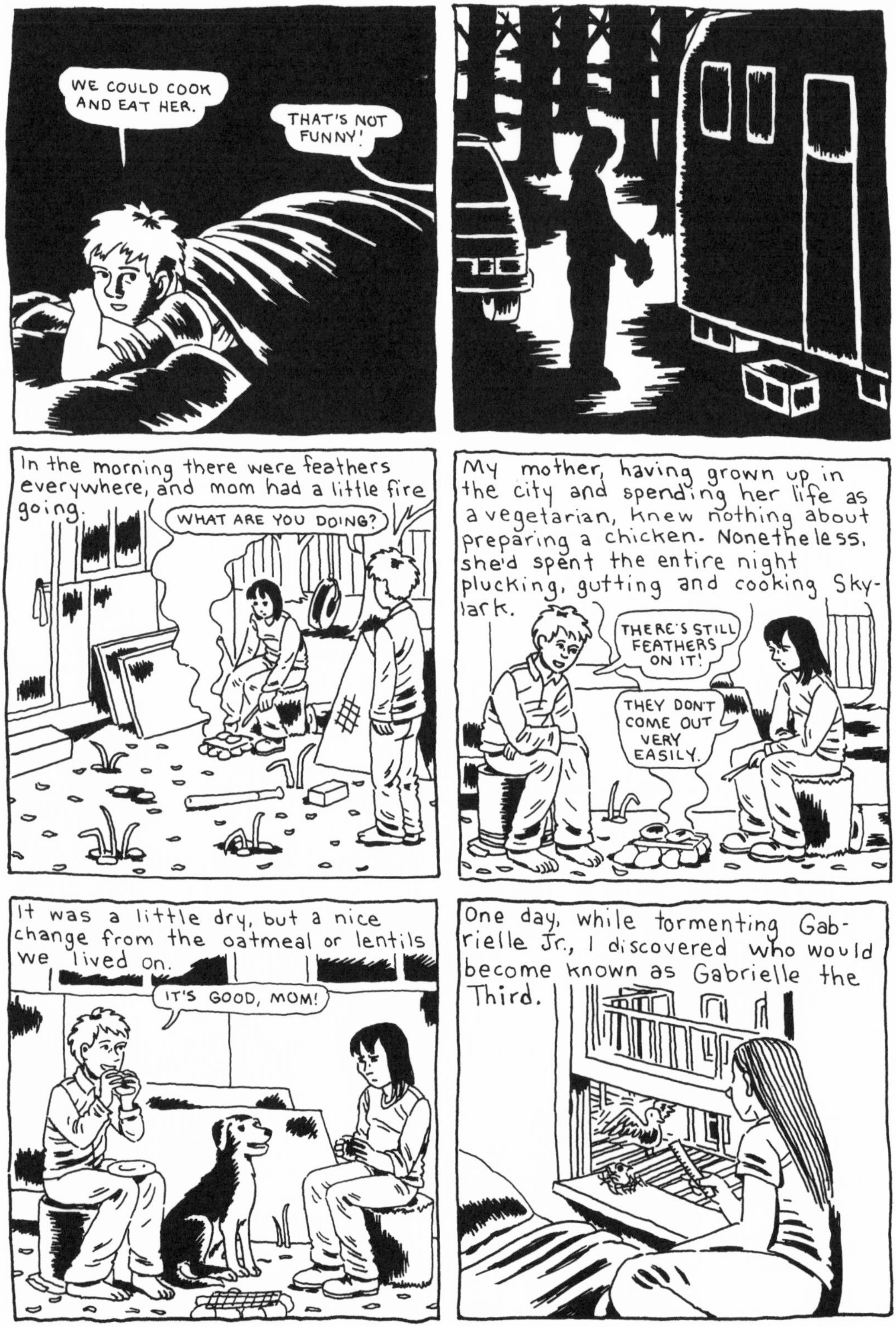
WE COULD COOK AND EAT HER.
THAT'S NOT FUNNY!
In the morning there were feathers everywhere, and mom had a little fire going.
WHAT ARE YOU DOING?
My mother, having grown up in the city and spending her life as a vegetarian, knew nothing about preparing a chicken. Nonetheless, she'd spent the entire night plucking, gutting and cooking Skylark.
THERE'S STILL FEATHERS ON IT!
THEY DON'T COME OUT VERY EASILY.
It was a little dry, but a nice change from the oatmeal or lentils we lived on.
IT'S GOOD, MOM!
One day, while tormenting Gabrielle Jr., I discovered who would become known as Gabrielle the Third.

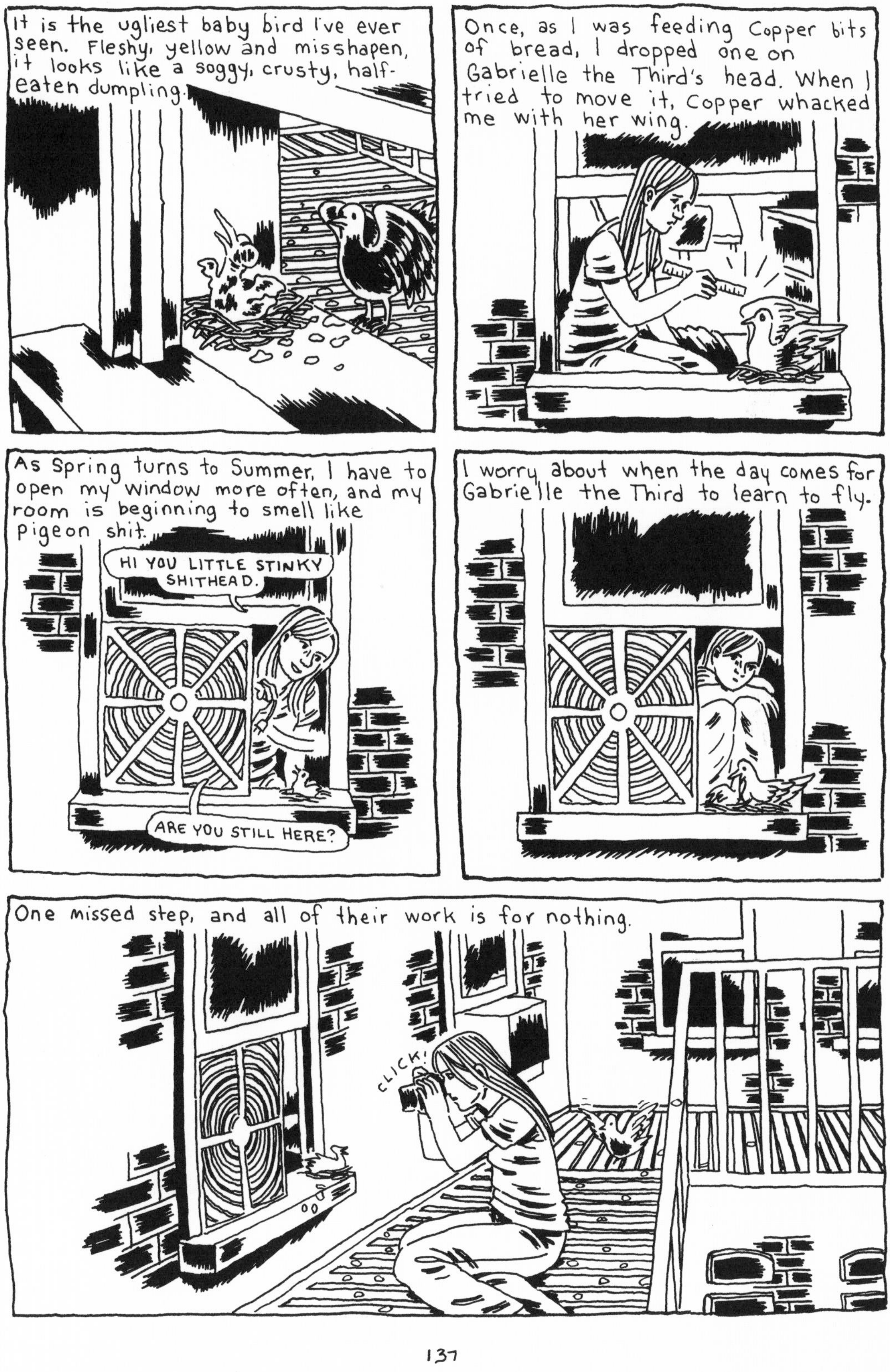
It is the ugliest baby bird I've ever seen. Fleshy, yellow and misshapen, it looks like a soggy, crusty, half-eaten dumpling.
Once, as I was feeding Copper bits of bread, I dropped one on Gabrielle the Third's head. When I tried to move it, Copper whacked me with her wing.
As Spring turns to Summer, I have to open my window more often, and my room is beginning to smell like pigeon shit.
HI YOU LITTLE STINKY SHITHEAD.
ARE YOU STILL HERE?
I worry about when the day comes for Gabrielle the Third to learn to fly.
One missed step, and all of their work is for nothing.
CLICK!

Helpless

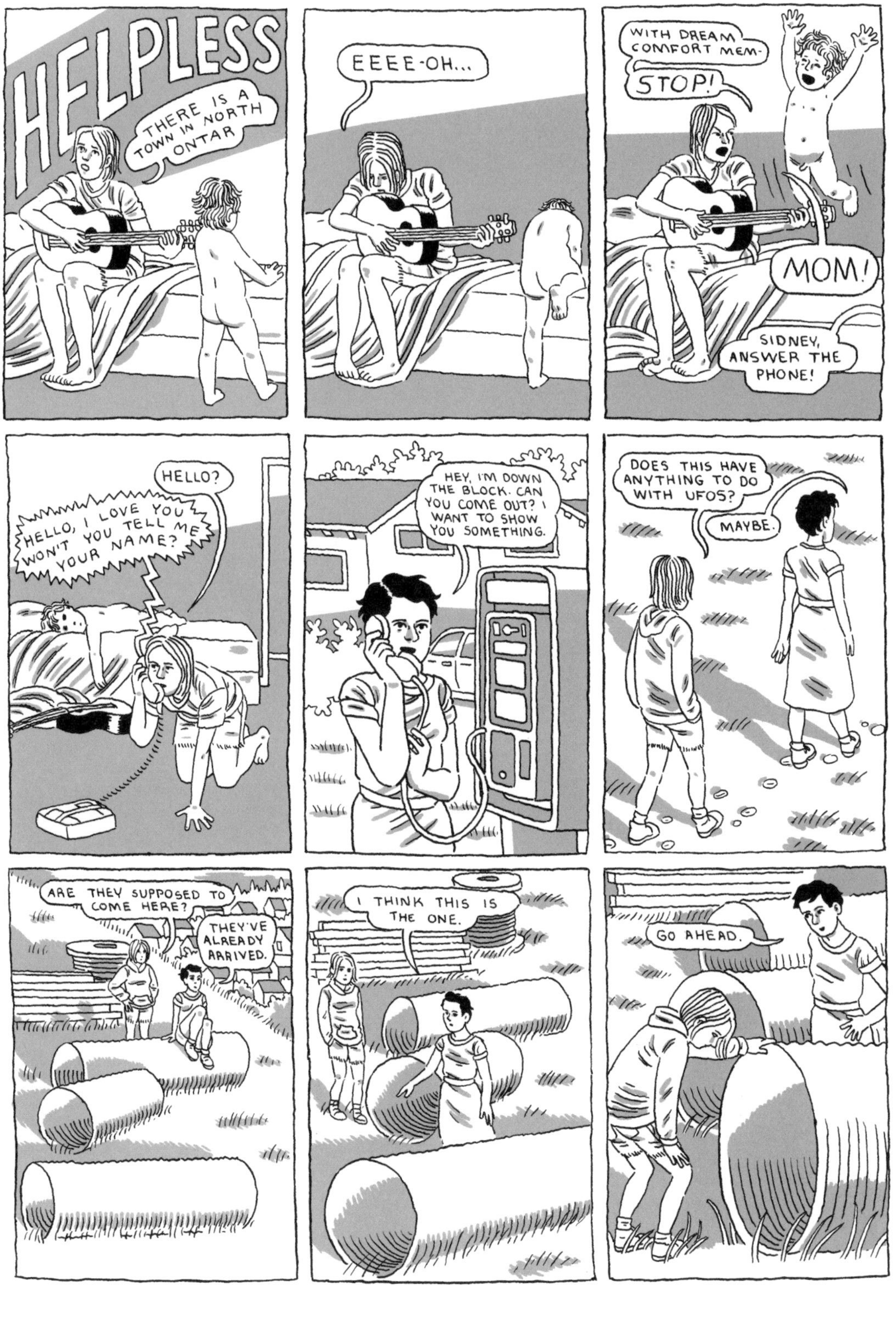
HELPLESS
THERE IS A TOWN IN NORTH ONTAR
EEEE-OH...
WITH DREAM COMFORT MEM-
STOP!
MOM!
SIDNEY, ANSWER THE PHONE!
HELLO?
HELLO, I LOVE YOU WON'T YOU TELL ME YOUR NAME?
HEY, I'M DOWN THE BLOCK. CAN YOU COME OUT? I WANT TO SHOW YOU SOMETHING.
DOES THIS HAVE ANYTHING TO DO WITH UFOS?
MAYBE.
ARE THEY SUPPOSED TO COME HERE?
THEY'VE ALREADY ARRIVED.
I THINK THIS IS THE ONE.
GO AHEAD.

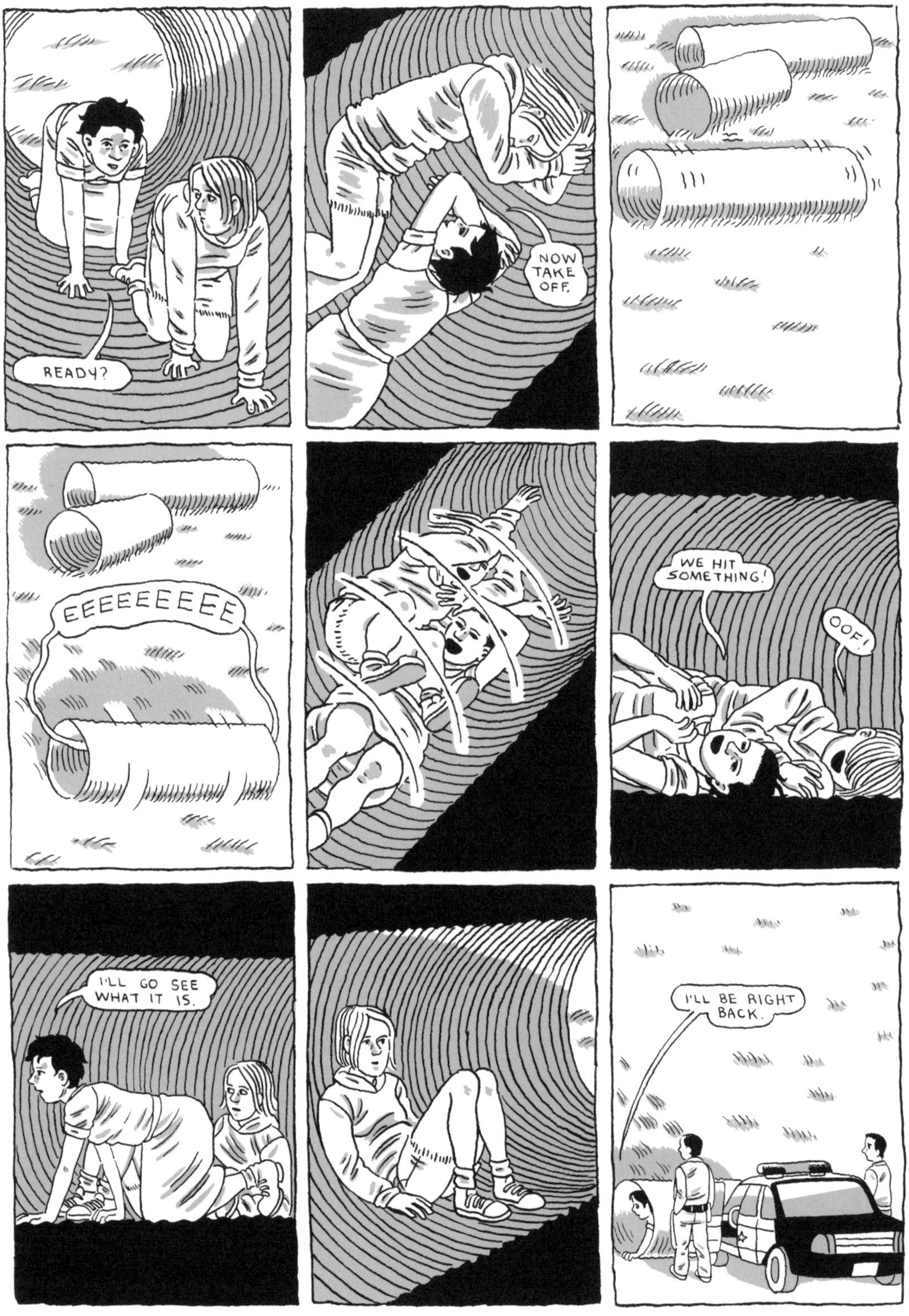
READY?
NOW TAKE OFF.
EEEEEEEEEE
WE HIT SOMETHING!
OOF!
I'LL GO SEE WHAT IT IS.
I'LL BE RIGHT BACK.

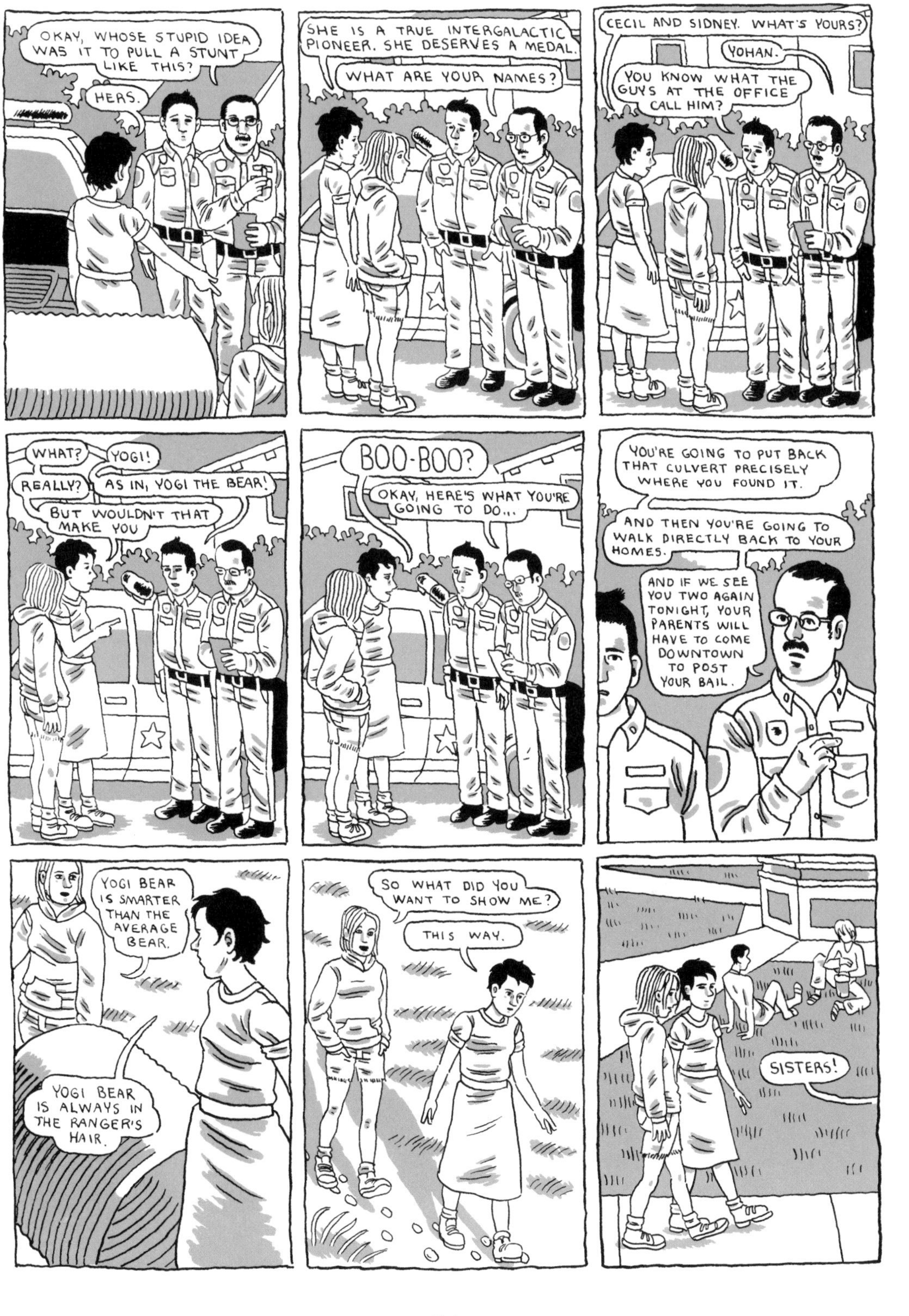
OKAY, WHOSE STUPID IDEA WAS IT TO PULL A STUNT LIKE THIS?
HERS.
SHE IS A TRUE INTERGALACTIC PIONEER. SHE DESERVES A MEDAL.
WHAT ARE YOUR NAMES?
CECIL AND SIDNEY. WHAT'S YOURS?
YOHAN.
YOU KNOW WHAT THE GUYS AT THE OFFICE CALL HIM?
WHAT?
YOGI!
REALLY?
AS IN, YOGI THE BEAR!
BUT WOULDN'T THAT MAKE YOU
BOO-BOO?
OKAY, HERE'S WHAT YOU'RE GOING TO DO...
YOU'RE GOING TO PUT BACK THAT CULVERT PRECISELY WHERE YOU FOUND IT.
AND THEN YOU'RE GOING TO WALK DIRECTLY BACK TO YOUR HOMES.
AND IF WE SEE YOU TWO AGAIN TONIGHT, YOUR PARENTS WILL HAVE TO COME DOWNTOWN TO POST YOUR BAIL.
YOGI BEAR IS SMARTER THAN THE AVERAGE BEAR.
YOGI BEAR IS ALWAYS IN THE RANGER'S HAIR.
SO WHAT DID YOU WANT TO SHOW ME?
THIS WAY.
SISTERS!

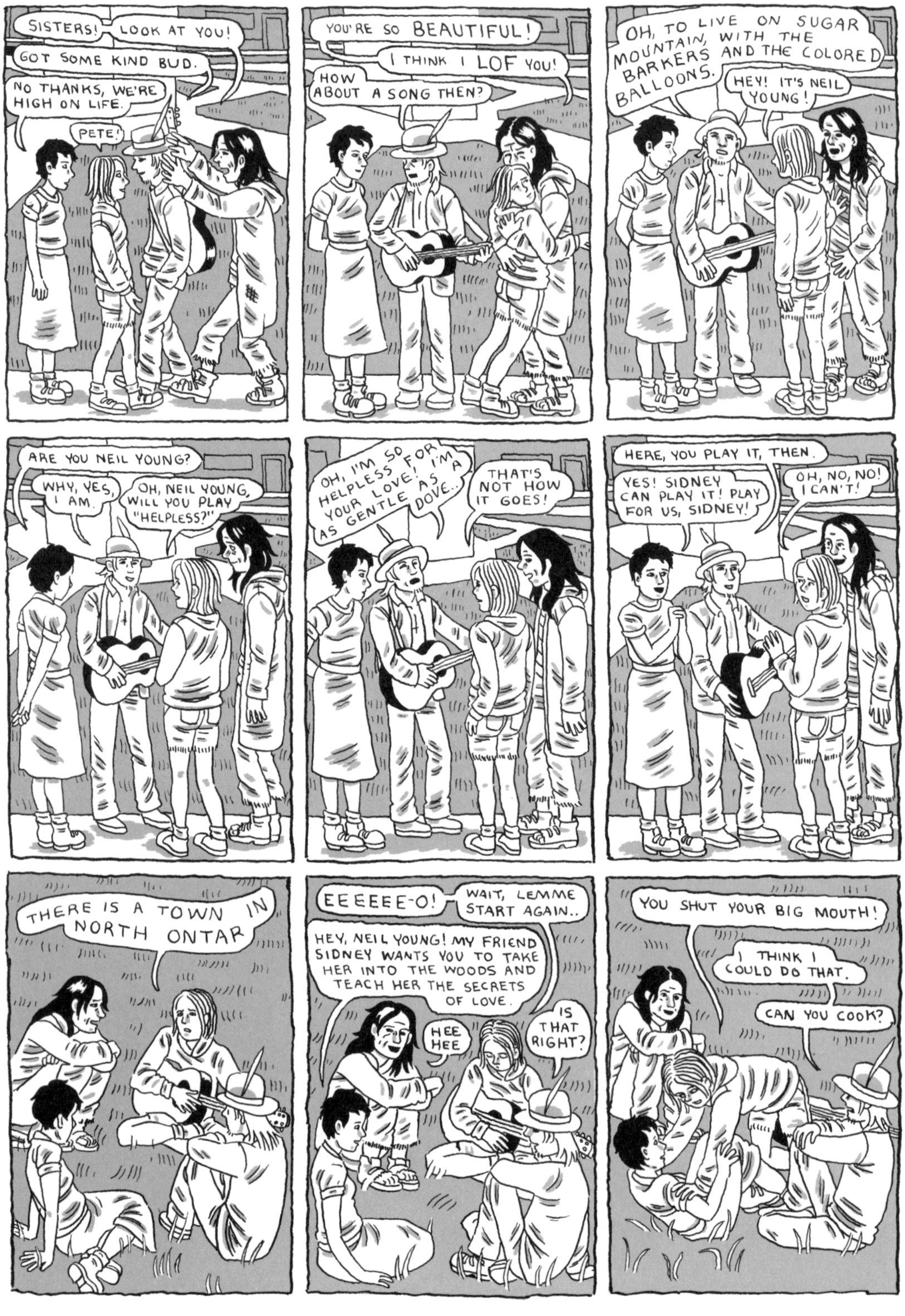
SISTERS!
LOOK AT YOU!
GOT SOME KIND BUD.
NO THANKS, WE'RE HIGH ON LIFE.
PETE!
YOU'RE SO BEAUTIFUL!
I THINK I LOF YOU!
HOW ABOUT A SONG THEN?
OH, TO LIVE ON SUGAR MOUNTAIN, WITH THE BARKERS AND THE COLORED BALLOONS.
HEY! IT'S NEIL YOUNG!
ARE YOU NEIL YOUNG?
WHY, YES, I AM.
OH, NEIL YOUNG, WILL YOU PLAY "HELPLESS?"
OH, I'M SO HELPLESS FOR YOUR LOVE! I'M AS GENTLE AS A DOVE..
THAT'S NOT HOW IT GOES!
HERE, YOU PLAY IT, THEN.
YES! SIDNEY CAN PLAY IT! PLAY FOR US, SIDNEY!
OH, NO, NO! I CAN'T!
THERE IS A TOWN IN NORTH ONTAR
EEEEEE-O!
WAIT, LEMME START AGAIN..
HEY, NEIL YOUNG! MY FRIEND SIDNEY WANTS YOU TO TAKE HER INTO THE WOODS AND TEACH HER THE SECRETS OF LOVE.
HEE HEE
IS THAT RIGHT?
YOU SHUT YOUR BIG MOUTH!
I THINK I COULD DO THAT.
CAN YOU COOK?

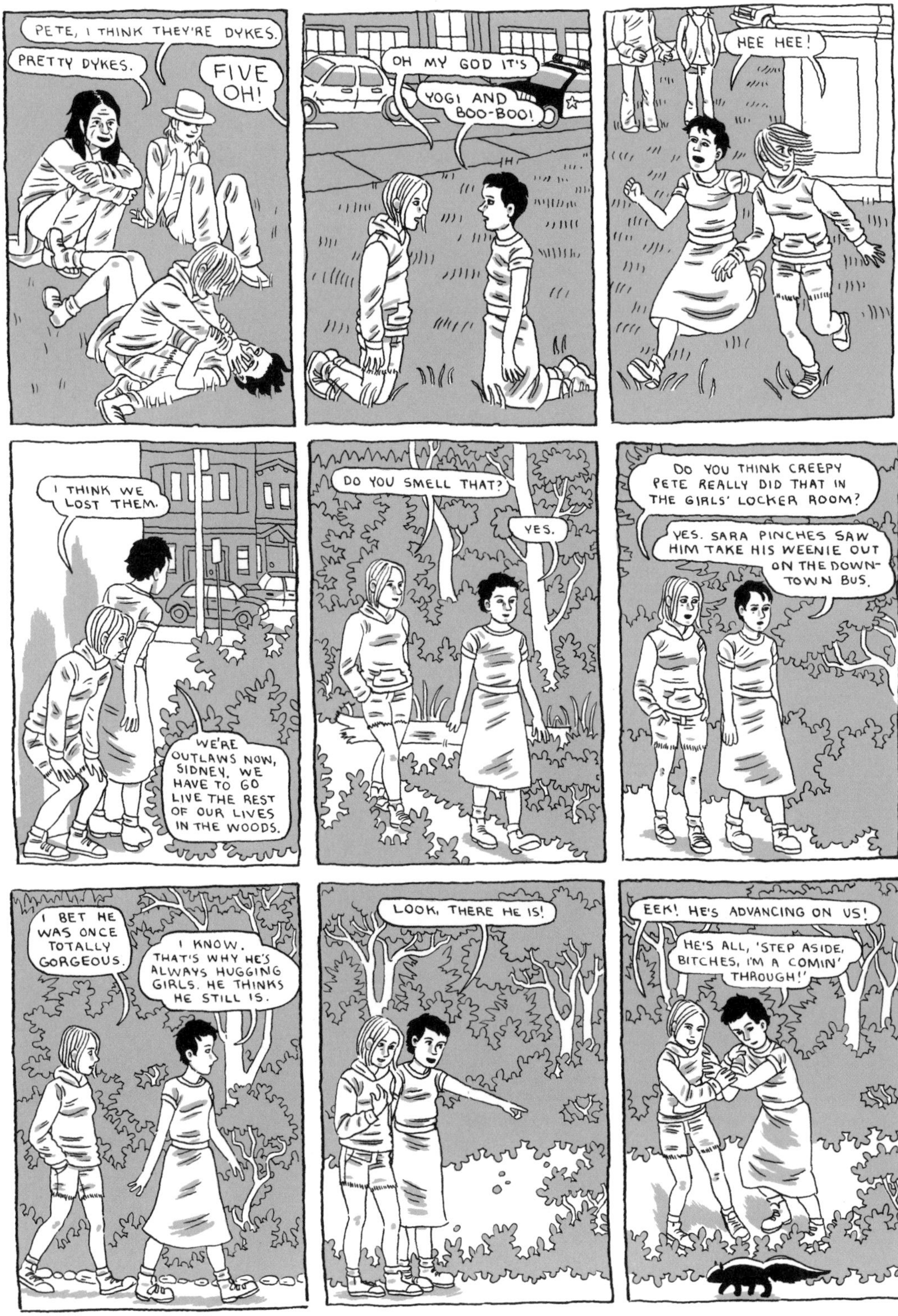
PETE, I THINK THEY'RE DYKES.
PRETTY DYKES.
FIVE OH!
OH MY GOD IT'S
YOGI AND BOO-BOO!
HEE HEE!
I THINK WE LOST THEM.
WE'RE OUTLAWS NOW, SIDNEY. WE HAVE TO GO LIVE THE REST OF OUR LIVES IN THE WOODS.
DO YOU SMELL THAT?
YES.
DO YOU THINK CREEPY PETE REALLY DID THAT IN THE GIRLS' LOCKER ROOM?
YES. SARA PINCHES SAW HIM TAKE HIS WEENIE OUT ON THE DOWN-TOWN BUS.
I BET HE WAS ONCE TOTALLY GORGEOUS.
I KNOW. THAT'S WHY HE'S ALWAYS HUGGING GIRLS. HE THINKS HE STILL IS.
LOOK, THERE HE IS!
EEK! HE'S ADVANCING ON US!
HE'S ALL, 'STEP ASIDE, BITCHES, I'M A COMIN' THROUGH!'

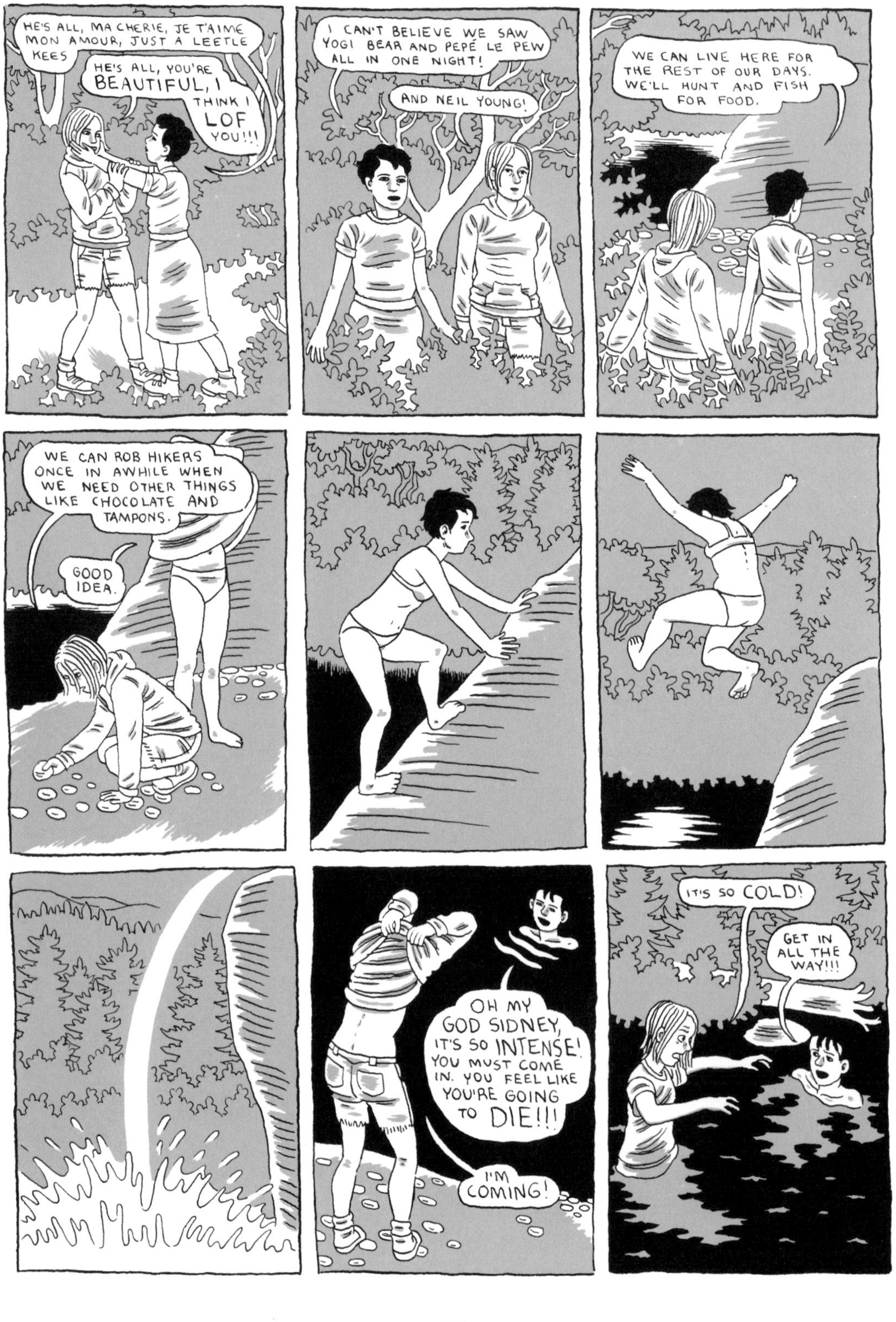
HE'S ALL, MA CHERIE, JE T'AIME MON AMOUR, JUST A LEETLE KEES
HE'S ALL, YOU'RE BEAUTIFUL, I THINK I LOF YOU!!!
I CAN'T BELIEVE WE SAW YOGI BEAR AND PEPÉ LE PEW ALL IN ONE NIGHT!
AND NEIL YOUNG!
WE CAN LIVE HERE FOR THE REST OF OUR DAYS. WE'LL HUNT AND FISH FOR FOOD.
WE CAN ROB HIKERS ONCE IN AWHILE WHEN WE NEED OTHER THINGS LIKE CHOCOLATE AND TAMPONS.
GOOD IDEA.
OH MY GOD SIDNEY, IT'S SO INTENSE! YOU MUST COME IN. YOU FEEL LIKE YOU'RE GOING TO DIE!!!
I'M COMING!
IT'S SO COLD!
GET IN ALL THE WAY!!!

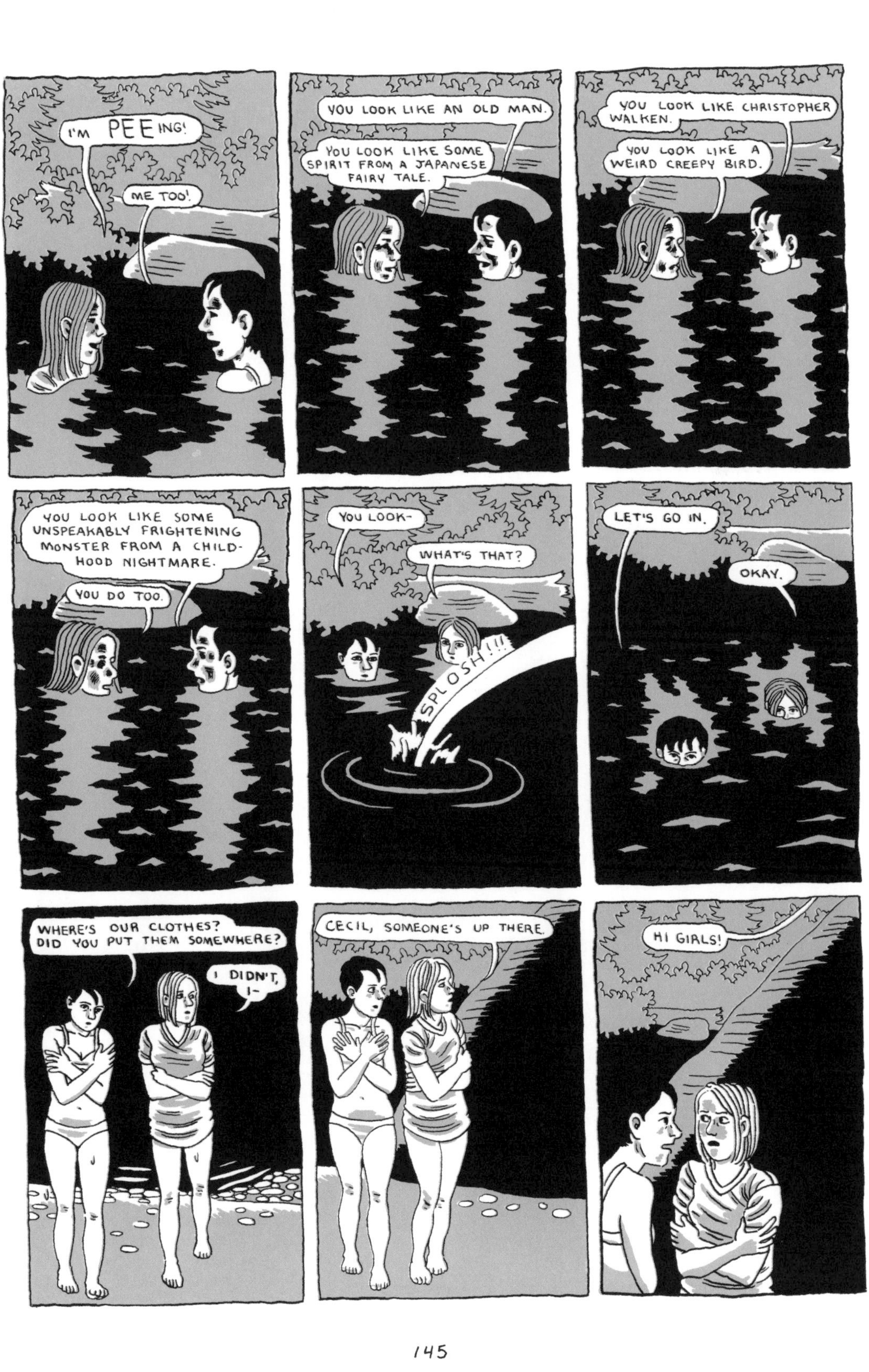
I'M PEEING!
ME TOO!
YOU LOOK LIKE AN OLD MAN.
YOU LOOK LIKE SOME SPIRIT FROM A JAPANESE FAIRY TALE.
YOU LOOK LIKE CHRISTOPHER WALKEN.
YOU LOOK LIKE A WEIRD CREEPY BIRD.
YOU LOOK LIKE SOME UNSPEAKABLY FRIGHTENING MONSTER FROM A CHILDHOOD NIGHTMARE.
YOU DO TOO.
YOU LOOK-
WHAT'S THAT?
SPLOSH!!!
LET'S GO IN.
OKAY.
WHERE'S OUR CLOTHES? DID YOU PUT THEM SOMEWHERE?
I DIDN'T, I-
CECIL, SOMEONE'S UP THERE.
HI GIRLS!

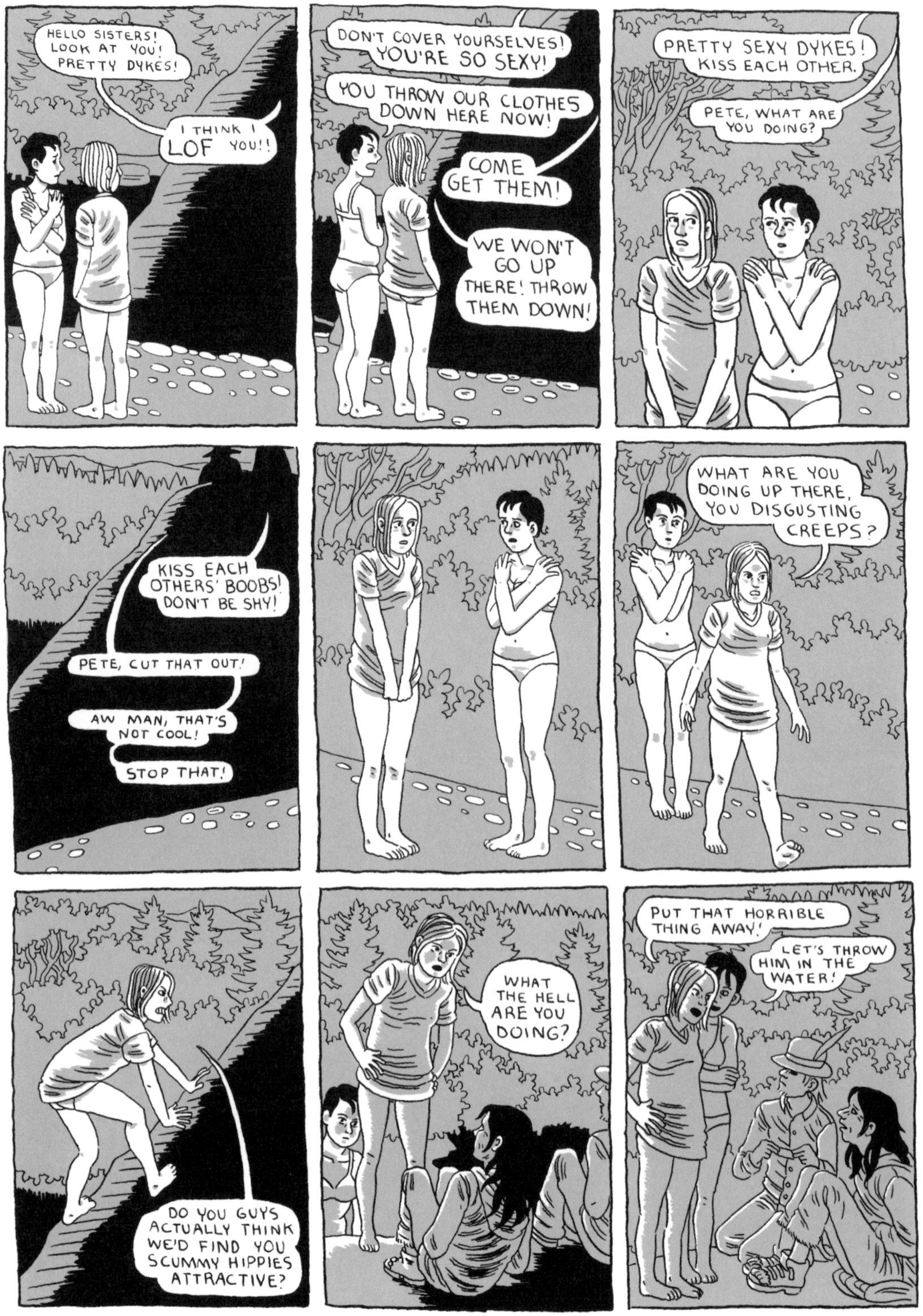
HELLO SISTERS! LOOK AT YOU! PRETTY DYKES!
I THINK I LOF YOU!!
DON'T COVER YOURSELVES! YOU'RE SO SEXY!
YOU THROW OUR CLOTHES DOWN HERE NOW!
COME GET THEM!
WE WON'T GO UP THERE! THROW THEM DOWN!
PRETTY SEXY DYKES! KISS EACH OTHER.
PETE, WHAT ARE YOU DOING?
KISS EACH OTHERS' BOOBS! DON'T BE SHY!
PETE, CUT THAT OUT!
AW MAN, THAT'S NOT COOL!
STOP THAT!
WHAT ARE YOU DOING UP THERE, YOU DISGUSTING CREEPS?
DO YOU GUYS ACTUALLY THINK WE'D FIND YOU SCUMMY HIPPIES ATTRACTIVE?
WHAT THE HELL ARE YOU DOING?
PUT THAT HORRIBLE THING AWAY!
LET'S THROW HIM IN THE WATER!

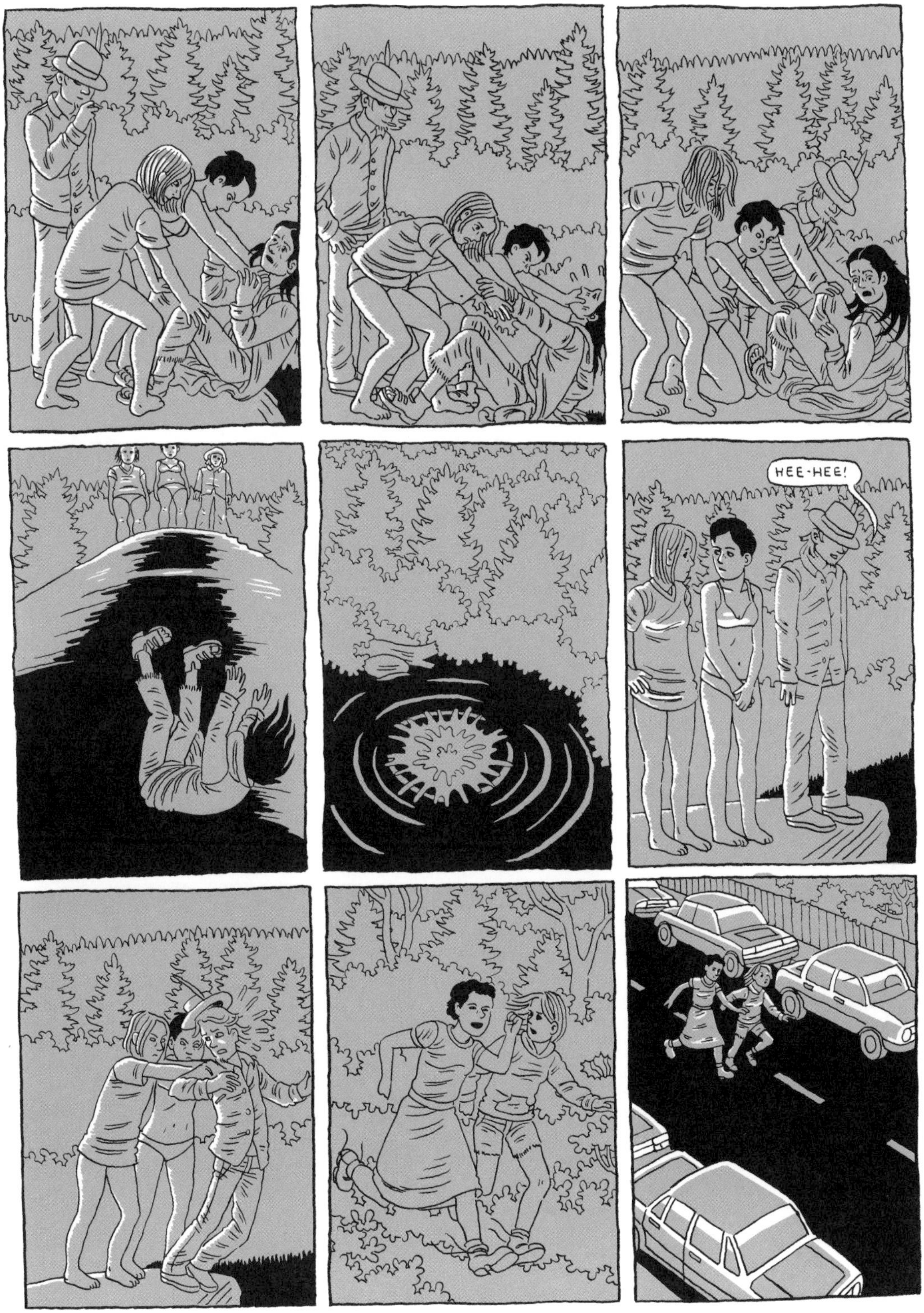
HEE-HEE!

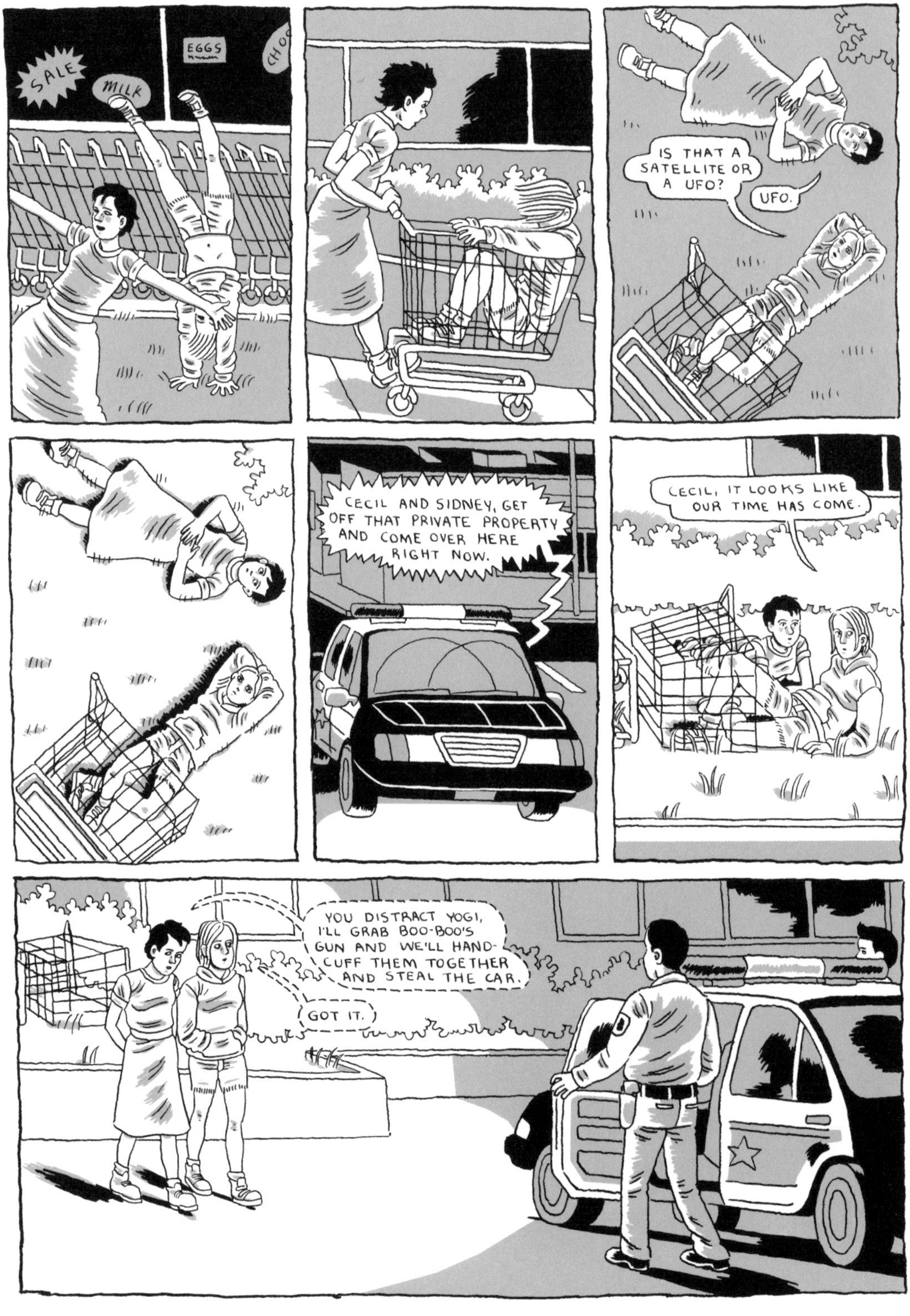
SALE
MILK
EGGS
IS THAT A SATELLITE OR A UFO?
UFO.
CECIL AND SIDNEY, GET OFF THAT PRIVATE PROPERTY AND COME OVER HERE RIGHT NOW.
CECIL, IT LOOKS LIKE OUR TIME HAS COME.
YOU DISTRACT YOGI, I'LL GRAB BOO-BOO'S GUN AND WE'LL HAND-CUFF THEM TOGETHER AND STEAL THE CAR.
GOT IT.

"Hit Me" was originally published in *Stuck in the Middle: 17 Comics From an Unpleasant Age.* (Viking Juvenile)

"Cecil and Jordan in New York" was originally published in *Kramers Ergot 5* (Gingko Press) and was based on an idea by Sadie Hales.

"One Afternoon" was originally published in *Scheherazade: Stories of Love, Treachery, Mothers and Monsters* (Soft Skull Press)

"I Feel Nothing" was originally published in *Mome: Summer 2005* (Fantagraphics Books)

"Robot DJ" was originally published in *Mome: Spring/Summer 2006* (Fantagraphics Books)

"Gabrielle the Third" was originally published in *Mome: Winter 2007* (Fantagraphics Books)

"Year of the Arowana" was originally published in *The Comics Journal Special Edition* 2005 (Fantagraphics Books)

"Felix" was originally published in *Drawn & Quarterly Showcase: Book Four* (Drawn & Quarterly)

"My Affliction" was originally published in *Lucky, Volume 2, number 1* (Drawn & Quarterly)

"Summer Camp" was originally published in *Lucky, Volume 2, number 2* (Drawn & Quarterly)